Table of Contents

—ɯɯ—

Introduction

—ᄿᄿ—

I usually never read the preface, acknowledgements, or introduction of a book because they are too boring, but I hope you will read mine. I want you to know who I am and what this book is about.

My name is Patrick Muenchen but most people call me "Coach." I am not the kind of coach you had in school who barked at you, tortured you, or made your PE experience miserable. I am the kind of Coach you remember fondly, the one who taught you how to play sports and got you excited about your fitness. When I walk down the halls of my school I get a lot of smiles, high fives and greetings-"Hi Coach." I guess my students like me pretty well because in 2004 I was nominated for "My favorite PE Teacher" and was selected and honored by *Sporting Kid Magazine* in Alpharetta, Georgia. My selection was passed on to the national level and I was chosen again and honored in Washington, D.C. during a *PE For Life* convention. I treasure these awards because kids are brutally honest, if they say it they mean it. If you have food in your teeth, your breath stinks, or your underwear are showing-they will let you know. When they told me they liked me I was pretty proud. I hope a big part of the reason they liked me was because I motivated them to become healthier-my main purpose in writing this book.

I am married to my lovely wife Susan and have two pretty cool kids, Sam and Molly. I am currently a physical education teacher in North Georgia. I love my job because I get to wear shorts and tennis shoes to work every day, I get paid to make a difference in young people's lives, and I get summers off. I have a Master's degree in Health Studies from the University of Alabama. I coach Little League baseball, basketball, and soccer. I love the Lord, my family, my community, my job, and my hobbies.

I am 40 years old at the writing of this book and have lived the past twenty years of my life (since I surrendered my life to the Lord) passionately by five priorities: Faith, Family, Fitness, Friends, and Fun. This book is a collection of some of the lessons I have learned about faith and fitness that have changed my life. Besides my formal education in PE school and graduate school, my educational endeavors in the "school of life" include working as a fitness trainer at the YMCA, serving as a fulltime campus and youth minister, participating in two overseas mission trips (Czechoslovakia and Honduras), serving as an adult Sunday school teacher, and teaching for over thirteen years in elementary and middle school. I wrote this book because I am passionate about my faith in the Lord and I am passionate about fitness.

If you have ever received a message or a piece of advice for someone that just burned in your heart until you shared it with them-that's how I feel about the thirty one devotions in this book. Each chapter unravels a faith principle in God's word and how it can be used to change your fitness. I have also shared some compelling stories and some pertinent research that I hope will inspire and motivate you to change.

I would like to thank the many people who have supported me along life's journey especially my wife, children, parents, extended family, friends and co-workers. They have shared their lives and stories with me and I have learned so much from them. Where would we be without family and friends to make life meaningful and worth living? I would like to thank my sister-in-law, Patti Muenchen, for her incredible editing and excellent suggestions. I would also like to thank Biblegateway.com for helping me locate scripture quickly as well as all the cited cool websites which have provided valuable and valid information.

I hope you will enjoy reading this book and will be motivated and inspired to change your life for the better in the areas of faith and fitness. God is so good and you will be able to enjoy life so much more if you are healthy in body and spirit. May God bless you!

Psalm 34:8 "O taste and see that the Lord is good…"

How to Use This Book

—◊—

Only read this page if you are serious about changing your life and developing your faith.

Jesus said that faith could move mountains and that anything was possible to him who believes. Your faith can change the way you live, but it must be developed to a point where it is an effective force of change in your life. Faith comes (or is developed) by hearing and speaking. If you want to develop the faith that moves mountains you must hear and speak the greatest truth on the planet-God's Word.

Each chapter in this book expounds on a scripture verse from God's Word that is a life principle that is applicable both to your faith and to your fitness. Each scripture is supported by other powerful scriptures that are formed into a message designed to change your perspective about your life and health. Read a chapter each day and discover how to apply your faith to God's Word. Read and speak the scriptures in each chapter over and over again. They are not my words, but God's words. The more you hear them the more they will change the way you think and believe.

If you want to call it brainwashing, then go ahead. A lot of people need their brain washed of all the negative thoughts they have come to believe. You don't become negative or pessimistic overnight. You hear negative things being spoken to you over and over again and eventually you begin to believe them. Then you begin to speak them yourself. "I can't do this. I will never lose this weight. I will never quit smoking. I don't have any friends. I am a failure." The more you hear and speak the words, the more you believe it. A negative faith is developed and you are able to fulfill your words and beliefs.

As a coach I tell my players over and over what to do. When they do it right I praise them. When they do it right in a game, I really praise them and the crowd goes nuts for them. They do something right and they get a happy feeling inside because I am speaking praise to them and they are beginning to believe in themselves. Even the kids with the lowest self-esteem begin to believe in themselves when they hear good things over and over again in a meaningful context. They develop confidence (or faith) in their abilities and they experience a level of success in the sport that they have never had before. Their faith changes their abilities and so can yours.

You can change your faith, your life, and your health by getting a hold of the principles in this book and making them yours. Believe in them and practice them. At the end of the book you will find the appendix where I have listed all the scripture verses from the chapters. Read and speak aloud these scripture verses over and over again. Meditate on them and let the Holy Spirit speak to you about how they apply to your life. Faith is not merely a mental under-standing or agreement but a belief in the heart. As you speak the words over and over again they will make the transition from head knowledge to heart faith. If you want to walk by faith you have to point your faith in the right direction. Let God's Word be the light to your path.

Finally, don't forget that faith without works is dead. At the end of each chapter you will find a *Faith in Action* tip designed to get you started on your road to a healthier life. Just do it! Do the tip so you can praise yourself for making a step in the right direction. As you exercise your faith and your body you will become a new person, no mountain will stand in your way, and nothing will be impossible for you.

By reading this page you already made a step in the right direc-tion. Way to go! You declared by your actions that you are serious. Now, let's do this!

1.

My Personal Fitness Journey

—ɯ—

Faith

Mark 5:19-20 "Go home to your people and report to them what great things the Lord has done for you, and how He had mercy on you." And he went away and began to proclaim in Decapolis what great things Jesus had done for him; and everyone was amazed."

Everyone has a story, a series of events that have happened in your life that have changed you for good or bad. As long as you live and breathe you are on a journey through this life and your journey is the story of what got you to where you are at this moment in time. Your story may include triumphs and tragedies, heavy burdens and smooth sailing, strong confidence and utter confusion, faith and fear, love and loneliness, laughter and heartache. As the poem *"Footprints"* suggests, the Lord has been with you every step of the way. He has promised in **Psalm 94:14 "For the Lord will not abandon His people, nor will He forsake His inheritance."**

Your journey has been marked with influential people, unique circumstances, and lessons that have helped you develop ideas about your faith and about who you are on the inside. Your responses to life's challenges have formed your character, defining your strengths and revealing your weaknesses. Victories and mistakes have been your tutors. Faith, family, and friends have given you the courage and strength to continue on your journey through life.

If you could write down some of the lessons you have learned, what would you say? Who provided you with inspiration, encouragement, and motivation to make it through? What forces guided you? What values helped you find your way? What was the hardest part of your journey? What marked your sweetest successes and rewards?

As I look back on my last 40 years, I see a journey that has taught me some very valuable lessons, especially in the areas of faith and fitness. *For We Walk by Faith* is a collection of some of the lessons I have learned. In future chapters I will share some highlights of my faith journey but first please allow me to share for a few minutes, my personal fitness journey. As you read my story, take some time to think about your own journey and what has brought you to your present level of fitness. As I reminisce, please contemplate what measures you have taken in regards to your own health and fitness over the years.

Fitness

I was born in Cincinnati, Ohio in 1966, the second of seven children. My parents had three boys in a row, all one year apart. After a two year break, they had two girls, one year apart, then another break, and two boys 11 months apart. Their family planning involved seven kids in 10 years.

My early childhood involved outdoor adventures and my introduction to sports. I spent my first eight years in Cincinnati where my daily exercise included playing baseball, kick the can, or hide-and-seek in our cul-de-sac. Sometimes we crossed the creek behind a friend's house to have mud ball fights in the woods near our tree fort. In the summer months, we would swim at Coney Island (a nearby water park) once or twice a week. In the fall, we would rake leaves for hours, and jump into the huge piles we created. During the winter, if it snowed, we would stay up till 10 or 11 p.m. riding sleds down the street with all of the neighborhood families. The lucky kid on my dad's back usually made the 150-yard trek to the bottom first.

In first and second grade I usually walked the half mile distance to school. In third grade I began attending a private, Catholic school and would sometimes hike about 2 miles through the Jesuit monastery and the surrounding woods and creeks back home with my brothers and neighbor. One of my first sports experiences was on a soccer team with my older brother, John. I remember on the first day of practice the coach asked for a volunteer to dribble the soccer ball down field, around the cone and back. My brother raised his hand and came forward. He picked up the soccer ball and dribbled it down field like a basketball to the sound of raucous laughter. We had a lot to learn. On some lucky weekends, when my mom was preoccupied with my younger siblings, we would convince her to let us ride our bikes the three miles to the United Dairy Farmers' convenience store to spend the money we had earned doing chores—emptying dirty cloth diapers in the toilet, cleaning the Venetian blinds, doing dishes, sweeping the floor—on candy. The trip was complicated and involved crossing a four-lane road, but we always came back with our paper sacks of Dip sticks, foot-long taffy and bubble gum with comics. Between the ages six and eight, I was probably five to ten pounds overweight and had a little pot belly. I was sometimes called fat boy and besides being a little uncomfortable with some flab hanging over my belt, it hurt my feelings to be teased by my friends.

My middle childhood was a sports lover's paradise. When I was eight we moved to Columbus, Ohio and I spent the next eight years of my life becoming a sports superstar (at least in my own mind). My dad actively participated in coaching us in all sports. By then there were six of us with another one on the way. Dad often coached two teams. Our mainstay sports were fall and spring soccer and summer baseball. I was a pretty good player and we had many successful teams. My brothers and I tried basketball one winter but we had such a tough season, we hung it up quickly. In addition to organized sports, we spent many afternoons playing ball in the neighborhood or riding our Huffy bikes along the paved trails next to the Olentangy River. Summers were spent cutting grass for extra money, delivering papers on bicycles (at 6 a.m.) and riding our bikes to the pool to hang out.

From third to eighth grade I attended St. Michael's Catholic School. I often rode my bike the three-a-half miles to school, through busy intersections and along four-lane roads. At school, we had PE once a week and recess every day for about 45 minutes. We played red rover, kill the man with the ball, or kick ball. I remember being picked last more than once and I remember how much it hurt. My eighth grade nickname, used secretly by the girls, was butt juice, apparently because my bottom was a little rounder than the other guys.

As you can see, my childhood was marked by lots of outdoor activity, walking and riding bikes, and sports. In the 70's we did not have television stations dedicated to children's programming and we did not have video games on CDs (although Atari was not bad). My mom chased us out of the house if it was nice outside and my dad was instrumental in getting us into sports. (**Proverbs 22:6** says **"Train up a child in the way he should go, even when he is old he will not depart from it."** Parents must be instrumental in setting fitness standards for their children). Although some of the adventures and independence we did in those days could not be done now because of societal changes, kids still need to get away from the television and get outside and get active. Fortunately, opportunities abound for children in the area of sports, karate, gymnastics, and a host of other activities.

Although my teenage years were influenced by the social issues of the 1980's I would like to focus on the fitness aspect only, although it is very sad to say, other components absorbed much of my time. By the start of high school, my body composition was fairly average. Once the kids my age started pitching curveballs in baseball, I quit playing and devoted myself full time to soccer, playing outdoors in the fall and spring and indoors during the winter. I lettered for four years in varsity soccer. At the end of tenth grade, I spent the summer with my uncle on a construction site (mainly in the trailer) where I gained about 15 pounds. I returned to soccer camp with curly hair (and looking like Richard Simmons). It took a while to lose the weight. My eating habits didn't help. A normal after school sweet tooth attack consisted of two or three Little Debbie oatmeal crème pies chased down with a 20-ounce Mountain Dew. If inhaled too fast, it was guaranteed to give you the "eebie geebies" (a sick feeling of sugar overload). Attending football games didn't help either because we always finished the evening with a late night hangout at McDonald's or a six-pack of square White Castle's cheeseburgers with mustard. When I was seventeen, we moved to Atlanta, Georgia and I spent my senior year at a new school. Soccer was my only means of fitness and my last senior game was my last game for about seven years.

My college years marked my introduction to recreational fitness and strength training. In fall of 1984 I began college at Georgia Tech. To compensate for my social life and my consumption of liquid calories, I began playing pick-up basketball games, tennis, and racquetball. I also started haphazard weight training in the student athletic center. I pretty much followed my college friend around and did whatever he did, except with a lot less weight. I think I began to bench press with about 65 lbs. I weighed 160 lbs. I also took as many PE courses as possible including volleyball, racquetball, swimming, strength training and fitness, tennis, basketball, and aerobics (to meet girls). The courses raised my grade point average and made me a little better tennis player. In strength training we were graded on weight improvement so I actually was forced to push it and get stronger. After some workouts, my arms and chest would be so stressed I could not get my hands up to my head to wash my hair in the shower. At one point in that particular class we were required to run a timed mile. I remember going out on campus one afternoon to run. I only made it about four blocks before my side hurt so bad and I was so winded that I had to walk. A few more attempts and a slower pace eased my bruised ego.

After a year of steady training I had established a real weight training program and was able to run 2 miles around campus. **Job 8:7 says "Though your beginning was insignificant, yet your end will increase greatly."**

In the fall of 1986, while lifting weights, I met a Christian guy named Alex who invited me to a Bible study. After several refusals I finally attended and under the conviction of the Holy Spirit, I surrendered my life to Christ and received His salvation. My life was radically altered.

Alex was an avid runner and through him and a world-class Australian runner (who was training for the Olympics), I was inspired. One fall day I attempted my first long (approximately six miles) run with these guys to Piedmont Park and back. About halfway there, I felt as if I was about to die. However, the ease and focus of my running partners got me through and gave me something to shoot for. **Proverbs 27:17** says **"Iron sharpens iron, so one man sharpens another."** By the end of college I was jogging three miles, two or three times a week, and lifting weights two or three times a week. I felt I was in pretty good shape and I had made remarkable improvements on my weight lifting.

My first career out of college was a desk job estimating for a construction company. I was in the office for 8-9 hours a day and severely missed my freedom and active lifestyle. My post-college days were a juggle between establishing a career, enjoying time with friends, and trying to stay in shape. Since I could no longer work out at my beloved student athletic center, I joined a fitness club. It was the "meat market" type with cheesy salespeople and super huge guys doing more talking than lifting. I went through about three clubs before I found the YMCA, a more family-oriented facility. I became a little stronger than college days (probably because I gained a few pounds sitting behind a desk) and was able to lift more weight than before. I began to vary my workouts between free weights and Nautilus type equipment and continued to run regularly.

During my early twenties I signed up and ran my first 10K race—The Peachtree Road Race. I survived my first 4th of July race with a time under 60 minutes and was proud. The race was the largest 10K in the United States and is a big deal in Atlanta with over 50,000 runners. From that point on, I made it an annual tradition.

My desk job restrained me for one year before I made a career change and went into fulltime campus and youth ministry. My schedule became much more flexible and I enjoyed working out on the campus again between ministry pursuits. I roomed with some great Christian guys, one of whom had a profound affect on my diet. Bart was a former Tech football player who also was in fulltime ministry. He had a father fighting heart disease and made a resolute decision to eat healthy for life so he did not have to battle the same later on. Bart's resolve to avoid unhealthy foods and exercise daily made a profound impact on me.

After a year in ministry I decided to go back to school and get a teaching degree. I picked up some part time jobs working at a fast food restaurant and then the YMCA. I was able to use the university fitness facility again to keep in shape. At age 24, I met my sweetheart while working at the YMCA. We shared a strong faith and love for the Lord, we both loved working with children, and we both worked out regularly. These three passions would become the source of many adventures. In a year we married. And unlike many of my friends who settled down to fat and comfortable bliss after tying the knot, we continued our commitment to fitness. I became a certified strength trainer at the YMCA and added a little knowledge to my fitness routine. We both worked several jobs at the YMCA including fitness training, the after school program, and summer camp.

After completing my education degree I was able to land a job teaching. To make extra money during the summer I worked the summer camp program. Working at the YMCA provided a free membership to the fitness center which was a great plus. After working with the kids either at school or during summer camp, I was able to get a nice workout in at the Y and meet other fitness enthusiasts.

I taught elementary school for five years as a fifth and sixth grade math and social studies teacher. To supplement my pay I also taught summer camp. I found the latter more rewarding because the children enjoyed activities more than academics. I realized my teaching career may be more enjoyable in the area of Physical Education so I returned to school again for an additional teaching certificate. To pay the bills I started a lawn maintenance company and walked my hiney off. I would mow between eight and fifteen yards a day, five days a week, besides attending classes in between. I estimated that I was walking about 15-20 miles per day just cutting grass. Because of the wear on my legs, I cut running out of my exercise routine. I continued to lift weights to maintain muscle strength and I also took up roller-blading and mountain biking. At close to 30, I wanted to prove I wasn't too old to try something new.

As I entered my thirties I took the leap into parenthood and homeownership. Balancing new responsibilities with fitness and fun were the landscape of the day. Mountain biking became the ultimate rush. Not only did I get the thrill of speedy downhill sections, but also intense cardio hill climbs and straight-aways. Although the trails were a 15 minute drive from home, I tried to make it a regular practice. I even entered a few mountain bike races. My second race proved too much for my cheap bike which sustained a broken chain and bent rim. For my next birthday, my wonderful wife upgraded my ride and bought me a beautiful new Trek which I enjoyed for many years. What a great gift idea-something to promote fitness!

When I returned to teaching after receiving additional certification I cut back on my lawn cutting business and returned to a regular regimen of running. I had to teach in the regular classroom for one more year before I received my dream job-PE teacher. I wore shorts and a t-shirt everyday to the job (except sweats from December to mid-March). I began to teach students how to take care of their bodies and to find sports and activities that would help them do so. I also started playing sports again. I played on an amateur soccer team for about three seasons and on a softball team for a few more than that. Although many of my teammates considered our practices and games "a good workout," it really didn't do as much for me as my running.

By my mid-thirties, I had returned to my running regiment of three miles every other day, with weight lifting or biking in between. I continued to run the annual Peachtree Road Race, and even started running a pre-qualifier so I could get a good starting number. In 2001, I recorded my fastest time of around 42 minutes and was one of the top 1000 finishers. This finish was a big deal since there were more than 50,000 runners and the first several hundred were among the world's elite runners. I received a mug from Nike for my accomplishment. I was able to achieve this feat two more times, a little slower each time.

Life in metropolitan Atlanta became too crowded for my family so we moved to the country. I purchased a used Schwinn road bike from a pawn shop, and took up road biking, since the mountain biking trails were now a 30-minute drive away and I can't stand to waste time driving to work out and then driving back. Over the previous ten years I had begun to accumulate fitness equipment for this very reason. I acquired a bench and Olympic barbell and weights, various dumbbell sizes, a stationary bike, a treadmill, a stair master, a recumbent bike, and a free weights tower with about 20 exercises you can do on it. Why waste money joining a gym when you can slowly buy your own stuff? There is no wasted travel time to and from the gym, no waiting for a piece of equipment, no stinky bodies or sweaty equipment, no obnoxious music, no closing time, and in between sets you can wash the car or do chores around the house instead of talking to another meathead.

Road biking proved to be as beautiful and as exhilarating as mountain biking. I live in the North Georgia Mountains within riding distance of the start of the Appalachian Trail. Aside from the occasional close call with a logging truck or chicken bus, my rides are gorgeous and a good burn

When my son turned six years old and was able to enlist in youth sports I hung up my own sports (softball) pursuits to focus on his budding career. Coaching him in his Little League endeavors became an interesting pastime passion. As I moved toward my later thirties I looked for new challenges to stay young and fit. To continue on my fitness journey I enrolled in a team adventure race at age 36. It was the sprint variety that lasted 5 hours for my team. We mountain biked, trail ran, kayaked, mountain biked some more, and did some team challenges in between. It was a blast albeit exhausting. It was great to see 300 other teams out there with us, enjoying nature, fitness, and personal challenge. I also learned to snowboard although I don't see the X-games in my future.

Now at age 40, my workout consists of cardio one day and lifting weights the next day. My cardio workouts are usually running 5 miles or road biking about 15 miles. My resistance training consists of two sets of each of my six exercises, and I can lift as much as I ever have in my life. I have run my first ½ marathon (13 miles), and my first marathon (26.2 miles). My regular job for the last seven years has been as a physical education teacher, starting with middle school, and later elementary school. I wear shorts or sweats to work and teach children about my second favorite subject, fitness (Jesus is #1).

Life is good. I have enjoyed every moment of my time here on earth. As I continue on my journey I will strive to take care of myself so that I can live a long and healthy life. Check out the life expectancy chart below. You have made it this far. How far will you go and what will be the status of your health?

Life Expectancy, United States, 2003 All races			
Age	Total	Male	Female
0	77.5	74.8	80.1
1	77.0	74.3	79.6
5	73.1	70.4	75.7
10	68.2	65.5	70.7
15	63.2	60.6	65.8
20	58.4	55.8	60.9
25	53.7	51.2	56.0
30	48.9	46.5	51.2
35	44.2	41.9	46.4
40	39.5	37.3	41.6
45	35.0	32.8	37.0
50	30.6	28.5	32.4
55	26.3	24.4	28.0
60	22.2	20.4	23.8
65	18.4	16.8	19.8
70	14.9	13.5	16.0
75	11.8	10.5	12.6
80	9.0	8.0	9.6
85	6.8	6.0	7.2
90	5.0	4.4	5.2
95	3.6	3.2	3.7
100	2.6	2.3	2.6

From National Vital Statistics Report, CDC

I hope my fitness journey has triggered some memories in your mind and heart about your own childhood, adolescent, and adult experiences. Unfortunately, I have found that too many people let their fitness experiences end in high school or college. My response is…you can't live in the past. Your body needs exercise and your health depends on it. I hope this book will help motivate you to continue on a journey of lifelong fitness.

Faith in Action: Today make a small investment into your fitness journey. Buy some good running shoes or some comfortable workout clothes and get ready to use them.

2.

The Call of God

—∿∿—

Faith

Philippians 3:13-15 "Brethren, I do not regard myself as having laid hold of it yet; but one thing I do: forgetting what lies behind and reaching forward to what lies ahead, I press on toward the goal for the prize of the upward call of God in Christ Jesus."

We are all called by God to do something important in life. We have been designed uniquely by Him for a specific purpose. Many of us have more than one calling. We may be called as a spouse, a parent, a businessperson, a fireman, a teacher, a politician, a banker, a doctor, a store clerk, a delivery person, or a Sunday school teacher. Our callings reflect who we are and what we do with our lives. Not everyone is called to the same thing. Our callings our based on the gifts, talents, and anointing the Lord has given us.

I believe God called me to be a husband, a father, an ambassador of Christ, a PE teacher, an ambassador of fitness, an uncle, a son, a brother, a Coach, a writer, and a vacation Bible school teacher. I love my callings and I pursue them with passion. My callings keep me very busy. I believe that God has ordained me to do these things so there are no wishy-washy feelings about the authority I have in Him to move forward and act as if I am on an important mission, commissioned by the King. I believe He has given me the grace and the gifts to fulfill these callings. **1Peter 4:10-11 says "As each one has received a special gift, employ it in serving one another as good stewards of the manifold grace of God. Whoever speaks is to do so as one who is speaking the utterances of God' whoever serves is to do so as one who is serving by the strength which God supplies' so that in all things God may be glorified through Jesus Christ, to whom belongs the glory and dominion forever and ever. Amen."** When I am feeling insecure I remind myself that this is what God has called me to do and He will help me find a way to make it through.

I find great comfort in the fact that Jesus called simple fishermen to become His disciples. It is also interesting to note that some of the first witnesses to His birth were simple shepherds. **1 Corinthians 1:26-27 says "For consider your calling, brethren, that there were not many wise according to the flesh, not many mighty, not many noble; but God has chosen the foolish things of the world to shame the wise, and God has chosen the weak things of the world to shame the things which are strong...."** Jesus saw Peter and his brother and said "come follow Me and I will make you fishers of men." The Bible tells us that they immediately left everything and followed Him. This tells me that you don't have to be extraordinary to be called by God. You don't have to be athletic, popular, or good looking. You only have to be obedient. If you are willing to answer His call and obey Him, you can be used by God.

Sometimes it is very easy to identify the call of God and other times it may take getting knocked off your horse (like the apostle Paul). If you are married then you are called to be a good spouse. If you have children, then God chose you to be a parent. If your parents are alive then He called you to "honor your father and mother" as a good son or daughter. If you are the head of the household then you are called to provide for your family by working an honest job. If you work hard at your job and have a good attitude then the Lord will move you up or move you on. If you are working hard with a good conscience that desires to serve the Lord, He will not allow you to get off track for very long. When Saul (later named Paul the Apostle) was persecuting the Christians while thinking he was serving God, the Lord knocked him off of his horse, blinded him for a couple of days, and revealed to him God's plan of salvation in Jesus. Once he got on the right track he made some serious progress for the Lord and His kingdom. If you pray for His will to be done, He will hear and answer you in His timing. Be faithful in your current calling and He will move you on.

You might remember the Bible story about Joseph. Joseph had a dream that God called him to rule over his brothers and even his parents. When he shared this dream one too many times he was sold by his brothers into slavery. He never gave up on his dream and believed God that one day it would come to pass. When he became a slave at Potipher's house he was so faithful and diligent that after a while he was put in charge of everything Potipher owned. Later he was thrown into jail after a false accusation and after more diligence and faithfulness he was put in charge of the jail. Finally he was brought before the king and interpreted a dream. The king was so impressed that he put him in charge of the entire kingdom. Many years later his brothers came and unknowingly bowed down before him, because he was ruler over them. God's calling was fulfilled through Joseph's obedience, diligence, and faithfulness.

As we fulfill God's calling there should be some sense of accomplishment and joy. There should be an inner peace and satisfaction in knowing that we are doing what God has called us to do. I love being a parent and take great joy in watching my children grow. Although I often fall short of perfection, I try my best to take care of them and teach them how to live life the right way. Some of our callings will bring us great joy and others will seem like a frequent battle and burden. It is important to find and strive in those callings that bring greater glory to God. Your occupational calling may not be very fulfilling but while you are there you can answer the call of being a light in the midst of darkness because we are all called to be His witnesses. When you are off the clock you can passionately pursue the other callings that God has placed on your life. There are many callings to be fulfilled whether it is preparing meals, teaching a Bible study, youth ministry, or serving in your community.

Jesus talked about the call of God in **Mark 10:43-45** when He said "**.....whoever wishes to become great among you shall be your servant; and whoever wishes to be first among you shall be slave of all. For even the Son of Man did not come to be served, but to serve, and to give His life a ransom for many.**" As we take up the greatest calling of being a servant to others, we will be a blessing to others and God will bless us as His Spirit works through us touching others.

We must adopt a servant attitude towards God and others. If we decide to serve others instead of desiring to be a ruler, we will disarm pride and any selfish motives. A servant merely wants to assist others. With this attitude we will discover and fulfill the call of God if we are obedient, diligent, and faithful.

Fitness

Have you had the flu recently? How about a serious sinus infection, a bad backache, or a stomach virus? When I experience a bad bout with sickness it can really knock me down and leave me disabled. Sometimes I am down right helpless. I am at the mercy of my wife to take care of me and pray me back to good health. When I have resisted the sickness all I can and I still can't shake it I feel like I will die if the Lord or some medicine doesn't work.

It's hard to be very effective at anything when I am sick. I feel awful, I am irritable, I am often tired, and I am not very spiritual. The thought of being a light to the world is pretty far from my mind.

If we don't take care of our body it will be difficult to fulfill the call of God. Lack of diligent care can lead to frequent sickness and chronic disease. Abuse of our bodies can lead to bodies that are dependent on medicine to survive or function normally. If we don't actively practice disease prevention including exercise and proper nutrition we can be more susceptible to things like heart disease and cancer. Heart disease and cancer can lead to premature death. You can't fulfill the call of God if you are six feet under.

Sickness or death from chronic disease can cut short the call of God on your life. A friend of ours smoked for years. Rather suddenly she developed a serious cough that laid her up in bed. A visit to the doctor revealed that she had an advanced stage of lung cancer and only weeks to live. She didn't live much longer after the diagnosis and left behind a husband and ten year old twins.

During my early thirties I taught an adult Bible study at my church. We had a regular group of about six people. One of the young ladies who attended was single and in her late twenties. She had survived breast cancer and one day she shared her battle with our group. Something she said made a profound impression on me. She told us about radiation treatments and how all her hair fell out. She talked about chemotherapy and how the doctors injected poison into her system to basically kill the cells in her body. She described how she would vomit and have diarrhea for days and how she would just sit in bed and wail. And worse, just as she would start to feel a little bit better, she would have to go back in for another injection. This went on for a period of six weeks. I really can't do justice to the words of pain that she described and how she felt as if 'her insides were being puked out.' But the one thing she did say that I will never forget is this, "If the cancer comes back I will not go through treatment again. I would rather die than have to go through that torture again."

Since hearing of her experience I have witnessed more than one friend going through the same battle. They describe the same pain, misery, discomfort, lack of energy, and uselessness. Some have survived and others have gone on to be with the Lord. While in the midst of the struggle for life itself, it is hard to think about the call of God. It is hard to be an effective parent, it is many times impossible to go to work, and it is too draining to serve or minister in any capacity. Recovery time is slow and takes full concentration. When you are fighting to survive it is hard to glorify God with your life, but it is not impossible. I have had some friends who have greatly inspired others by their faith and fighting spirit. Their personal battle brought many together in prayer and helped them focus on what is truly important in life.

The table below lists the leading causes of death for different age groups. As we travel through life, pursuing the call of God, we will face different challenges to our health and existence. It is important that we know what we are up against.

Ten Leading Causes of Death by Age Group
All races, both sexes, 2002

Cause	All ages	1-9	10-19	20-29	30-39	40-49	50-59	60-69	70-79	80-89
Diseases of heart	1	5	5	5	3	2	2	2	1	1
Cancer (malignant)	2	2	4	4	2	1	1	1	2	2
Cerebrovascular disease	3	10	9	9	8	7	5	4	4	3
Chronic lower respiratory	4	8	7			10	7	3	3	4
Accidents	5	1	1	1	1	3	3	6	8	9
Diabetes mellitus	6			8	9	8	4	5	5	7
Influenza and pneumonia	7	6	8	10	10			10	6	6
Alzheimer's disease	8								9	5
Kidney disease	9							8	7	8
Septicemia (blood disease)	10	7	10				10	9	10	10
Assault/homicide		4	2	2	6	9				
In situ neoplasms, benign		9								
Congenital malformations		3	6	7						
Suicide			3	3	4	4	8			
HIV disease				6	5	5	9			
Chronic liver disease					7	6	6	7		

From CDC, National Vital Statistics System

If we take active measures to increase our fitness level we will reduce the incidences of sickness and disease. An active body that is fed good nutrients stays healthy.

Cancer, heart disease, and other chronic diseases are not 100% preventable but there are measures we can take to greatly reduce our chances of susceptibility. Smoking for example is about the worst thing you can do for your health. Anyone who smokes is inviting catastrophe into his or her life. Anyone who smokes is taking a serious risk of not fulfilling the call of God on their life. We must eliminate risks and practice good habits to promote our health. We each have a holy and unique calling from God. We must embrace it as such.

I believe there is an act of disrespect for the call of God if we don't do everything in our ability to honestly prepare and protect our bodies for the work of His service. Only you can be the best mom or dad in the world for your kids. They want you and not a substitute. Only you can be the best child to your parents. Only you can fulfill the specific call and plans God has for your life. Take care of your body and practice some preventative measures so that you will greatly reduce your risk of disease and live a long healthy life while fulfilling the call of God.

Faith in Action: Identify one negative habit that is hindering your maximum potential in regards to your call from God. Destroy that habit today, forever!

3.

The 5 F's

—ɯ—

Faith

Matthew 6:21 "for where your treasure is, there your heart will be also."

What are the treasures of your life? What do you most often think about, dream about, and most earnestly desire? Whatever consumes your mind, emotions, and heart are your true treasures. These treasures are what we place a high value on in life. They become our values and we direct our priorities in life to achieve these values.

As I have matured in life, I have been able to more clearly identify what things are important to me and how I must rank them in importance in my life. Time is a precious commodity. Each day we are faced with demands that pull us in many directions (working, sleeping, eating, traveling, spending time with friends, church, children, extended family, housework, yard work, recreation, television shows, exercise, vacation, education, romance time, leisure, and the list goes on). I have had to learn to establish my priorities and use them to direct my path. I have set up the 5 F's to navigate my life. They are Faith, Family, Fitness, Friends, and Fun. When faced with a decision on what to do next or how I will plan my day and week, I refer to the 5F's. I then decide what will be scheduled, rescheduled, or eliminated. I don't have time to do everything, so I have to make some wise choices on what needs to be done and what can wait.

My faith in God is always first. The Lord gave me life, He saved me from my sins and changed me on the inside, He has blessed me abundantly, and if everything else in life fails I know He won't. Jesus made it clear when He told His disciples in **Matthew 6:33 "Seek first His kingdom and His righteousness; and all these things shall be added to you."** If we make God our number one priority in life, everything else will fall into place. As we focus on Him, He shows us what is truly important in life and gives us the ability to enjoy and focus on those things. As we put the Lord first by reading the Word, spending time in prayer, going to church to worship with other believers, and doing other spiritual things everything else falls into place. I believe the Lord is even able to bless the rest of our day and make it more productive.

The first commandment says in **Exodus 20:2-3 "I am the LORD your God, who brought you out of the land of Egypt, out of the house of slavery. You shall have no other gods before Me."** Anything that comes before the Lord, or takes preeminence in our life before Him is an idol. Whether it is work, or a girlfriend or boyfriend, or money, or status, or possessions, or whatever… the Lord and His kingdom, must come first. Even our family can become an idol if we put them before the Lord. He wants to be first place in our heart and have our highest love, affection, and devotion.

Family is my second priority. The Bible says in **Exodus 20:12"Honor your father and your mother, that your days may be prolonged in the land which the Lord your God gives you."** I was born into a family that has loved me very much and has taken care of me. We have had a wonderful life growing up together, supporting one another, playing with one another, encouraging one another, loving one another, enjoying one another. I love my parents and brothers and sisters and there is nothing we wouldn't do for one another.

Besides the family I was born into, I now have my own family that is a priority in my life. I love my wonderful wife and children and enjoy spending time with them and growing together. We are a tight group and we are committed to loving and supporting one another no matter what. My family is a very important part of my life and my God-given responsibilities as a husband and father include leading my family, loving my wife, teaching and raising my children, providing financially for them, and spending time with them. **Proverbs 22:6 says "Train up a child in the way he should go, even when he is old he will not depart from it."** Being a good father means I spend time with my children and teach them about life, about loving the Lord, and about loving your neighbor. Being a good husband means I show Christ's love to my wife. My attempts to be a good husband include sharing my life with her, showing interest in her life, praying together, planning together, supporting her goals and pursuits, giving her a break from the kids so she can have some free time, and helping out around the house with the cleaning chores. I fall short many times, but often let her know how much I love her.

Fitness

Fitness is my third priority in life. I have decided that I want to live a long and healthy life and I am going to do whatever it takes to fulfill this goal. I don't plan on getting heart disease, cancer, diabetes, or some other chronic disease because I am taking several diligent steps to promote my health. **1Corinthians 6:19-20 says "Or do you not know that your body is a temple of the Holy Spirit who is in you, whom you have from God, and that you are not your own? For you have been bought with a price: therefore glorify God in your body."** We must honor our body as the temple of the Lord and take care of it. Fitness has been a priority of mine for twenty years. I can say it is a priority because I regularly schedule time each day for fitness-related activities. I plan what my workout will include, when I will do it, and how long it will take. Fitness must be a priority in our lives so that we can live a long and healthy life. If our body is healthy and we are free from sickness and disease, we will have more time to devote to our other priorities.

We must make a one hour investment each day to stay physically fit. One of the favorite quotes of teachers is "If you fail to plan, you plan to fail." Taking time to exercise each day will bring many benefits into our lives including maintaining a healthy weight, maintaining a strong heart, frame and muscles, relieving stress, increasing self esteem and confidence, staying mentally alert, and guarding against the negative effects of aging.

Statistics show us that fitness is not a priority for a *growing* segment of our population (pun intended). Most people make eating a priority. My dad, who is in pretty good shape, has the alarm on his watch set for dinner time. It chimes at 6:00pm and he walks to the dinner table. Most people wouldn't dare neglect their body by not feeding it. However, many people neglect their body everyday by not exercising it. Quite a few people take better care of their dog, by letting it out to exercise, than they do their own body.

Friends are another priority of mine. The Bible says in **John 13:35 "By this all men will know that you are My disciples, if you have love for one another."** If we display the love of Christ to our neighbors, coworkers, and those in our church and community, we will be recognized as disciples of Christ.

My wife and I take specific steps to serve our friends and neighbors and let them know that we love them. She regularly hosts a women's study group on Tuesday mornings. They gather together to talk, encourage one another, solve the world's problems, study the Bible, and pray for one another. They are a loving group that always welcomes visitors. If a neighbor needs help, a tool, a truck, or another point of view on a project, I try to lend a hand. If our friends seem as if they are stressed about something we try to take their kids so they can have a little down time. There is no magic formula to making friends- spend time with them, show them you care, help them when they need it, and encourage them to be all they can be in Christ. Friends are one of life's great investments.

On November 16, 2004 I learned more deeply the value of friends. My wife was teaching aerobics and I was coaching basketball at the local Park & Rec. The attendant brought me the phone while I was on the court and it was my neighbor who told me to hurry home, my house was on fire. When my son and I turned the corner of our driveway we saw our house engulfed in flames and a couple dozen firefighters battling the blaze with three fire trucks. My wife joined me shortly and we watched our house and thirty eight years of possessions burn up. By the time the blaze was extinguished you could see through the house to the backyard. While our worldly possessions perished and we stood with the clothes on our back, we learned a valuable lesson-the most important possession in life is family and friends. Our friends stood with us into the night and cried and prayed with us. They cheered as I carried our dog to safety from underneath the stairs. Neighbors brought clothes and stuffed cash in our hands. They offered a place to stay and help in whatever way they could. Neighbors, church friends, families from the school I taught at, community friends and family members showered us with so many blessings that we were overwhelmed. Their overwhelming support helped us through a difficult time and made us realize how rich we were in the one of life's greatest treasures-friends.

Fun is the final priority in my life. Carpe Diem (seize the day) is a concept we should all live by every day. Everyday should be lived with zest, as if it was our last. We should savor every moment and enjoy it to the fullest.

I met a friend in college who taught me how to have fun. My friend may be on the far left of the fun spectrum. He plans his life around adventures and weekends. At work he punches the clock and does his job adequately. But when it is five o'clock he is out the door and on his way to dinner with a friend, a movie, shopping, or a night on the town. This friend has joined my family for summer vacation and this is where I really saw his passion for having a good time. The week before vacation he went home and got to bed early every night. He was resting up so he could "party hard" and have a good time on vacation. Most of the rest of the world uses vacation as a time to relax and recoup. Not him, he was ready to have some fun.

I love to have fun. My workplace is one of my domains of fun. I love my job and the people I work with. I go out of my way (sometimes too much) to joke around with my co-workers and keep things light. **Proverbs 17:22** says **"A joyful heart is good medicine..."** Studies have shown that stress can detrimentally affect our health. If we can keep things light and in perspective, we can live longer and happier. We must enjoy our career and those we work with.

Besides having fun during our every day routine in life, we must also schedule fun things in our life. Family vacations are a great way to enjoy life. They can be simple like going camping, or extravagant like skiing the Rockies or visiting Disney. Whatever the case, budgeting fun times together is a great investment that you will never forget. You won't remember or look fondly upon finishing that extra project at work for a few extra bucks, but you will remember your son or daughter's first ride down the waterslide at the campground you stayed at during a family outing.

Sometimes my priorities of faith, family, fitness, friends, and fun conflict with one another. Although fitness is a priority in life, it doesn't come before the Lord or my family. I have passed on many bicycle races and road races because they are scheduled on Sunday during church time. Sometimes family duties conflict with my workout schedule. When conflicts arise I have to put off my exercise plans until later, or another day. A rigid workout schedule is not worth the price of your wife walking out on you or your kid ending up on drugs because he never knew you cared.

Sometimes friends can conflict with family and fitness priorities. If my wife agreed to half of the things all her lady friends wanted to do, she would never be at home and she would never work out. While friends are important, they should not come before your family or before taking care of your body. It is hard to be a good friend if you are sick all the time.

Time Management Facts and Figures
By Dr. Donald E. Wetmore

- The average working person spends less than 2 minutes per day in meaningful communication with their spouse or "significant other".
- The average working person spends less than 30 seconds a day in meaningful communication with their children.
- 80% of employees do not want to go to work on Monday morning. By Friday, the rate only drops to 60%.
- The average person gets 1 interruption every 8 minutes, or approximately 7 an hour, or 50-60 per day. The average interruption takes 5 minutes, totaling about 4 hours or 50% of the average workday. 80% of those interruptions are typically rated as "little value" or "no value" creating approximately 3 hours of wasted time per day.
- 95% of the books in this country are purchased by 5% of the population. 95% of self-improvement books, audio tapes, and video tapes purchased are not used.

- 20% of the average workday is spent on "crucial" and "important" things, while 80% of the average workday is spent on things that have "little value" or "no value".
- In the last 20 years, working time has increased by 15% and leisure time has decreased by 33%.
- 90% of those who join health and fitness clubs will stop going within the first 90 days.
- It takes approximately 30 days to establish a new physical or emotional habit.
- The average American watches 28 hours of television per week.
- 78% of workers in America wish they had more time to "smell the roses".
- 49% of workers in America complain that they are on a treadmill.
- Angry people are twice as likely to suffer a heart attack as a person in better control of their emotions.
- 75% of heart attacks occur between the hours of 5:00 a.m.-8:00 a.m., local time.
- More heart attacks occur on Monday than on any other day of the week.
- 25% of sick days are taken for illness. 75% of sick days are taken for other reasons.
- 75% of American workers complain that they are tired.
- The average worker gets 6 hours and 57 minutes of sleep per night.
- The average worker spends 35 minutes per day commuting.
- Good Time Managers do not allocate their time to those who "demand" it, but rather, to those who "deserve" it.
- The most powerful word in our Time Management vocabulary is "no".
- It almost always takes twice as long to complete a task as what we originally thought it would take.
- "A project tends to expand with the time allocated for it." If you give yourself one thing to do, it will take all day. If you give yourself two things to do, you get them both done. If you give yourself a dozen things to do, you may not get 12 done, but you'll get 7 or 8 completed.
- Delegation is an unlimited method to multiply time for achieving results.
- The hardest part about delegation is simply letting go. "If you want a job done right, you have to do it yourself."

- 1 hour of planning will save 10 hours of doing.
- Time Management is not doing the wrong things quicker. That just gets us nowhere faster. Time Management is doing the right things.
- "If you always do what you've always done, you always get what you've always got." To change our output, we must change our input.

Dr. Donald E. Wetmore, a full-time Professional Speaker, is one of the foremost experts on Time Management and Personal Productivity and the author of "Beat the Clock".
Productivity Institute-Time Management Seminars, Copyright 1999
http://www.balancetime.com/

It is cool when priorities overlap. The Lord wants us to live a long and healthy life. Part of honoring the Lord then is taking care of our body by eating right and exercising. My wife doesn't want me in a cranky mood when I get home from work. Part of alleviating the stress of the day, for my family's sake, is taking a 45-minute run after work. My kids want me to see them grow up. If I don't take care of my body through daily exercise, I greatly increase my chances of dying from America's #1 killer-heart disease. Exercising with family and friends can be a fun way of building relationships and keeping fit.

As you strive to establish priorities in your life remember that if you are not physically fit, you will not be able to function at **full** capacity in any area of your life, whether it is related to your faith, family, friends, work, or recreation. Your health affects every area of your life. Determine what your priorities are in life and live by them. Set up a schedule filter that allows you to put the most important things first. Live by your priorities and you will live a healthy and fulfilling life.

Faith in Action: After prayerful consideration make a list in your Bible of what you want the values in your life to be. Set them in order of importance and use today as a day where you prioritize everything you do by your values. Make a running list of things that need to change or be throw out to make room for your new values.

4.

Check up Time

—〰—

Faith

Psalm 26:2 "Examine me, O LORD, and try me; test my mind and my heart."

D avid cried out in Psalm 26 for the Lord to check him out. He wanted to make sure his mind and heart were clean before the Lord. He wanted to know that he was in a right standing with God and that no sin was blocking his prayers or relationship with the Him.

In **Psalm 19:12-14** David said **"Who can discern his errors? Acquit me of hidden faults. Also keep back Your servant from presumptuous sins; Let them not rule over me; Then I will be blameless, and I shall be acquitted of great transgression.**

Let the words of my mouth and the meditation of my heart be acceptable in Your sight, O LORD, my rock and my Redeemer." He was deliberate and thoughtful about his spiritual condition. He prayed for a spiritual checkup. He even asked that the Lord would keep him away from sins that he didn't even know were wrong or offensive to the Lord.

The Bible says that David was a man after the Lord's own heart. What a great testimony to be written down for all of eternity! David's name lives on today in infamy and many Jews, including Jesus, refer to their ancestry as 'the house of David.'

How often do you give yourself a spiritual checkup? Do you cry out to the Lord to examine you to make sure you are mentally and spiritually clean? Most people do not. In fact, most people are like Adam, and run and hide their sin from the Lord. Some people deny their sin, while others rationalize it. Hiding, denying, and rationalizing are all inappropriate responses to sin in our life. They are great tools of man that he uses to self destruct and stay in bondage to sin. As long as you practice one of these, you will live in defeat, and will never change. These are prideful responses that say 'I have it under control' or 'I am entitled to this.' Pride comes before the fall.

The correct response to sin is to come into the light of the Lord, humble yourself, confess your sins, ask for forgiveness, and ask in FAITH for His power to change. Only then can you be free, and walk in His forgiveness and victory. **1John 1:9** says **"If we confess our sins, He is faithful and righteous to forgive us our sins and to cleanse us from all unrighteousness."**

The way to forgiveness and spiritual healing is through examination. We must, at certain times in our walk with the Lord, take time to do a spiritual inventory. We must get quiet before the Lord and reflect on where we have been, where we are now, and where we are going. Any humble heart that searches before the Lord will find answers. If you are honest before the Lord and admit your shortcomings and wrongdoings with a sorrowful and repentant heart, He will hear you. After all, do you really think you can fool Him or lie to Him and get away with it? He is the Truth. He is the Light. And He wants you to come to the Light and expose the darkness. Nothing you can say will shock Him, since He already knows everything anyway. All He wants to do is forgive you and help you change. There is no sin that is more powerful than the blood of Jesus. His blood is the ultimate cleansing power. When David was rotting away with the sin of adultery and murder he turned to the Lord in deep sorrow and repentance. Here are the words of David in the **Psalm 51** as he cried out to the Lord:

> **"Be gracious to me, O God, according to Your loving-kindness; According to the greatness of Your compassion blot out my transgressions.**

Wash me thoroughly from my iniquity and cleanse me
  from my sin. For I know my transgressions, and my
  sin is ever before me.
Against You, You only, I have sinned and done what is
  evil in Your sight,
So that You are justified when You speak and blameless
  when You judge.
Behold, I was brought forth in iniquity, and in sin my
  mother conceived me.
Behold, You desire truth in the innermost being, and in
  the hidden part You will make me know wisdom.
Purify me with hyssop, and I shall be clean; wash me,
  and I shall be whiter than snow.
Make me to hear joy and gladness, Let the bones which
  You have broken rejoice.
Hide Your face from my sins and blot out all my
  iniquities.
Create in me a clean heart, O God, and renew a stead-
  fast spirit within me.
Do not cast me away from Your presence and do not
  take Your Holy Spirit from me.
Restore to me the joy of Your salvation and sustain me
  with a willing spirit.
Then I will teach transgressors Your ways, and sinners
  will be converted to You.
Deliver me from bloodguiltiness, O God, the God of my
  salvation;
Then my tongue will joyfully sing of Your righteousness.
O Lord, open my lips, that my mouth may declare Your
  praise.
For You do not delight in sacrifice, otherwise I would
  give it;
You are not pleased with burnt offering.
The sacrifices of God are a broken spirit;
A broken and a contrite heart, O God, You will not
  despise.

**By Your favor do good to Zion; Build the walls of
  Jerusalem.
Then You will delight in righteous sacrifices,
In burnt offering and whole burnt offering;
Then young bulls will be offered on Your altar."**

I have found at certain times during my walk with the Lord that
I have drifted astray. I feel dryness in my spirit and a separation
from the Lord. During these times I have had to search my heart and
do a check up. I heard some good advice that has proved invaluable to me in getting back on track with the Lord. The advice: each
morning pray Psalm 51 for 30 days. As I have prayed this Psalm and
offered my heart to the Lord, I have found refreshment from Him. I
hope you will find the same. Take time to do a spiritual checkup and
examine your heart before the Lord.

Fitness

How often do you give yourself a physical checkup? What is
your general fitness level? Are you physically fit? Are you an active
person or are you a couch potato? When is the last time you went
to the doctor for a check-up? What is your blood pressure? What
is your BMI (Body Mass Index)? Would you consider yourself too
skinny, average weight, overweight, or obese? How is your diet?
Do you eat too much junk? How many calories do you consume?
Do you get enough fruits and vegetables every day? Do you take
vitamin supplements? Do you get enough fiber in your diet?
These are all questions we should periodically ask ourselves.
These are also questions we should know the answer to. In fact, if
you haven't asked these questions to yourself, or you don't know the
answer, it is time for a little check up.
Here are some indicators that may suggest that you need to
become more physically fit:
You can't see your feet. You have more than one set of clothes in
your closet for different body sizes. The thought of running a mile
is absolutely absurd to you. You have chronic pains in your body.
Your bowels are not functioning properly. You can't fit comfortably

into a regular-sized chair. You can't tie your shoes without great difficulty. Getting the mail or taking out the trash is a workout. You can pinch more than a few inches around your waist. Your arms jiggle when you wave. You circle the parking lot several times when visiting the grocery store, and then drive off because there is not a spot close enough to the entrance. You postpone or cancel outside activity because it is too hot outside.

Most people don't want to address their health. They hide from going to the doctor because they don't want to hear a bad report. Other folks deny that they have an eating problem or exercise problem. They think they can stop whenever they want and go on a diet or begin to exercise again whenever they get in the mood. Some people rationalize their poor health status by blaming others or by blaming environmental conditions or physical problems. While barriers may exist we are all responsible for our own health.

Recently I announced to my elementary school that we would be fitness testing the parents along with the children, during a PTO meeting in the fall. I told them I was warning them now so that they could get in shape. Their reaction was laughter, frightful laughter. Many wives came up and said, "My husband will be doing that one, not me." The parents did not want to be tested on their fitness status. Most said they would die if they had to run a mile. Yikes! That is not a healthy reaction.

If we are going to live a healthy life, we must regularly assess our health to know where we are at. There are three things that are great indicators of our health status: activity level, body composition, and diet. These three items greatly affect our health (of course, so do unhealthy habits like smoking, drugs, etc.). A periodic check up in these areas will give us a good idea of our current health practices.

Your activity level can easily be determined by figuring out how much time you spend being active. The CDC (Center for Disease Control) recommends that people should engage in moderately intense activity for 30 minutes, 5 or more times a week. This is in addition to regular movement during the day. The CDC goes on to define moderate activity as things like walking briskly, biking at 5-9mph, boxing, weightlifting, playing tennis or golf, and other exercises. A simple diary and knowledge of your activity is an easy way to check up your activity level.

Body composition is another way to assess your health. Your body composition is the amount of water, fat, protein, carbohydrates, and other vitamins and minerals in your body. If your body has too much fat, you are at risk for heart disease and other chronic illnesses. It doesn't take rocket science to know whether you are overweight or obese. Most people can look in a mirror and get a good idea of where they are at. However, finding your Body Mass Index (BMI) is a more scientific way to assess your body composition. There are several websites that will calculate and score your BMI by entering your height and weight. Your BMI will describe your weight status which is an indicator or your health. The following table will help you determine your BMI.

Body Mass Index Calculation	
Kilograms And Meters	Formula: weight (kg) / [height (m)]^2 Calculation: [weight (kg) / height (m) / height (m)]
Pounds And Inches	Formula: weight (lb) / [height (in)]^2 x 703 Calculation: [weight (lb) / height (in) / height (in)] x 703 Calculate BMI by dividing weight in pounds (lbs) by height in inches (in) squared and multiplying by a conversion factor of 703.

BMI	Weight Status
Below 18.5	Underweight
18.5-24.9	Normal
25.0-29.9	Overweight
30.0 and above	Obese

Assessing your diet is another key factor in determining your health. Your diet may be a little more difficult to assess. The amount of calories you consume, your portion sizes, and the types of foods you eat may be a good indication of how healthy your diet is. How much you eat in terms of calories, and how much you burn off will directly affect your weight. Nutritional facts may be obtained on most of the foods you eat. You also may want to consider the variety of foods you consume as well as the amounts of fruits and vegetables, whole grains, fats, proteins, and carbohydrates you eat on a daily basis. The Dietary Guidelines for Americans published by the Department of Health and Human Services is a great place to start analyzing your diet. The Dietary Guidelines makes some key recommendations that everyone should follow: consume a variety of nutrient dense foods and beverages within and among the basic food groups while choosing foods that limit the intake of saturated fats, cholesterol, added sugars, salt, and alcohol. Periodic assessment of what we eat is crucial to a healthy lifestyle.

Estimated Calorie Requirements (in Kilocalories) for Each Gender and Age Group at Three Levels of Physical Activity

			Activity Level	
Gender	**Age (Years)**	**Sedentary**	**Moderately Active**	**Active**
Child	2-3	1,000	1,000-1,400	1,000-1,400
Female	4-8	1,200	1,400-1,600	1,400-1,800
	9-13	1,600	1,600-2,000	1,800-2,200
	14-18	1,800	2,000	2,400
	19-30	2,000	2,000-2,200	2,400
	31-50	1,800	2,000	2,200
	51+	1,600	1,800	2,000-2,200
Male	4-8	1,400	1,400-1,600	1,600-2,000
	9-13	1,800	1,800-2,200	2,000-2,600
	14-18	2,200	2,400-2,800	2,800-3,200
	19-30	2,400	2,600-2,800	3,000
	31-50	2,200	2,400-2,600	2,800-3,000
	51+	2,000	2,200-2,400	2,400-2,800

From Dietary Guidelines for Americans 2005
USDA

Don't avoid giving yourself a check up in the areas of physical activity, body composition, and diet. Be thoughtful, realistic, and honest when assessing your lifestyle habits. If you can't be objective, then ask a friend or loved one to report what they have noticed about your habits. When you have made a realistic assessment about your habits, do something about it! If you need to improve on your amount of exercise then make plans to do so. If you are overweight or obese don't rationalize, justify, or make fun of yourself—do something about it. If you have a bad diet, change your eating habits. The purpose of giving yourself a check up is so that you can develop a strategic plan to change unhealthy habits if you discover that are problems. **Proverbs 14:16** says **"A wise man is cautious and turns away from evil, but a fool is arrogant and careless."** Once you have assessed your health take some diligent steps to change.

Faith in Action: Calculate your BMI. For the next three days calculate the amount of calories you consume. Analyze your results and make some changes if necessary.

5.

Glorify God in Your Body

—∿—

Faith

1 Corinthians 6:19-20 says "Or do you not know that your body is a temple of the Holy Spirit who is in you, whom you have from God, and that you are not your own? For you have been bought with a price: therefore glorify God in your body."

Our body was designed to be the temple of the Lord. What an awesome thought! The God of heaven and earth wants to live inside of us. He does not want to dwell in a church or in the Ark of the Covenant. He wants to live inside of us and have intimate fellowship with us.

Before Jesus left earth He promised His disciples that He would send a Helper to lead them and guide them into all the truth. The Helper is the Holy Spirit. He said in **Luke 24:49 "And behold, I am sending forth the promise of My Father upon you; but you are to stay in the city until you are clothed with power from on high."** The disciples received the baptism of the Holy Spirit on the day of Pentecost. They were filled with God's Spirit and power. As they went out and preached, others were saved and filled with God's Spirit as well. **Acts 2:17 says "'And it shall be in the last days' God says 'That I will pour forth of My Spirit on all mankind'…"**

God's plan for our lives is salvation and the filling of His Spirit. He desires for us to be His temple. **2 Corinthians 6:14-18 says "Do not be bound together with unbelievers; for what partnership have righteousness and lawlessness, or what fellowship has light with darkness? Or what harmony has Christ with Belial, or what has a believer in common with an unbeliever? Or what agreement has the temple of God with idols? For we are the temple of the living God; just as God said, "I WILL DWELL IN THEM AND WALK AMONG THEM; AND I WILL BE THEIR GOD, AND THEY SHALL BE MY PEOPLE. "Therefore, COME OUT FROM THEIR MIDST AND BE SEPARATE," says the Lord. "AND DO NOT TOUCH WHAT IS UNCLEAN; And I will welcome you. "And I will be a father to you, And you shall be sons and daughters to Me," says the Lord Almighty."** God wants to dwell in us and walk among us. His favorite dwelling place is a heart that hungers and thirsts for Him. As we become filled with His Spirit we must surrender wholly to Him. We must seek after truth, righteousness, love and peace. Our temple must be a holy temple for the Lord. We must fill our spirit with good things that honor and glorify the Lord. There is no room for junk, sin, or darkness in the temple of God. As the scripture states, there is no fellowship with light and darkness. God does not wink His eye at sin. He does not condone drunkenness and carousing. He is not the God portrayed in the movies that smokes cigars or causes the wind to blow up ladies skirts to reveal their panties. He is true light and is looking for hearts that want the light.

When the scripture says "glorify God in your body" it is requesting specific action be taken on our part to magnify the Lord. The act of glorifying God may be one of prayer, praise, worship, or adoration. We must make an effort to worship and praise our King. Glorifying God means always honoring Him in our actions. Glorifying God also means denying sin a place in our mind, heart, body, or life. We can glorify God in our temple by keeping it holy and pure.

Jesus ran the money changers out of the temple. He turned over their tables and beat them with a whip as they fled. He saw that they were perverting the temple of God. He said that His Father's house was a house of prayer. If we want to be the temple of God we must run the sin out of our lives. We must be careful what we watch, listen to, read, and speak. We must set our mind and our heart on God's things and not the ways of the world. The closer we draw near to God, the more of Him we will experience.

Jesus said in **Matthew 7:6 "Do not give what is holy to dogs, and do not throw your pearls before swine..."** If He told His disciples to treasure what is precious and don't just give it to anyone, don't you think the Father will do the same. He will not pour out His Spirit on an unclean vessel. He will look for vessels that are hungry and thirsty for Him alone. Glorify God in your body and He will fill you to overflowing with the power and sweetness of His Holy Spirit.

Fitness

As I stood in the line at a convenience store, a young man in front of me dumped his purchases onto the counter for the clerk to ring up. The young man was about 20 years old, dressed in jean shorts and a white tank top. He was ruddy, and slender. His evening snacks consisted of three Hostess snacks, a bag of chips, and an extra large (64ounce), bladder buster soda. He was probably on a road trip as I was and needed a little energy to drive into the night. I imagine his selections contained over 1000 calories, over 50 grams of fat, and ZERO nutrients (sorry, caffeine and sugar are not considered nutrients; they will keep your body running, but in a hyped up, jacked up state). Unless the light bulb comes on soon, his temple will begin to deteriorate and enlarge in an unhealthy manner.

The charge to glorify God in your body means we should take care of the physical structure of our temple in such a way that the Lord is glorified. In other words, when people look at you they should be thinking 'Glory to God, what a beautiful creation of the Lord.' Your temple should look neat, healthy, and fit. Your temple should in some way represent the character of God. It should not be a rundown, falling apart, shabby temple. It should not be a temple that could at any moment implode from a heart attack due to serious neglect. Is your body physically fit and able to serve the Lord in full capacity?

When the Lord gave instructions for His temple to be built, it was magnificent and detailed. The best materials and craftsmanship were used. Those who contributed to the building of it were honored to be able to glorify the Lord in its construction. It was breathtaking. When the disciples toured the temple with Jesus they marveled at its beauty.

If the Bible told us to glorify God in our car what would you do? Hopefully, you would take care of your car. You would wash and wax it regularly. You would get the French fries out of from under the seat and vacuum the carpet. You would Windex the windows and wipe down the dashboards and doors and spray a little Armor-All on them to make them shiny. You would keep good tires and brakes on your car. You would make all the necessary scheduled maintenances like oil changes, timing belts, etc. You would put good fuel in your car that is free from contaminants. It is sad that so many people take much better care of their car than they do their own body.

Maintaining a glorious temple means that we have adopted a resolute attitude that states two important things: our temple is honorable and we must make purposeful steps to care for it. Your body is a tremendous gift from God. It is a remarkable creation that is able to make incredible adjustments to its environment so that it can sustain itself. Your body is able to store energy, regulate its temperature, fight stress, adapt to extreme conditions, fight sickness, and basically heal itself just to name a few functions. God has blessed you with this temple so you may honor Him with your life. Your temple is more valuable than your diamond ring, your car, your computer, or your plasma television set. It is more valuable than your home, because it is your spirit's home (and God's Spirit) for your entire life. You should greatly honor your body as such.

If you take care or your body (temple) it will take care of you. Basic care for the temple includes feeding it good nutrients, providing it with plenty of water, exercising it, cleaning it, and protecting it from harmful stimulus (drugs, smoke, radiation, junk food, etc.) Care is a verb. Your temple needs active and deliberate plans for its upkeep. The more you take care of it, the longer it will last and perform at maximum potential. (It almost sounds like a car, doesn't it?) When you reach 50, 60, 70, and well into your 80's your temple can remain strong and vital. Honoring and caring for your temple are two things you can do to glorify God.

Harmful Effects of Smoking

Among currents smokers, 57% of male deaths and 50% of female deaths are due to the effects of smoking.

30% of all cancers are smoking related including cancer of the lungs, larynx, oral cavity, esophagus, bladder, pancreas, uterus, cervix, kidney, and stomach.

Smokers increase their chances of death from emphysema or bronchitis by 10 times.

21% of all heart disease in the country is smoking related. Smoking triples the risk of heart disease.

Smoking increases the risk of infertility and impotence, and increases the risk of cataracts, hearing loss, vision loss, bone weakening, and rheumatoid arthritis.

Cigarette smoke contains over 4,800 chemicals, 69 of which are known to cause cancer. Nicotine is one such chemical that is highly addictive.

Smoking causes premature wrinkling of the skin, discoloration of the teeth and fingertips, premature graying, bad smelling breath, clothes, and hair, poor sense of taste and smell, and persistent coughing.

From Tobaccofreekids.org and the American Lung Association

Glorifying God in your body is a stewardship assignment. A wise steward will diligently follow the command of the Lord and be blessed by Him. A lazy steward may be chastised by the Lord for lack of faithfulness.

One of the ladies that attended my wife's aerobics class made a commitment to take care of her temple. Over the course of three years she experienced a trickle down effect in her health. She began to exercise and got hooked and lost over thirty pounds. Next she quit smoking. Then she began to eat right. Her love for her temple and taking care of herself finally resulted in her going back to college to finish her degree and honor the Lord with her life and talents. The trickle down effect of health and wellness created a desire in her to glorify God in her body and life.

Don't settle for a rundown, beat up temple. Don't struggle through this life being overweight and plagued by health problems. Decide today that you are going to be like Nehemiah and rebuild the temple of the Lord. If you begin today to care for your temple maybe you can fulfill the word in **Haggai 2:9 "The latter glory of this house will be greater than the former...."**

Faith in Action: Go buy a case of water and put it under your desk at work. Drink two bottles per day. Don't drink any other beverages until you have consumed your water.

6.

Abundant Life

—ɯ—

Faith

John 10:10 "The thief comes only to steal and kill and destroy; I came that they may have life, and have it abundantly."

What is abundant life? What would the ultimate lifestyle entail? What components would make your life truly successful, rewarding, and fulfilling? What is life really about? Some people may define abundant life as winning the lottery and being able to do whatever they want. This view may suggest that material things will bring abundant life. Obviously, you can't buy happiness, or love. Others may define abundant life as being able to travel to many places and see the world. Others may define abundant life as being able to enjoy hobbies like hunting, fishing, or sun bathing all the time. Our concept of abundant life will determine our goals in life and our motivation to achieve this higher standard of life.

The Bible actually defines life, or more importantly, eternal life, as a state of being in God's presence. Jesus came so that we can have abundant life-fellowship with the Heavenly Father. Being in God's presence is a spiritual place where we enjoy the good things of His character and Spirit: love, joy, peace, patience, goodness, kindness, faithfulness, and self-control. Abundant life involves knowing God and making the journey through life hand in hand with our Creator. Can you imagine a life where stressful situations just bounce off you because you have this inner peace and joy that just radiates from within because you know that everything is going to be alright because God is on your side? Can you imagine waking up every morning and saying "It's a great day on planet Earth and I can't wait to get out there and experience life?" How about not only saying it, but also meaning it? Life with the Lord is filled with hope, joy, and peace.

In 2001 my wife and I became foster parents to three children who lost their mother in a car accident. The children were staying with their grandparents until some alleged abuse occurred and Family Services stepped in and took custody. Within a few weeks they ended up with us. The two girls were ages seventeen and thirteen, and the boy was eleven. They had seen enough of the bad side of life to last a lifetime. They never knew their father, the mother was in and out of their life and allegedly on drugs, and there was other reported abuse that took them from their home. Their concept of life or abundant life was not a very bright one. They had hurts, fears, mistrust, doubts, and emptiness resulting from their losses. Helping them cope with the past and look forward to a brighter future was a daunting task.

We tried to show them the possibilities that life had to offer by sharing our lives and our faith with them. We stressed the importance of trusting in the Lord, valuing their education, making wise choices, and using their God-given talents. We introduced them to our loving families and showed them what family life could be like. We took them on a vacation to the beach and even took the boy snowboarding in the Rockies to show them the beauty that lay beyond our small county. We gave the oldest girl a job at our business and tried to teach her the value of hard work. We did everything we could to expand their horizons and instill values and seeds of possibility in them. In the year that they were with us we tried to help them define abundant life.

No one has a perfect life. Many people have experienced rejection, disappointment, humiliation, sorrow, and pain. These negative experiences cannot be the building blocks that form our concepts about life. Abundant life is more than the absence of negative experiences. It is more than monetary gain. It is more than experiencing things that exist in this world. Abundant life involves fellowship with eternity. Abundant life involves a spiritually fulfilling life that transcends the five senses. Abundant life is walking hand in hand with the Lord. Jesus came so that we could all experience abundant life through faith in Him and a relationship with the Father.

As we grow in our relationship with the Lord we begin to trust Him more as our Shepherd, Provider, Healer, Protection, Peace, Victory, Love, Hope, and Life. Jesus said in **Mark 9:23 "All things are possible to him who believes."** The more we know Father God, the more we trust in Him, and experience the abundant life that He has prepared for us. The possibilities of life with God are endless.

Fitness

Not only does the Lord want us to experience abundant life through a relationship with Him, but He also wants our bodies to experience abundant life. He wants our body to be healthy and strong. Did you know that Jesus was in the health ministry? The Bible goes to great detail of how He went about healing the sick. **Acts 10:38** says **"You know of Jesus of Nazareth, how God anointed Him with the Holy Spirit and with power, and how He went about doing good and healing all who were oppressed by the devil, for God was with Him."** Jesus desired for everyone to be healthy and whole. His ministry agenda consisted of preaching the gospel and healing the sick. He would stay up well into the night praying for the sick. He would walk miles to pray for a dying girl or raise the dead. He sent a very clear message to the world— 'I WANT MY PEOPLE TO BELIEVE IN ME, AND I WANT THEM TO BE HEALTHY SO THEY CAN SERVE ME.' **In Mark 1:40-41** it says **"And a leper came to Jesus, beseeching Him and falling on his knees before Him, and saying, "If You are willing, You can make me clean." Moved with compassion, Jesus stretched out His hand and touched him, and said to him, "I am willing; be cleansed."** If you were ever wondering if it was God's will for you to be healed, you can rest assured on the words of Jesus. He said very clearly that HE IS WILLING.

God never desired for you to be sick or unhealthy. His plan is not for sickness to rule in your body. He is the Healer. His Son made a clear statement about His will and purpose. **3John 1:2** says **"Beloved, I pray that in all respects you may prosper and be in good health, just as your soul prospers."** Why would the apostle John pray for health if it was contrary to the will of God?

The abundant life that the Lord wants us to have involves a healthy one. If we know the Lord wants us to be healthy, then we must align our actions to fulfill His will. We must take steps to live a healthy life so that we can experience the abundant life He has prepared for us. Just as we don't want sin to reign in our life and take away the abundant spiritual life, we must also be diligent to keep unhealthy habits out of our life so that we can experience abundant life in respects to our physical health.

Carrying extra weight around, for example, makes you uncomfortable or miserable and does not reflect the abundant life that the Lord wants for us. Just the fold at the belt line is downright annoying. Shortness of breath from a brief walk, nagging mouth sores from smokeless tobacco, arthritis, diabetes, high blood pressure, migraine headaches, backaches, emphysema from smoking, cancer, and so many other health problems are not the abundant life that the Lord has for us. Physical ailments that come upon us due to no fault of our own are one thing, but if we become ill due to neglect then we are to blame. Poor choices and laziness can interfere with the abundant life.

While I was living with my parents in high school and college our neighborhood had a walking man. The walking man was a tall slender gentleman who was always out walking the neighborhood. He walked at a brisk pace and could usually be caught out cruising two or three times a day. When I was in college during a run one day I stopped and asked him how far he was walking today. His response was, "the usual, 6-8 miles."

I was impressed that someone in their sixties could walk that far everyday. Nearly 20 years later, during a visit to my parent's house, I saw him again, walking. He looked nearly the same and had the same brisk pace. I pulled my car over and asked him how he was doing. He stopped to chat through my car window. I reached out and shook his hand and he returned a vice grip handshake. He was the picture of health. I told him that I remembered him walking during my high school years and was glad to see him still going at it. I told him I was a PE teacher and would like to share his story with my students. He informed me that he had recently turned 80 and was walking 2-3 miles a day when it was cool outside. I praised him for his commitment and told him I would see him in another 10 years. Wow, he looked great! I was inspired in the fact that walking is a great way to maintain your health way into your senior years. I am sure the walking man is living the abundant life.

Popular Factors Considered to Define Abundant Life

- Faith and a relationship with God
- A happy marriage
- Close friends and personal relationships
- Having children
- Personal health and physical fitness
- Financial security
- Fulfilling occupation
- Enjoyable hobbies and leisure time
- A good sense of humor and the ability to laugh easily
- A sense of purpose, destiny, and usefulness
- A satisfactory sex life
- Material comforts and possessions
- Volunteering, helping others, and making a difference in the world
- Education level and intellectual stimulation
- Creativity and personal expression

From various sources

Please realize the Lord wants you healthy. He wants you to get up every morning and feel great. He wants you to look in the mirror after the shower and smile because you are looking and feeling good. He wants you to have the energy and stamina that you need to have a fulfilling day. He wants you to be able to get out and enjoy His creation, and enjoy your children without any health restrictions. He wants you to fulfill the ministry that He has for you with joy and zest for life. He wants you to live a long and blessed life. Seize the abundant life that Christ has for you. Take steps every day to promote a healthy life.

Faith in Action: Make plans today for a fun-filled, active vacation with the ones you love. No business, no stress, just fun and activity.

7.

Wisdom is Crying Out

—ɯ—

Faith

Proverbs 1:20-33
²⁰Wisdom shouts in the street, She lifts her voice in the square;
²¹At the head of the noisy streets she cries out;
At the entrance of the gates in the city she utters her sayings:
²²"How long, O naive ones, will you love being simple-minded?
And scoffers delight themselves in scoffing
And fools hate knowledge?
²³"Turn to my reproof, behold, I will pour out my spirit on you;
I will make my words known to you.
²⁴"Because I called and you refused, I stretched out my hand and no one paid attention;
²⁵And you neglected all my counsel And did not want my reproof;
²⁶I will also laugh at your calamity; I will mock when your dread comes,
²⁷When your dread comes like a storm And your calamity comes like a whirlwind,
When distress and anguish come upon you.

²⁸"Then they will call on me, but I will not answer; they will seek me diligently but they will not find me,

²⁹Because they hated knowledge, and did not choose the fear of the LORD.

³⁰"They would not accept my counsel, they spurned all my reproof.

³¹"So they shall eat of the fruit of their own way, and be satiated with their own devices.

³²"For the waywardness of the naive will kill them, and the complacency of fools will destroy them.

³³"But he who listens to me shall live securely, and will be at ease from the dread of evil."

The Bible is loaded with wisdom and instruction about how we should live our lives. Sunday school lessons teach us how we all should act. The preacher will also expand on the scriptures and point us in the direction of God's ways. There are preachers on the television and preachers on the radio. There are thousands of good Christian books that teach us how to live for God. Godly mothers, fathers, grandmas, and grandpas have also told us how we are supposed to act. "Say your prayers. Go to church. Don't talk like that. You better wait until you are married. Stay away from drugs. Give your life to the Lord and live for Him."

WISDOM IS CRYING OUT IN THE STREETS. SHE IS MAKING KNOWN THE PATHS OF LIFE. Are you listening?

When I read Proverbs chapter one, it brings the fear of the Lord on me. I have great concern because of the lack of attention that too many people give to wisdom. People who don't listen to wisdom have a certain and unhappy ending. The Bible calls folks who don't listen to wisdom fools. **Proverbs 1:7** says that **"fools despise wisdom and instruction."** Have you ever met someone who is a know-it-all? How about someone who says—"you can't tell me what to do"? How about someone who just doesn't care too much about anything? These are dangerous folks who are headed in the wrong direction. Caution—stay away from them. Some people don't want to hear sound advice or wisdom. Some people think they know everything there is to know in life. **Proverbs 13:20** says

"He who walks with wise men will be wise, But the companion of fools will suffer harm." Choose your friends wisely and try to choose friends who are wise.

When you hear the truth and it weighs heavy on your heart, you are getting your chance to respond and do something about it. If you are wise you will greatly treasure new wisdom and knowledge. Part of treasuring knowledge is ACTING upon it. Jesus said in **Matthew 7:24-27 "Therefore everyone who hears these words of Mine and acts on them, may be compared to a wise man who built his house on the rock. And the rain fell, and the floods came, and the winds blew and slammed against that house; and yet it did not fall, for it had been founded on the rock. Everyone who hears these words of Mine and does not act on them, will be like a foolish man who built his house on the sand. The rain fell, and the floods came, and the winds blew and slammed against that house; and it fell—and great was its fall."** Those who hear wisdom and act upon it are wise. Wise people are blessed and live a life that is protected from the destruction of the world.

I frequently heard a quote from my dad about school and grades as I progressed from grade school to high school to college. He used to say "You might as well give it 100% of your effort because you have to put the time in anyway." About the time report cards came out I would really wish I had followed his advice. The meaning of the words wouldn't really dawn on me until it was often too late. Now I frequently use those words with my son and the children I teach and coach.

The wise act...and the foolish do nothing. Which are you? **Proverbs 1** above says that **"the complacency of fools will destroy them."** Apathy is a terrible bondage that can ruin your life. If you know the right thing to do and don't do it, it can come back to bite you later. The consequence of being foolish is destruction. Don't be lazy about getting your life together and acting on sound wisdom.

Have you ever heard a message in church and thanked the Lord because you knew that message was divinely prepared for your friend who has been going through some difficulties and is sitting two pews down from you? You celebrate because he is getting the word he needed to inspire his faith to make it through his trials.

After the service you greet your friend and say, 'wasn't that a great message?' and he just shrugs and says 'it was alright.' You smile and move on but later shake your head in utter disbelief because your friend must not have heard a word the preacher said. Some people just aren't paying attention or they just don't want to get up and act.

Pray that the Lord will give you ears to hear His wisdom from whatever source He chooses, and feet to act upon what you hear.

Fitness

Eat your vegetables. Buckle up. You had better take that weight off. Do your homework. Why don't you go outside and get some exercise? Don't drink and drive. Smoking is hazardous to your health. Be careful about the friends you make. Watch the speed limit. Take your vitamins. Wear your helmet. Drink responsibly. Put on your sunscreen. Quit eating all that junk. Put your jacket on, it's cold outside. Wisdom is crying out.

Most folks know what the right thing to do is; they just don't do it. They know they shouldn't eat a bunch of chips, sodas, and excess sugar. They know they should eat their five helpings of fruits and vegetables every day. They know it is unhealthy to carry extra weight on their bodies. They know it is important to exercise. However, they just don't act on their knowledge. They live in some fantasy land with a teenage mentality that believes they are invincible.

Most teenagers think they can do anything and there will be no consequences or ramifications. They don't think anything bad will happen to them. They think the sky is the limit. They drive 90 miles per hour on country roads and don't ever consider the possibility of a crash. They drink excessively or do drugs and never stop to think that they might get caught or worse yet, die. They sleep around and don't think they will contract an STD or get pregnant. They point a gun at someone and shoot them and don't realize the gravity of their actions or the fact that they are cutting someone's life short. Too many people are the same way about their health. They eat and drink way too much, or they continue to smoke, they carry around too much weight, they don't exercise, and they naively think there will be no consequences. Diabetes, high blood pressure, heart disease, cancer, liver disease, lung disease, accidents, and AIDS are real consequences that are most often the result of lifestyle behaviors. Health experts have concluded that the following lifestyle choices are the leading health indicators: physical activity, overweight and obesity, tobacco use, substance abuse, responsible sexual behavior, mental health, injury and violence, environmental quality, immunization, and access to health care. Our actions in all these categories determine our health. It is time to wake up and use the knowledge we have acquired to practice healthy behaviors. Paul said in **1 Corinthians 13:11 "When I was a child, I used to speak like a child, think like a child, reason like a child; when I became a man, I did away with childish things."** People need to stop thinking like teenagers and grow up in their outlook on life and realize that their behavior has real consequences for their health. Unless you have had your head buried in the sand for years, you can't hide from the fact that there are things you can do to improve your health.

Every ten years the experts from 400 national agencies evaluate the health of our nation and prepare a report with health goals and objectives for the next ten years. The chart below lists 28 major goals.

Besides these major goals, the experts have created 467 objectives in 28 focus areas. Many objectives focus on interventions designed to reduce or eliminate illness, disability, and premature death among individuals and communities. Others focus on broader issues, such as improving access to quality health care, strengthening public health services, and improving the availability and dissemination of health-related information. Each objective has a target for specific improvements to be achieved by the year 2010. The entire document is several hundred pages long.

The collective wisdom of all these agencies is crying out that there is something you can do to change your health status. In fact, there are a lot of things you can do to change your health. The experts have done the research, determined the causes of health problems, and discovered how to prevent or correct many of those problems. All we have to do is follow their advice. We must be diligent to listen to wisdom regarding our health and act upon it.

Healthy People 2010 Goals

1. Improve access to comprehensive, high-quality health care services.
2. Prevent illness and disability related to arthritis and other rheumatic conditions, osteoporosis, and chronic back conditions.
3. Reduce the number of new cancer cases as well as the illness, disability, and death caused by cancer.
4. Reduce new cases of chronic kidney disease and its complications, disability, death, and economic costs.
5. Through prevention programs, reduce the disease and economic burden of diabetes, and improve the quality of life for all persons who have or are at risk for diabetes.
6. Promote the health of people with disabilities, prevent secondary conditions, and eliminate disparities between people with and without disabilities in the U.S. population.
7. Increase the quality, availability, and effectiveness of educational and community-based programs designed to prevent disease and improve health and quality of life.
8. Promote health for all through a healthy environment.
9. Improve pregnancy planning and spacing and prevent unintended pregnancy.
10. Reduce food borne illnesses.
11. Use communication strategically to improve health.
12. Improve cardiovascular health and quality of life through the prevention, detection, and treatment of risk factors; early identification and treatment of heart attacks and strokes; and prevention of recurrent cardiovascular events.
13. Prevent HIV infection and its related illness and death.
14. Prevent disease, disability, and death from infectious diseases, including vaccine-preventable diseases.
15. Reduce injuries, disabilities, and deaths due to unintentional injuries and violence.
16. Improve the health and well-being of women, infants, children, and families.
17. Ensure the safe and effective use of medical products.
18. Improve mental health and ensure access to appropriate, quality mental health services.

19. Promote health and reduce chronic disease associated with diet and weight.
20. Promote the health and safety of people at work through prevention and early intervention.
21. Prevent and control oral and craniofacial diseases, conditions, and injuries and improve access to related services.
22. Improve health, fitness, and quality of life through daily physical activity.
23. Ensure that Federal, Tribal, State, and local health agencies have the infrastructure to provide essential public health services effectively.
24. Promote respiratory health through better prevention, detection, treatment, and education efforts.
25. Promote responsible sexual behaviors, strengthen community capacity, and increase access to quality services to prevent sexually transmitted diseases (STDs) and their complications.
26. Reduce substance abuse to protect the health, safety, and quality of life for all, especially children.
27. Reduce illness, disability, and death related to tobacco use and exposure to secondhand smoke.
28. Improve the visual and hearing health of the Nation through prevention, early detection, treatment, and rehabilitation.

From U.S. Department of Health and Human Services

When I was a child and adolescent I remember spending time, sometimes overnights at my grandparents' house. My grandma would nag my uncle about all his snacking. I can still hear her words crystal clear—"You had better lose that damn weight or it is going to kill you." (She was Irish and feisty.) She must have said it hundreds of times over the years. My uncle would laugh it off and say "Oh Mom." My uncle is a hard worker and spent many hours on construction sites. He had little time for exercise and would often stop at the convenience store for chips, a candy bar, and a Coke. Through poor snacking, bad eating habits, and lack of exercise, he gained weight. About a year and a half ago he was diagnosed with cancer of the rectum. The cancer was large in size and radical measures had to be taken. Through surgery and chemotherapy, the cancer was removed. However, the operation was not without incident. My uncle has lost the function of his rectum and now must wear a colostomy bag for the rest of his life. He has to deal with a literal pain in the side for the rest of his life. Wisdom was crying out but he didn't listen. Gran told him to lose weight but he didn't act on her pleadings. Now he is facing some tough consequences. I am pleased to say that he is a fighter and has a very positive outlook on life. He has now begun exercising and says, "I never thought I could look forward each day to getting up and walking a few miles." He loves it. He has also promised that if my book ever makes it and I make the Oprah show, he will be the skinny guy in the back!

Listen to the voice of wisdom and take care of your body. Do the healthy things that you know are right and have heard over and over again. Your body will love you for it and you will greatly reduce your chances of developing a disease related to unhealthy lifestyles.

Faith in Action: Put on your running shoes and go to the street. Walk or jog in one direction for ten minutes, turn around, and walk or jog back. Repeat this every other day. Each week add one minute to your direction until you get to 30 minutes each direction for walkers (20 minutes each direction for joggers).

8.

Love Yourself

—⚬—

Faith

Psalm 139:13-16 "For You formed my inward parts; You covered me in my mother's womb. I will praise You, for I am fearfully and wonderfully made; Marvelous are Your works, and that my soul knows very well. My frame was not hidden from You, when I was made in secret, and skillfully wrought in the lowest parts of the earth. Your eyes saw my substance, being yet unformed. And in Your book they all were written, the days fashioned for me, when as yet there were none of them."

God made you special. He carefully crafted you in the womb. You are a master work of His. You are unique in every way and no one has your gifts, talents, temperament, and personality. He thought you were special enough to create and prepare a plan for your life. He loved you enough that He sent His Son to pay the price for your sins by dying on the cross in your place. Even though you were hostile towards God in the rebellion of your sins, He put the blame and punishment of His wrath on Jesus. He loved you so much He wanted to provide a plan of salvation for you. God loves you enough that He wants to spend this life and eternity with you in close fellowship. **John 3:16** says **"For God so loved the world that**

He sent His only Son, that whosoever will believe in Him will not perish but have everlasting life."

Jesus was crucified with His arms wide open. They were wide open to receive you into His family. Jesus said in **Matthew 11:28 "Come unto me all you who are weary and heavy laden and I will give you rest."** He came to earth to seek and save you because you are valuable to Him. He even told a parable about you in **Luke 15:4-7** saying **"What man among you, if he has a hundred sheep and has lost one of them, does not leave the ninety-nine in the open pasture and go after the one which is lost until he finds it? When he has found it, he lays it on his shoulders, rejoicing. And when he comes home, he calls together his friends and his neighbors, saying to them, 'Rejoice with me, for I have found my sheep which was lost!' I tell you that in the same way, there will be more joy in heaven over one sinner who repents than over ninety-nine righteous persons who need no repentance."** You are the one sheep He finds of great value. He wants to find you. Now if God loves you as His child, and thinks you are so special, don't you think you should love yourself? If He finds great value in you, don't you think you should find great value in yourself?

When I became a parent I understood more fully God's love for me as His child because I have a profound love for my own children. During the birth of my son there were some complications. His forehead was hitting my wife's tailbone in face presentation and he had to be delivered by C-section. When he came out his forehead had some swelling and he looked like Cro-magnum man. The post op nurse said the protruded forehead would probably never go away. I could care less. He was the most beautiful creature I had ever seen. I was in love with him and could care less if he had six toes or four fingers. He was a beautiful gift from the Lord. (The nurse turned out to be wrong, and the swelling went away after a couple of days.) The more I grow as a parent the more fully I understand God's unconditional love for all of His children. I have come to comprehend that He loves me as much as I love my own children. I love them for who they are as special and unique creations that are a little part of me. As I convey my love to my children I hope that they are able to understand how valuable they are. As I shower love and blessings on them I hope they are able to understand that they are special, unique, wonderful, and worthy of love. If they understand my love for them they will have confidence in who they are and will be able to love themselves and recognize their value. They will have a confidence in life that says 'I am worth something because my dad thinks I am special. He loves me for who I am so I am worthy of love. I will love my self and take care of my self and make something special of my life because he believes in me and loves me."

Your self worth and self value are vital keys to a joyful and successful life. Your self worth is developed from your ability to love yourself. Can you honestly say "I love myself"? Self love is developed by the understanding that God loves you and thinks you are valuable. If He loves you, then you are lovable and must love yourself. Loving yourself means accepting who you are and taking care of yourself. Loving yourself means valuing your life and making it the very best that you can. How you take care of yourself and what you do with your life are two very strong indicators of how much you love yourself.

Jesus said in **Matthew 22:39 "You shall love your neighbor as yourself."** Your ability to love others is contingent upon your ability to love yourself. If you do not truly love yourself then you will have a difficult time loving others. Jesus said the entire Bible can be summed up in two things: loving God with all your life and loving your neighbor as yourself. If you truly desire to make something of your life then you have to do two things: accept God's love for you as His special and wonderful child, and begin to love yourself. There is only one you. Love yourself for who you are and share yourself with the world.

Fitness

Many of the ways that a person abuses his or her body begin as a lack of self esteem and lack of self love. Subjecting your body to excessive alcohol, drugs, overeating, smoking, or unprotected sex are all signs of lack of self worth. People who willfully damage their body by self-inflicted abuse have psychological issues that are rooted in some type of lack of self worth and lack of self love. Think about it. Why would you abuse and defile something you love? It doesn't make sense.

Most smokers began smoking when they were teens. Whether they will actually admit it or not, most began because of peer pressure and lack of self esteem (self worth). They wanted to be accepted or look cool so they copped a rebellious attitude and began to smoke. They did not love themselves enough for who they were and see enough value in themselves so they tried to win acceptance by smoking. They subconsciously thought they would be a more loveable person if they identified with a gang of people who were also unlovable and were demonstrating it by abusing their bodies. Maybe it sounds a little far fetched but I can promise you that nobody begins smoking, or drinking, because it tastes great. I tried a cigarette in the back of my dad's car and nearly coughed my lungs and throat out. I was also green and nauseous for an hour because of all the toxins I had just introduced to my body.

Most people begin drinking alcohol for the same reasons as smokers. They also find out that alcohol enables them to mentally escape their feelings of insecurity and sometimes even become someone they are not. Their lack of self love causes them to constantly get drunk to escape who they are.

Overeating is another example of a lack of self love and lack of self worth. Most people who overeat confess that they find some comfort in food. They have experienced some kind of rejection in the world and have allowed that rejection to seep into their heart and cause them to doubt their self worth. They comfort themselves with food. Their lack of love for their self and body causes them to seek comfort in food and they become overweight or obese. Since they don't love themselves they continue to mistreat their body and subject it to health concerns brought on by excessive weight.

Having multiple sex partners and practicing unprotected sex are other indicators of lack of self love. Young men and women who search for love and acceptance by trying to sexually satisfy a boyfriend or girlfriend or even a stranger are searching for love in the wrong place. Society has misguided us into thinking that sex equals love. Often young people who have no self love feel that if they offer sex to someone, that person will love them and then

---

Twelve Steps to Recovery as defined by Alcoholics Anonymous

1. We admitted we were powerless over alcohol—that our lives had become unmanageable.
2. Came to believe that a power greater than ourselves could restore us to sanity.
3. Made a decision to turn our will and our lives over to the care of God as we understood Him.
4. Made a searching and fearless moral inventory of ourselves.
5. Admitted to God, to ourselves, and to another human being the exact nature of our wrongs.
6. We're entirely ready to have God remove all these defects of character.
7. Humbly asked Him to remove our shortcomings.
8. Made a list of all persons we had harmed, and became willing to make amends to them all.
9. Made direct amends to such people wherever possible, except when to do so would injure them or others.
10. Continued to take personal inventory and when we were wrong promptly admitted it.
11. Sought through prayer and meditation to improve our conscious contact with God, as we understood Him, praying only for knowledge of His will for us and the power to carry that out.
12. Having had a spiritual awakening as the result of these steps, we tried to carry this message to alcoholics, and to practice these principles in all our affairs.

---

they will love themselves because someone else loves them for the sexual satisfaction they have provided. Having sex does not bring about love. Sex is a gift from God that was meant to be shared by two people who would spend the rest of their life together, enjoying one another. When this special gift is given outside of marriage and commitment it causes even more rejection because something special was given away without any enduring love attached. Two hearts are sown together and then ripped apart and rejection and lack of self love result. Frantic searching and multiple experiences yield emptiness, rejection, and bitterness. Eventually sex is practiced unprotected because the owner no longer respects his or her own body enough to keep it free from sexually transmitted disease.

Our health habits are determined to some degree by our love for our self and our body. It is a good thing to love your self and your body enough that you want to take care of it and honor it. God loves you and He wants you to realize that you are loveable and that your body is worth taking care of.

Many people who begin bad habits at a young and vulnerable age become addicted to their vice. Insecurity and lack of self love cause them to fall into a bad habit that has highly addictive qualities. The good news is that many people wake up and see the light and decide that they love themselves enough to change. They decide that their health is important, that their life is more valuable than this present state, and that they want to be around for their family and children because they are VALUABLE. Because they love themselves enough, they are able to break their addiction, the bad habit, and walk free for the rest of their life.

Realize God's love for you and the value that He has placed on your life. Develop a love for yourself and practice it by caring for yourself. As you realize that you are lovable, see the worth in every one of God's creations and begin to love others as you love yourself.

Faith in Action: Make an investment into taking care of yourself by purchasing some vitamins and supplements: For vitamins try a multivitamin, C, E, and beta-carotene. For supplements try garlic and fish oil. Take the recommended dose for one bottle cycle and see if you notice a difference.

9.

Desire, Discipline, Delight

—ᴠᴠ—

Faith

Matthew 16:24-25 ""If anyone wishes to come after Me, he must deny himself, and take up his cross and follow Me. For whoever wishes to save his life will lose it; but whoever loses his life for My sake will find it."

The Christian life is one of sacrifice. The power of true life comes by dying to your self and living for and with Christ. Just as Jesus went to the cross and died for the sins of the world, and rose again, to bring eternal life to all, we too must experience a similar death to sin, and new life with Him. This death to sin and self is what the Bible refers to as repentance. It is when you turn away from living for yourself and begin to live for the Lord. The new life that you experience as you believe in His forgiveness and power to be free from sin is what the Bible calls being born again. Jesus said in **John 3:3 "Truly, truly, I say to you, unless one is born again he cannot see the kingdom of God."** The death to self and new life in Christ is the beginning stage of a fulfilling Christian life.

After we experience this initial death to self and life with Christ there will be many other times in our Christian life where we will experience the need to die to a bad habit and form a new one. This process is called sanctification. It is where the Lord begins to clean up our life and make us more like Him. No one is perfect and we all have need of improvement in some area. If you are not sure of where you need to improve ask your spouse or a close friend. I'm sure they can point you in the right direction.

Sometime in the 1990's Dr. Larry Lea developed an awesome teaching on the Lord's Prayer. In his series he described three stages of change that people go through when they are developing a new habit. The stages are desire, discipline, and delight. Dr. Lea used these stages to describe what you will go through when you develop a new prayer life with the Lord.

The first stage in developing a new habit is desire. Desire means to long or hope for with a strong intention or aim. In this stage you will recognize an area of your life that is in need of change and you will desire something better. Desire should never be scorned upon. If its flames are fanned properly it will provide the fuel for change. In college, after seeing Dr. Lea's seminar I recognized a void in my own prayer life-it was largely absent and I had no power in my prayer time. I knelt honestly before the Lord and told Him (like He didn't know) that my prayer life was dismal. I told Him I wanted things to change-I desired an intimate relationship with Him and I wanted more power in my prayers.

The next stage of developing a new habit is discipline. This is where the rubber meets the road. In the discipline stage we must take up our cross and follow Jesus. We must die to our fleshly nature and bad habits and make positive steps in a new direction. When I began my quest for a new prayer life I encountered many struggles. I set a time in the morning to meet the Lord for prayer. When my alarm sounded at 6am my flesh threw out objections immediately. I fought sleepiness, boredom, distractions, lack of time, and desire for other things. I battled my own excuses and justifications but eventually discipline was victorious. After months of struggle a new prayer life and habit emerged.

My desire and discipline yielded a delightful prayer life. When I entered my prayer chamber (a study hall room at the end of my dormitory hall) it was like I was entering the throne room of God. I could drop to my knees and worship my King or put on my head phones and dance and celebrate before Him. The presence of His sweet Spirit would fall upon me and I would delight in fellowship with the Lord. I had found the power in prayer that I was so desperately longing for.

The stages of desire, discipline, and delight can help develop an intimate relationship with the Lord in prayer, as well as many other good spiritual habits like reading the Bible, confessing the word, sharing your faith, or serving others.

Fitness

The stages of desire, discipline, and delight are not just applicable to spiritual habits. They are also applicable to many other habits like exercising and eating right.

My wife loves to get people's stories on their 'light bulb moment.' It is a moment in time when they realize their health is a mess and they need to do something about it. It might be a time when they experience a severe illness such as a heart attack, cancer, or pneumonia. It might be looking at themselves in a photograph with friends and realizing, 'Oh my goodness, I look awful.' It might be a pair of jeans or a dress that is just too tight to wear anymore. It might be the realization that they are not going to be around for their children if they don't take serious measures to protect their health. It might be the sudden death of a close friend.

The light bulb moment opens up the door for the desire to change. People recognize their current situation and desire a change. It is a wonderful thing to recognize the need for change and desire a new you. If you experience a light bulb moment seize the opportunity as a message from the Lord to CHANGE. Fall on your knees and cry out for His help. Not taking care of your body (temple) is sin. Smoking, overeating, being lazy by not exercising, consuming too much alcohol, or doing drugs is damaging your body, and it is sin. Confess your sin to the Lord. Ask for His forgiveness. Express to Him your desire to change. Ask for His power to come into your life and help you change. Don't rely on your own strength to change. Make the Lord an active part of your equation. **Psalm 37:5 says "Commit your way to the LORD, Trust also in Him, and He will**

do it." With God on your side and a firm resolve to change, you are on your way to a new you.

Stages of Change Model For Physical Exercise

1. **Not ready for change-** consider the pros and cons of physical exercise.

2. **Thinking about change-**identify interests, develop small specific goals, develop long term vision

3. **Preparing for action-**develop support, find time, create a plan of action

4. **Taking action-**create balance, support yourself in thought and action, pat yourself on the back

5. **Maintaining a good thing-**plan for setbacks, maintain your confidence

(From the Centers for Disease Control)

But don't under estimate the incredible battle ahead. Discipline is definitely a battle. It is your spirit and mind against your defiant flesh. Your flesh has an innate desire to take it easy and be pampered. If you don't believe in the fleshly battle, begin a new diet and then walk into Chick-Fil-A and take a big whiff of the waffle fries. When you place your order, it probably won't be for a salad. Or make a batch of brownies and don't eat any. Then you will see what battling the flesh is like. Whether you are changing you're eating habits or beginning a new exercise routine-you will experience opposition. Paul the apostle said in **1 Corinthians 9:27 "I discipline my body and make it my slave, so that, after I have preached to others, I myself will not be disqualified."** Your spirit person must rise up on the inside of you and take charge. You must walk by the spirit and not by the flesh. You must decide that you are going to make a change and you are going to stick with it regardless of what you feel like. Don't even give your body the option of backing out by running a check of what you feel like today. Discipline is "training that corrects, molds, or perfects the mental faculties or moral character; an orderly or prescribed conduct or pattern of behavior." (Webster's Dictionary)

There will be obstacles to your plans for a fitness routine and a healthier lifestyle. Scheduling conflicts, hunger, weakness, temptations, soreness, cold weather, tiredness, and many other things will stand in your way. You must not surrender to the protests of the flesh and the enemy. Diligence and discipline must prevail. Be resolute, determined, and steadfast in your commitment to a new habit.

Most people who have been working out for six months or more will tell you that they are addicted. You will hear them say "I can't wait to get my workout in." If you are not a fitness 'player', you will think they are on crack or something. These folks have reached the delight stage of change. They experience the euphoria of adrenalin that is released when you exercise. Through my graduate studies I have learned that there are many healthy chemical reactions that take place when you vigorously exercise. These chemical releases provide your body with a healthy dose of a natural stimulant and pain killer. Not only will you feel great when you exercise, but also afterwards. Your body will de-stress itself and return to a level of homeostasis. Your resting heart rate will decrease, your mind will be cleared, and your aches and pains will subside. You will also experience other benefits like better rest and even more regular visits to the potty. As you continue on your exercise discipline, you will become an exercise junkie. You will delight in the feeling and benefits of regular exercise. Exercise will be something you look forward to and enjoy everyday.

About six years ago I decided to learn how to snowboard. My sister is an excellent instructor in Snowmass, Colorado and all of my brothers were picking up the new habit and bragging about how great it was. I wanted to prove I wasn't too old to learn something new and could still hang with the big dogs so I went out for a visit with a new desire. I am a pretty decent skier but my skills had absolutely no influence on my ability to snowboard. If you fall while you are skiing your boots snap out of the skis and you can manage your fall. When you snowboard you are locked on and you are one with the board. If you catch an edge you are hurled to the ground either face first or backwards. The discipline stage of developing this new habit is very painful. I wiped out several times just getting off the lift-a few times I knocked over other people and a few times I was run over after falling. While learning to make turns going from toe side to heel side I was vehemently thrown to the ground many times. I had my back and neck adjusted enough to equal many visits to the chiropractor. Eventually, as I stuck with it, discipline paid off and I was able to successfully complete some gentle runs. After a few years of fine tuning my skills I now delight in snowboarding. I can ride the lift to the top, make it off successfully without killing anybody, carve up the mountainside, and even catch a little air. A small seed of desire and some hard work gave me a delightful new hobby.

The journey of desire, discipline, and delight can help you develop some wonderful new habits.

Faith in Action: It's time to develop a new spiritual habit. For the next thirty one days you are going to read a chapter of the book of Proverbs each day. No watching television until you have read your chapter. Notice how your spirit goes through the stages of desire, discipline, and delight.

10.

The Weapons of Our Warfare

—∿∿—

Faith

Ephesians 6: 10-17 "Finally, be strong in the Lord and in the strength of His might. Put on the full armor of God, so that you will be able to stand firm against the schemes of the devil. For our struggle is not against flesh and blood, but against the rulers, against the powers, against the world forces of this darkness, against the spiritual forces of wickedness in the heavenly places. Therefore, take up the full armor of God, so that you will be able to resist in the evil day, and having done everything, to stand firm. Stand firm therefore, having girded your loins with truth, and having put on the breastplate of righteousness, and having shod your feet with the preparation of the gospel of peace; in addition to all, taking up the shield of faith with which you will be able to extinguish all the flaming arrows of the evil one. And take the helmet of salvation, and the sword of the Spirit, which is the word of God."

There is no doubt that life is a battle. We face struggles and conflicts every day. The turmoil may be within our mind or heart or it may be in the world around us. Some folks face a battle at home and others face a battle at work. Family and coworkers demand our time and assistance. We face more things in our schedule than we can handle. We must juggle family, work, sports, home maintenance, the bills, church obligations, friends, and other unforeseen time demands. We face challenges in relationships, decisions, financial struggles, and life's temptations.

The Lord Jesus Himself knows about facing battles and He is sympathetic to those who are engaged in them. The Lord was faced with people trying to kill Him from the time He was a baby until He was crucified on the cross. He was faced with crowds of people following Him, pressing in on Him, begging for His attention, and wanting something from Him. He was tempted by the devil himself.

The Lord promised and sent a Helper to give us power in life to overcome. His Spirit living on the inside of us is the resource we need to reign in life. His Spirit will lead us into the truth and teach us the things we need to do to overcome. His Spirit can teach us how to put on the armor of God and stand firm against the devil and the challenges of life. By taking active steps to "suit up" in God's power we can be prepared for everything the enemy has to throw at us.

The Lord has provided us with full battle armor to resist the devil and stand firm against him. He has given us the breastplate, the girdle, the boots, the helmet, the shield, and the sword. God's spiritual armor must be applied to our lives each day so that we are prepared for battle. This spiritual armor is applied by performing spiritual acts that dress us for battle in much the same way that we would prepare to go to work.

Before you go to work you wake up, clean up, dress up, and set up your priorities for the day. You pack up your tools for success-lunch, briefcase, laptop, cell phone, and head into battle. Preparing spiritually by putting on the armor of God is a similar routine but much more glorious and important. Putting on the armor of God involves establishing spiritual routines that enable us to be a warrior for God. These spiritual routines prepare us to battle the devil, temptations, and the struggles of life on an ongoing basis.

Putting on the armor of God involves applying the blood of Christ as our righteousness, thinking according to God's word and meditating on it, reading God's word, speaking God's word, spending time in prayer with the Lord, worshipping and praising the Lord, and witnessing for the Lord. If you do these seven things, you will not live a defeated life. You will be one who overcomes and you will put the devil to flight.

Following is a brief description of the application of the armor of God as I have practiced it over the years. I have listened to many teachings about the armor of God but have found these routines to be successful in strengthening me in the Spirit.

The breastplate of righteousness is a piece of the spiritual armor that protects us against self righteousness and condemnation. We can put on the breastplate of righteousness by applying the blood of Christ as our righteousness. We do this by reminding ourselves that we are saved by the grace of God. We must acknowledge that we are unable to save ourselves through our works and we must receive His gift of salvation and forgiveness through the death and resurrection of His Son. When we put our faith in Jesus paying the price for our sins we receive His forgiveness and gift of righteousness. There is nothing more powerful than the blood of Jesus. His blood covers our sins and we are forgiven and free. Start everyday by thanking the Lord for His salvation in Christ.

Putting on "the helmet of salvation" and our having "our loins girded with truth" refer to our ability to think according to the word of God. God's word is truth and the truth is able to set us free from the lies of the world and society. The wisdom of the world says one thing and God's wisdom says another. We must think according to the Bible. Society teaches us to look out for number one. Jesus teaches that the greatest among us is the servant of all. Thinking according to God's word requires first that you read it. I read two chapters of the Bible almost every day. I have read the gospels many times and the New Testament several times. Each time I read, the Holy Spirit inspires me and shows me something new. Sometimes I feel as if I have walked with the Lord on the shores of Galilee, listened to Him teach on the mountainside, seen Him heal the sick, and watched Him walk on water. Don't just listen to other people teach about the word of God. Open up the pages and live and walk with Jesus and the rest of His followers. He will make the Word alive to you. The more you read the more knowledge you will have to draw from. The Holy Spirit will remind you of things you have read and will show you real life applications of God's word. Reading God's word provides you with the helmet and the girdle.

Besides reading and thinking about the Bible it is also powerful to speak the Word. The spoken word is the sword of the Spirit. Jesus defeated the devil when He was being tempted in the wilderness by speaking scripture verses to him. God created the world by His spoken words. Jesus cast out the devil and often healed the sick with spoken words. Find your favorite scripture verses, type them up, and speak them out loud as you drive to work. As you practice this regularly you will memorize them, your faith will get behind them, and powerful things will happen. My daily confession scriptures pertain to being filled with the good things of God's spirit, being blessed by God, being protected by God, and being filled with power to minister to others. I can't begin to express the blessings I have received by speaking these verses on a regular basis. The power of the sword of the Spirit is activated by speaking God's word.

Jesus often arose early to pray. He also prayed late into the night. If He needed prayer then we certainly do. He was tapping into God's power, grace, mercy, healing, and strength. Prayer is nothing more than speaking honestly with the Lord. In reverence, sit or kneel and speak with the Lord. Confess your sins and weaknesses, praise and thank Him, ask for His grace, blessing and protection, ask for wisdom, commit your ways and plans to Him, remind Him of His promises (word). The Father knows you inside and out. He knows what you are going through. Nothing is hidden from His sight. He just wants to hear from you. You don't have to be eloquent, just real. He loves you and wants to spend time with you. As you pray and trust God you build a shield of faith around yourself by believing that He is in control of every aspect of your life.

Sometimes you just have to shout. Something in our being was made to sing and dance. Jamming to the world's music is okay, but there is nothing like dancing and singing to the Lord. There are many times in the Bible where God's people began to praise Him with song and dance and He would show up in great power and strength. When Paul was in prison He began to sing to the Lord and the place was shaken and the chains fell off and the gates were opened. How is that for deliverance? I have been in church services where the band starts jamming and we enter right into the throne of God and celebrate before Him. God is exalted and we are blessed. Singing and dancing are ways to put on our spiritual boots and use them to stomp the devil. Other times we have worshipped in holy reverence before the Lord with hands lifted high in surrender to Him. His powerful healing presence descends upon us like dew and everyone is refreshed in Him. Find a church where the believers gather together and praise and worship the Lord. Life is too short to attend a dead church. You can also spend time in your own room with a CD, singing and dancing before the Lord. He will show up.

A final step in applying the armor of God is witnessing for the Lord. **Revelations 12:11** says that the believers overcame the devil by the **"word of their testimony."** We must use our feet (spiritual boots) to bring the good news to others. When we are witnesses for Christ the devil is defeated. Jesus said if we confess Him before man then He will confess us before the Father. Every time we share about the Lord with those around us, God's kingdom advances and the devil is pushed back. When we witness about God's goodness and salvation we are fulfilling the great commission in **Mark 16:15** where Jesus said **"Go into all the world and preach the gospel to all creation."**

It would be close to impossible to perform every spiritual act, every morning. I believe the spiritual armor is durable and lasts for awhile before you have to renew it. As you get before the Lord during your quiet time you need to assess your spiritual condition and let the Holy Spirit lead you in what you need to focus on. Some days it might be reading and meditating on the word. Other days it may be prayer, praise, dancing, or confessing aloud God's word.

On the morning I was scheduled to cut down some trees around my house I set out to read the Bible and was urged by the Spirit to pray. I pressed into prayer and focused on God's protection for my family and my life. Later that morning my dad and I set out to cut down some trees that were leaning towards my house. One particular tree that posed a threat was supporting half of my son's tree house. After much consideration our plan was for me to stand on the roof of the tree house and cut the top two thirds of the tree off with the chainsaw while my dad pulled it with a tractor so it would fall between the tree house and our home. Twenty-five feet off the ground I made my wedge cut and then began to cut the tree from the back. When my final cut was mostly through the tree, it began to crack and fall. I put down the chainsaw in great fear and realized I would not make it down the ladder in time to safety. I scurried across the roof and hugged the other tree that was holding up the other side of the tree house. As my dad took off on the tractor the tree fell in the right direction but the heavy trunk hit the corner of the tree house roof and tilted the entire structure forward breaking things as it smashed to the ground. My saw slid off the roof and hit the ground twenty-five feet below with the rest of the tree. I was left hugging the other tree for my life. My friend, my dad, my sister-in-law, and niece and nephew shook their heads in utter disbelief. My friend scolded me and my sister-in-law made the comment that 'I must be living right.' I had narrowly escaped a serious injury or death because I had put on my spiritual armor that morning.

Taking little steps every day to put on the armor of God will enable us to become strong in the Spirit. We will be able to battle the challenges of life more effectively and use God's tools to overcome.

Fitness

There are certain weapons that we can use to battle sickness, chronic disease, and unhealthy aging. The weapons of a healthy lifestyle include aerobic exercise, strength training, proper diet, proper hydration, proper sleep, environmental management, and stress management. These mighty weapons, if used correctly and frequently, can put the enemies of your health on the run.

Aerobic exercise is the most important thing you can do for your body. I have often said that some folks are in much more need of daily exercise than they are of daily food. A well established routine of 30-60 minutes of vigorous physical activity can do wonders for your body. Aerobic exercise burns calories and helps you maintain appropriate body weight. Aerobic exercise will strengthen and increase the capacity of your heart and lungs. Aerobic exercise will increase circulation of blood, nutrients, and oxygen to the body. Aerobic activity will elevate your body temperature and percolate out roaming sickness in much the same way that your body spikes a fever to rid itself of a virus. It will also develop muscular strength. Aerobic exercise can increase and prolong mobility. Aerobic exercise can help de-stress your body. It can regulate bowel functions and decrease insomnia. Aerobic exercise is a powerful weapon in keeping your body healthy.

Strength training is another weapon that will fight off unhealthy aging. A regular moderate routine of weight lifting can help strengthen your frame and develop muscle mass. A strong frame will help you stay mobile well into your senior years. Developing muscles will help you perform more demanding tasks with fewer injuries. Developing muscle mass or lean muscle tissue will give you built-in calorie burners that consume calories even when you sleep. Muscles burn calories (even at rest) while body fat is excess stored energy that basically hangs on your body until it is needed. Strength training will burn body fat and increase lean muscle tissue.

Proper diet is a key weapon that soldiers of fitness can use to defeat the enemies of health. Proper diet involves consuming the appropriate amount of calories, eating a wide variety of foods, eating 5-7 servings of fruits and vegetables every day, avoiding fats, fried foods, and sugars, and avoiding a consistent diet of processed foods. Too many Americans make the mistakes of eating extra large portion sizes (too many calories), drinking too many sodas, eating too many snacks, eating too much fried food, and consuming too much fat. Pick a few of these dragons and slay them with a proper diet and you will see a great change in your body composition, cholesterol level, and even blood sugar level.

One of the easiest and cheapest things you can do to stay healthy is drink water. Approximately sixty percent of our body weight is comprised of water. Our cells are mostly water. Our blood is mostly water. When we don't drink enough water we experience dehydration. The Mayo Clinic reports that even a drop of 2% of our body water can lead to symptoms such as dizziness, fatigue, inability to concentrate, irritability, excessive thirst, muscle weakness, headaches, and lightheadedness. Dehydration can even slow your metabolism. The Institute of Medicine recommends that men drink about 13 cups (3 liters) per day and women drink about 9 cups (2.2 liters) per day to keep hydrated. Adequate hydration will kill hunger pangs, and decrease the risks of colon cancer by 45% and bladder cancer by 50%.

Getting enough sleep is an important weapon that must be used to enjoy a high quality of life. According to the Sleep Foundation sleep deprivation can lead to negative effects on performance and physical and mental health. A few problems include reduced energy, greater difficulty concentrating, diminished mood, and greater risk for accidents. These negative effects can further lead to poor work performance and problems with relationships. Sleep apnea can lead to high blood pressure, heart attacks, and stroke. The most common sleep stealers are stress, depression, and chronic pain. Students, travelers and shift workers also are at risk for sleep deprivation. Most adults need between 7-9 hours of sleep per night. If you aren't getting adequate sleep due to the issues of life, it is important for your health and mental and emotional well being that you resolve those issues so that you can catch up on your sleep and live an adequately rested life.

One of the most influential weapons of good health is managing your environment. To a strong degree we are a product of the environment around us. If we live in an unsanitary environment we will experience adverse health consequences. Secondhand smoke is extremely dangerous to your health. Living near or on top of radioactive or toxic waste can skyrocket your chances of various types of cancer. Mold and bacteria can promote various infections. Many of the leading causes of death in the early 1900's were a result of water, food, or air born illness (plagues, diarrhea, and pneumonia). Sound, air, and water pollution can introduce negative health cursors into your life. The more toxins that your body must fight, the more stressed your immune system will become. The cumulative effects of stress on your system will bring about health problems. Finding and maintaining a clean, healthy, and peaceful environment is important for the healthy development of your body.

Create a healthy home environment

To reduce asthma and allergies:
Achieve good indoor air quality by maintaining a well ventilated home free from pollutants such as tobacco smoke and carbon monoxide.
Use dust mite mattress and pillow covers. Wash bedding in hot water once a week.
Eliminate cockroaches and pest with gel baits, by sealing cracks, and by eliminating food and water sources.
Limit use of pesticides and other harsh chemicals.
To control mold and moisture:
Vent clothes dryers and bathroom exhaust vans to the exterior (not crawl space or attic).
Repair water leaks to plumbing and roof.
Replace water damaged materials.
Insulate cold water pipes.
Routinely check and clean gutters to divert water from the foundation.
Install a dehumidifier to pull excess moisture from the house.
To increase home safety and prevent unintentional injuries:
Install and routinely test smoke detectors and carbon monoxide alarms.
Eliminate tripping hazards and make sure travel pathways are well lit.
Poison-proof your home by installing child safety latches, locking medicine cabinets, and disposing of expired medicines.
Keep firearms in locked cabinets and use trigger locks.
Keep matches and lighters out of children's reach.
Use child proof fencing around pools and hot tubs.
To prevent lead poisoning:
Repair peeling and deteriorating paint.
Keep children, pregnant and breastfeeding women, pets, and others away from the dust of renovation or remodeling work areas.
Wash hands thoroughly and often.

Prevent dust from spreading. Use a HEPA filter on your vacuum.

To promote indoor air quality:

Service gas and oil appliances regularly.

Store solvent chemicals away from the home.

Air out new carpets and furniture.

Avoid smoking in your home or car and never smoke around children.

From U.S. Dept of Housing and Urban Development
    Office of Healthy Homes and Lead Hazard Control

Although other weapons of warfare exist that may be used to promote optimal health I want to conclude this list with stress management. We are all faced with daily challenges at home, work, school, or in the community that bring stress into our life. Additional challenges of changes, death, moves, or financial or other problems can put us over the top of the stress chart. Although some stress is good for the body, chronic relentless stress can lead to heart disease, cancer, lung ailments, accidents, cirrhosis, and even suicide. We must take active steps to manage our stress to promote our health. Things like time management, communication, prioritization, exercise, prayer, relaxation techniques, music, massages, and leisure time can help reduce and manage the stress in our life. Kill the stress before it kills you.

Using these and other weapons of a healthy lifestyle will give you the victory over sickness, disease, and the unhealthy aging process. Use them often and you will live a long and healthy life.

Faith in Action: Identify one problem area in you home environment and fix it. Purchase a dehumidifier, air filter, or HEPA vacuum. Fix a leaky pipe or clean up some mold, mildew, or dust. Do one thing to make your home a healthier place.

11.

Watch over Your Heart

—‿∿‿—

Faith

Proverbs 4:23 Watch over your heart with all diligence, for from it flow the springs of life.

The scripture encourages us to guard our spiritual heart against things that will damage it. Our spiritual heart is like our natural heart. It delivers the nutrients it has received to our mind and spirit. Our fuel for life will be whatever we put into our spiritual heart. Jesus confirmed this when He told His disciples that what you eat will not send you to hell but rather what comes out of your heart. He said in **Matthew 15: 17-19 "Do you not understand that everything that goes into the mouth passes into the stomach, and is eliminated? But the things that proceed out of the mouth come from the heart, and those defile the man. For out of the heart come evil thoughts, murders, adulteries, fornications, thefts, false witness, slanders."** If we put negative things into our heart, eventually they will come out.

Proverbs 4:23 is a command from the Lord to be careful what we spiritually consume. There is a lot of junk on TV, the radio, and the Internet that can ruin our heart (spirit). On any given television show or movie you can almost count on the fact that there will be multiple acts of violence, inappropriate sexual relationships or innuendo, and plenty of cursing or inappropriate talk. Most sitcoms and comedians thrive on taking it over the top and pushing the limits of shock and awe humor. This flood of garbage desensitizes us to what is right and wrong and fills our heart and mind with negative thoughts that will take root and affect us.

In radio, most show hosts don't mind saying whatever to whomever to get a laugh either. Some of the shock jocks go to great lengths to ridicule others, judge others, condemn others, or make lewd and inappropriate comments. They must not have heard the words of Jesus in **Matthew 12:36-37** where He says **"But I tell you that every careless word that people speak, they shall give an accounting for it in the Day of Judgment. For by your words you will be justified, and by your words you will be condemned."** This constant barrage of insults and negative "humor" causes our hearts to become callous to what is acceptable and what is out of line.

The Internet has become a source of negativity for many people as well. The Internet has become a purveyor of "porn at your fingertips" for far too many men. Men have become addicted to looking at pictures of naked women. They can no longer control their raging appetite for sexually explicit material. For others chat rooms and personal web pages like My Space have become a breeding ground for inappropriate relationships and child predators. People can spend hours upon hours reviewing web pages and fantasizing about relationships with people who are probably not accurately representing themselves. They can engage in written conversations that have no boundaries or consequences. The fantasy world of the Internet has caused their hearts to sink to all time lows.

"So-called friends" can ruin our hearts as well. Listening all day to someone complain or talk badly about others or tell dirty jokes and talk inappropriately or curse frequently can bring down any good man or woman. The companionship of fools is greatly frowned upon in the Bible. It is draining to be around negative people all day if you are trying to serve the Lord. Bad company corrupts good morals.

Jesus was very clear about how we should deal with the bad forces of life. **In Mark 9:47** He said **"If your eye causes you to stumble, throw it out; it is better for you to enter the kingdom of God with one eye, than, having two eyes, to be cast into hell..."**

In other words radically destroy and cast out anything that might cause you to stumble and lose out on eternal life.

If we fill our hearts with all the junk and negativity that the world has to offer, our spiritual light will not shine very brightly. It will be hard to be a witness for Christ if garbage flows in and out of our mouths and spirits. On the other hand, if we fill ourselves with the word of God and good Bible teaching, and surround ourselves with positive, faith-filled friends, we will have a power coming out of us that will be unstoppable. We will be salt and light to the world. We will be filled with everything that is good and holy and righteous and we will overflow with all the goodness of God to those around us. The fruit of God's spirit will be evident in our life: love, joy, peace, patience, goodness, kindness, faithfulness, gentleness, and self-control.

When our family moved out of the city to the North Georgia Mountains in 1999 we purchased a fixer-upper farm house in the boondocks. For the first year at our new residence we had no cable or satellite and no Internet service. We picked up about three stations on a television with rabbit ears antennae. The stations were fuzzy and sometimes you had to hold the antennae to get a good picture. The absence of the media and its barrage of social influences gave us a nice break and allowed us to focus on spiritual things, fixing up our house, and enjoying time with each other. What was happening in the rest of the world had no influence on us because we were out of the loop and loving it.

It is not too difficult to walk in the light. In fact, it is quite refreshing. The more we walk in it, the easier and more desirable it is to choose the light instead of the darkness. Read good books, listen to Christian music and radio stations, listen to preaching tapes or CDs, watch good, wholesome movies and videos that are inspiring, and spend time with quality people. Children are great to spend time with because they are pure and filled with joy. Jesus said the kingdom of God belonged to such as these.

Jesus said in **Matthew 7:17-20 "So every good tree bears good fruit, but the bad tree bears bad fruit. A good tree cannot produce bad fruit, nor can a bad tree produce good fruit. Every tree that does not bear good fruit is cut down and thrown into the fire. So then, you will know them by their fruits."** If we put good things into our heart, it will also be evident by what comes out of our life. Conversely, if we put bad things in our heart, it will be evident by what comes out of our life. We might fool people for a little while, but our true colors will eventually come shining through.

Get rid of the junk in your life. Fill your heart and mind with good things and you will have a healthy, vibrant, spiritual life.

Fitness

Our physical heart is very similar to our spiritual heart. The same principal, "Watch over your heart with all diligence, for from it flows the springs of life" applies to both of our hearts. Our physical heart pumps blood that provides nutrients and oxygen to our entire body. When our heart stops pumping, we die. The blood that flows from our heart, in essence, is a spring of life to our body. If we have put good nutrients into our system, they will be picked up by the blood and distributed throughout the body for energy and rebuilding. If we put excess fat and cholesterol into our system, these ingredients will begin to coat our veins and arteries with sludge. If we do not keep a close watch over our heart by paying attention to what we put into our body, its flow may become partially clogged or blocked. Clogging and blockage may lead to high blood pressure, stroke, or cardiac arrest. Heart disease is the number one cause of death in the United States for people over 50 years of age. More people die from heart disease than from any other cause. Heart disease is a chronic disorder that is highly preventable. The cost of prevention is DILIGENCE. We must be diligent in protecting our heart.

The computer industry used to have a saying: Garbage In=Garbage Out meaning what we program into the computer controls what we will get out of it. The body is the same way. If we put a bunch of garbage in our body, we will destroy it. Remember, Jesus said, "A good tree bears good fruit, and a bad tree bears bad fruit." Eating unhealthy junk-food will destroy our body. However, a healthy diet of fruits, vegetables, and fiber, along with a proper balance of carbohydrates, proteins, and fat will provide us with the appropriate nutrients we need to build a healthy body and supply us with ample energy.

We must make healthy choices every day that will benefit our heart and body. Our diet must be consistent and planned. When we are in the grocery store we must fill our cart with good food and pass by unhealthy food. We must plan and shop for five or six healthy dinners with fresh fruits and vegetables for breakfast, lunch, and dinner. We must develop a staple, healthy breakfast and lunch that is prepared and ready to go for the day. If we have purchased good foods in advance, we won't be left at the mercy of rummaging through the refrigerator for something that looks tasty or running out for fast food.

Lack of a plan usually results in putting bad food into our body which will in turn result in an unhealthy heart. If we eat a great deal of fried food or foods loaded with excess fat (butter, cheese, oils, grease), we can expect that the unhealthy deposits will begin to coat the insides of our arteries. Sugars, sodium, preservatives, additives, and excessively processed food have negative effects on the body. Without proper nutrients our body can experience many different meltdowns. Our immune system can be lowered and we can get sick often. Diabetes can develop. We can experience mental and emotional disorders. Cancer can develop. Liver or kidney disease can set in. These conditions are a direct result of poor diet and lack of exercise. If we don't get the necessary vitamins, minerals and fiber in our diet our body will function abnormally.

Sometimes the outward appearance of the body gives an indication of what things are like on the inside as well. The old saying, 'You can't judge a book by its cover' does not usually apply to the fitness of a person. If someone is carrying a lot of extra fat on their body, their arteries probably have an unhealthy deposit of fat in them as well. This is an alarming condition that does not seem to have much effect on many folks. As a PE teacher, I am alarmed by the weight of some of my students. I recognize it as an unhealthy condition on the inside, as well as on the outside. Unfortunately there is a new wave of acceptance about carrying some extra pounds that promotes the idea that it is normal and acceptable. Significant excess weight is an indicator that the heart and body may be in danger.

The safest way to a healthy heart is diligent care. Fad diets are not going to make us a good tree. Dieting to get ready for swimsuit

Enemies of the Heart

Saturated Fats, Trans Fats, and Cholesterol
Danger: Consuming high levels of fats equates to higher consumption levels of saturated fats, trans fats, and cholesterol. These unhealthy fats increase the levels of low-density lipoprotein (LDL) cholesterol which may increase the risk of coronary heart disease.
Recommended intake: Total fat intake should be between 20-35% of total calorie intake. Less that 10% of total calories should come from saturated fats (which mean 20g or less for 2000 calorie diet). Cholesterol intake should be 300mg/day or less.
Food examples: 1oz regular cheddar cheese (6g sat fat), 3oz regular ground beef, cooked (6.1g sat fat), 1 cup whole milk (4.6g sat fat), 1 medium croissant (6.6g sat fat)
1/2cup regular ice cream (4.9g sat fat), 1tsp butter (2.4g sat fat), fried chicken leg with skin (3.3g sat fat); **most serving sizes are 2-3 times larger than these examples**

Sodium
Danger: Consuming high levels of salt (sodium chloride) result in high blood pressure which is a risk factor for heart disease. Most Americans consume way more salt that is recommended.
Recommended intake: Consume less than 2300mg (1tsp of salt) of sodium per day.
Food examples (mg sodium): 1oz bread (95-210mg), 4oz frozen plain cheese pizza (450-1200mg), 1/2cup of frozen vegetables (2-160mg), 2Tbsp reg. salad dressing (110-505mg), 2 Tbsp salsa (150-240mg), 8oz canned tomato soup (700-1260mg), 1oz of potato chips (120-180mg), 1oz tortilla chips (105-160mg), 1oz pretzels (290-560mg)
Most serving sizes are 2-3 times larger than these examples

From USDA, Dietary Guidelines for Americans 2005

season is not a healthy way to go. Lifestyle change is what we need. We must plan a healthy diet of natural foods with plenty of fruits and vegetables as well as a balance of carbohydrates, proteins, and a little fat. We must avoid junk food and fast food. We must exercise every day to strengthen our heart and body.

Our spiritual heart and our physical heart are precious gifts from the Lord. We must watch over them with all diligence, for out of them flow the forces of life.

Faith in Action: For one week totally eliminate the following items from your diet: fried foods, cheese, non-lean meats, and table salt. Replace these foods with healthier choices, not junk.

12.

Enduring Tribulation

—m—

Faith

Romans 5:3-5 "And not only this, but we also exult in our tribulations, knowing that tribulation brings about perseverance; and perseverance, proven character; and proven character, hope; and hope does not disappoint, because the love of God has been poured out within our hearts through the Holy Spirit who was given to us."

Trials are what build a man or woman. Character is forged like metal, through fire and tamping. There is no easy road that brings perseverance. It is achieved through sweat and blood and turmoil. Tribulation is defined in Webster's Dictionary as "distress or suffering resulting from oppression or persecution; a trying experience." If you have ever lost a loved one, you have been through tribulation. If you have ever owned a business and others have relied on you for their family income, you have been through tribulation. If you have ever lost your job, lost your home, lost your spouse through an ugly divorce, or battled a life threatening illness, you have been through tribulation. No one is shielded in life from trials, and if you have lived any length of time on this planet, you have probably experienced your share of tribulation. Jesus told us clearly in **John 16:33 "In the world you have tribulation….."** There is no way around it. If you don't get hit at the job, you might get hit at home. If you don't get hit at home you may have your health attacked or the health of a dear loved one. If you wonder where this attack comes from, you can stop wondering right now….the Bible says in **John 10:10 "The thief (devil) comes only to steal and kill and destroy…."**

When tribulation comes upon you, what do you do? Your answer to that question says a lot about your character. Some people run away when trouble comes. They don't face it or deal with it, they just flee. Others curse God, curse others or rant and rave and act like a maniac. Some folks look for someone to blame and badmouth when they experience tribulation. And some drop to their knees, humble themselves before Almighty God, and ask for faith and strength to endure. These folks are the ones in whom the Lord not only builds great character and strength but also blesses in the midst of their trial. How do you handle your tribulation?

For my brother and his fiancée, the night before their wedding was unfortunately one of the most challenging times of their lives. After a nice rehearsal dinner at an Italian restaurant, my sister-in-law's aunt and uncle were both struck by a car while crossing the street. Their injuries were critical and they both passed away in the hospital. The next several hours that unfolded after the accident were unimaginable tribulation for my brother and sister-in-law. The anguish, pain, loss, confusion, and despair were greatly compounded by a looming decision they had to make-should the wedding be postponed? The most joyous day in their lives together faced being cancelled by a tragic accident. After much prayer and family consultation they decided to go through with the wedding. Their character and resolve to press on and focus on the joy of the day was a testimony to all of us about enduring tribulation and perseverance. The wedding was beautiful and the reception afterwards was one of the best parties I have ever attended. I know they are going to produce some wonderful children because their character and poise under tremendous pressure was nothing short of divine.

Like most folks, my family has been through our share of trials as well. Some were much longer than others. I know trials are not easy, and it is a battle to make it through. You fight and achieve some victory and then you fall down or make a mistake. Then you get back up and fight some more. Each time you get back up another notch of character is added to your belt. I believe falling is part of the process. **Proverbs 24:16 says "For a righteous man falls seven times, and rises again..."** When you get back up perseverance is being developed in your life. It is a component of faith that has that never quit attitude.

Perseverance is personified in the fictional fighter Rocky Balboa. Rocky had a 'never quit' attitude each time he was in the ring with Apollo Creed, and then with Clubber Lang, and then Ivan Drago, and then with Tommy Gunn. Rocky was the ultimate warrior and fighter. He would get pounded in the ring and then get back up at the bell to enter the next round. He had a stubborn fighting spirit that would not give up. No wonder Paul the apostle talked about 'fighting the good fight of faith'. We need to be like Rocky and get the eye of the tiger in regards to our faith and fitness.

Helen Keller, who lost her sight and hearing due to an illness when she was nineteen months old, had the following to say:

"Although the world is full of suffering, it is full also of the overcoming of it. My optimism, then, does not rest on the absence of evil, but on a glad belief in the preponderance of good and a willing effort always to cooperate with the good, that it may prevail. I try to increase the power God has given me to see the best in everything and every one, and make that Best a part of my life."

She learned to speak and read Braille in five different languages and became a famous speaker and writer. She learned how to endure tribulation and succeed despite the odds.

If you want to find someone who has Biblical character, find someone who has been through some trials. Character is developed by going through tough times, fighting the fight of faith, keeping your wits about you, and hoping in God for a better day. Trials are God's testing ground that enable you to prove that you have what it takes in your character to move on to the next level.

No one is perfect and you may stumble, become negative, curse, or do some things you wish you could take back immediately. But if you don't quit, and if you don't run out, you still have the opportunity to endure, persevere, and receive proven character. That's good news. If you quit, life is like boot camp for the Navy Seals, when you ring the bell to announce your resignation from training you are recycled and have to come back and try it again until you succeed. You will continue to face trials the rest of your life. The more successfully you handle them, the more character you develop, and the easier it is to win the next time you are faced with a challenge. David beat a lion and then a bear before he beat Goliath. He was no stranger to fights and he had developed a faith that said 'God will give me the victory, like He did before.' That is the proven character and hope that the Lord is looking for in all of us.

Now, let me finish the scripture above. In **John 16:33** Jesus said **"In the world you have tribulation, but take courage; I have overcome the world."** The Lord has overcome the world and tribulation, and with Him, we can also.

Fitness

I am totally amazed at how many people do not like to sweat, and think they are going to die if they do. I have met countless kids who won't go outside during the summer time because they might get sweaty. Sweating, to me is like breathing or drinking water, it is just something that happens. The great thing about it is, the more you do it, the more you get used to it.

Have you ever met anyone that has thought that running a half mile or even a mile might actually kill them? They laugh at the seeming impossibility and absurdity of the task. 'Why would I ever want to do that?' The thought of leaving the couch to go outside and actually exercise for personal health is as foreign as another language. It is like looking at Chinese letters and trying to make sense of what they mean.

Beginning a weight lifting or strength training program is equally a painful task. Most people who have thought about joining a gym have no idea what to do once they get in the door. If they are able to get through some type of workout program, they are so sore afterwards that they can't lift their arms or legs and think "Oh my God, what have I done?" It is weeks before they recover, because they don't go back to work the soreness out, and they associate strength training with some type of torture.

During one of my first attempts at beginning to run in college I had a rude awakening. I had eaten about two hours earlier and thought I was good to go. I laced up my black Converse All Star hi tops and headed down the campus loop for a possible one mile run. The great high school soccer player only made it a few blocks before I was severely winded and cramping badly. I had to pull up and walk. My ego was devastated and I was dumbstruck by these folks who say they run three, four, five, or six miles at a time. I thought it was truly impossible but I went back out and tried again. It took months for me to build up to a decent pace and distance. It took **years** for me to work up to three miles and more years to work up to six miles. I learned it is possible. I even went on to the ultimate challenge of running a marathon (26.2 miles.)

Exercise is just like tribulation. You must ENDURE some sweat and some pain before you get any endurance. The more 'pain' you endure, the stronger you get. I guess the principle of 'No pain, No gain' really is in the Bible- "tribulation brings about perseverance, and perseverance proven character." If you can endure about three or four weeks of sweat and a little soreness, you can become a lifelong fitness freak. It will take about that long for you to become acclimated to the heat, the sweating, the stress on your body, the gasping for breath, and of course the soreness. After the acclimation process something wonderful will happen... you will get addicted. You may not be able to go out and run a six mile race in under 60 minutes right away. But you will show gradual and consistent improvement over weeks and months. You will become one of those fitness freaks who look forward to getting home so you can go work out. You will plan your day around what workout is coming up that afternoon. I know it sounds crazy but it is true. You will also begin to get in better shape (developing that proven character). You will begin to set higher goals for running and lifting. You will begin to invest money in workout clothes and equipment. You will start to recruit others to come and join the pain. You will begin to talk about your great run. You will start flexing and showing off your muscles to your kids.

Strength Training 101

Strength training will provide the following benefits:
- Increased strength of bones, muscles, and connective tissues
- Increased muscle mass which will result in increased basal metabolic rate or BMR (your body will burn more calories).
- Enhanced quality of life.

Work all the major muscle groups to prevent imbalances and postural problems.

Exercise	Muscle Group
Leg Press	quadriceps, gluteals
Leg Curl	hamstrings
Chest Press	pectorals
Lat Pull Down	latissimus dorsi
Lateral Raise	deltoid
Triceps Press	triceps
Biceps Curl	biceps
Curl-up	abdominals
Back Extension	erector spinae

One set of 8-12 repetitions, working the muscle to the point of fatigue, is sufficient. Breathe normally and perform a slow lift through the full range of motion. When you are able to perform 12 repetitions correctly increase the amount of weight by 5-10 percent. Warm up and stretch before lifting.

Exercise each muscle group at least twice per week with one or two days off for rest between workouts. Try a variety of machines and free weights to enhance your progress.

From: American Council on Exercise
Check out: www.acefitness.org/getfit/freeexercise.aspx for pictures of how to perform many strength training exercises.

When my wife is out exercising and hits a point of resistance from her body where it does not want to go on she kicks into a "mind over matter" battle mode. She has adopted a slogan "make up your mind and your body will do the rest." When she becomes fatigued she focuses on someone who is going through a much more difficult struggle than her. Sometimes she thinks about our troops overseas who have left everything to fight for freedom and the safety of our country. Other times she thinks about friends who are battling sickness or cancer or disabilities. She is able to make it through by dedicating her run to them and focusing on the inspiration of their fighting spirit to overcome their challenges.

One such inspirational fighter is our friend Billy. Billy is a pole climber for an electrical company. About ten years ago he fell off a pole and struck his head on a pole. It left a nice lump on his skull and put him out of work for a few months. Ten years later he began to experience blackouts in his vision and dizzy spells. The cause was a brain tumor at the sight of the contusion. After brain surgery to cut out what they could of the tumor, Billy was left with blurry vision and a prescription of radiation treatments and steroids. Billy is a man of faith and always declared that it didn't matter how bad it was, he would get better and God would get more glory. On his first radiation visit the doctor told him that they were going to focus so many thousands of watts of light, in the form of a laser, on his tumor to destroy the rest of it. After correcting the doctor on the amount of watts (because he checked out the electrical input at the street) he rephrased what the doctor told him-"So you are telling me that light is going to heal my brain. The Bible says God is light, so God is going to heal my brain. Glory to God let's get started." After months of treatment and battle, Billy's faith in God and perseverance paid off. He was healed of the brain tumor, his vision has been restored, and he drives himself to work everyday to climb poles for the electrical company. The other day I saw him race and beat his son to the car after a basketball game.

Enduring tribulation during daily exercise will produce perseverance in you. It's scary but a little daily sweat and soreness can transform you into a new person.

Faith in Action: Drop and give me twenty. It is time to begin a strength training routine. Do three sets of pushups and three sets of crunches. Each set should include twenty repetitions. If you can't do regular pushups do modified pushups from your knees but keep your backside straight. Take a five to ten minute break between each set. Continue this routine every other day.

13.

Don't Follow the Crowd

—∽—

Faith

Matthew 7:13-14 "Enter through the narrow gate; for the gate is wide and the way is broad that leads to destruction, and there are many who enter through it. For the gate is small and the way is narrow that leads to life, and there are few who find it."

You can't follow the crowd and expect that you are going the right direction. "Everybody is doing it" is not a good defense. A lot of people speed on the highway. A lot of people cheat on their taxes. A lot of people engage in sex outside of marriage, whether pre-marital or extra-marital. A lot of people do drugs. A lot of people are alcoholics. A lot of people are in bondage to pornography. A lot of people are bound up in the love of money and greed. A lot of people don't honor the Lord with their life, time, talent, and money. A lot of people heartily or passively approve of sin by accepting it as 'life.' A lot of people are on the road to destruction. Societal norms cannot be our guide on the road of life.

Jesus called His disciples to be a light in the midst of a dark world. He said in **Matthew 5:16 "Let your light shine before men in such a way that they may see your good works, and glorify your Father who is in heaven."** If we walk in the light with Him, because He is the light, we will follow a different path than others. His path is the path of righteousness. When you chose to follow Jesus you die to yourself and your own wants and desires, and live for Him. You begin a life of service to God and others. That does not sound like most of society, does it?

When we follow the narrow path that leads to life we walk like Jesus walked. He told those around Him in **John 6:38 "For I have come down from heaven, not to do My own will, but the will of Him who sent Me."** We must be people who are on a mission. We must be people of destiny that are taking a different road than the rest of society. When people think or talk about you, they should recognize that you are unique. You are not the average Joe. You walk to the beat of a different drum, a heavenly one.

Imagine for a moment, if you lived every day like it was your last. Imagine if you knew the end of time was near and soon you were going to the throne of God and were going to give an account of your life before the judgment seat of Christ. How would you live your life? Hopefully you would set out on a course to make a difference in as many people as you can. You would love and bless those around you. You would give freely of your time and possessions, because you knew you couldn't take them with you. You would love your family and tell them how special they were to you. You would seize every moment: roll in the green grass, dance in the rain, drink in the last rays of sunshine, and let the wind blow through your hair and across your face. You would see to it that every moment had purpose and was greatly treasured. You would make peace with the Lord, and ask forgiveness of those you had offended. You would hopefully clean the slate of the past, cut off the excess baggage of worldliness that weighs you down, and FOCUS on the things that are really important. I don't think you would watch one moment of television.

The narrow road that leads to life is one of focus. It is a life that is focused on the Lord and His kingdom. It is a life that is focused on loving and serving others. It is a life that is focused on making a difference in the lives of others. Wouldn't it be a great world if everyone had the desire in their heart to use their God given talents to make this world a better place? That is what we are all called to do.

Fitness

Most folks don't take care of themselves. Our nation is increasingly headed in the wrong direction in regards to our health. We are one of the richest and most well educated countries in the world, and we have very bad health habits. Out of 19 developed nations, the United States has the lowest life expectancy. Heart disease continues to be the number one killer. The National Health and Nutrition Examination Survey from 1999-2002 found that more than 30% of Americans over age 20 are obese and over 65% of Americans over age 20 are either overweight or obese (CDC website). More than 50% of Americans do not get enough physical activity, and 25% engage in no leisure time activity at all. One third of children in grades 9-12 do not regularly engage in vigorous physical activity. The mainstay of our nation is fast food or unhealthy food, and we are not exercising.

One of the funniest or perhaps most pathetic things I have ever seen was at a campground in Virginia. The campground rented golf carts for about $40 per day (more than the cost of a campsite) and they were sold out. The campers who went to enjoy the great outdoors were riding their golf carts to the pool, the restroom, putt-putt, and the play area. One lady even packed up her dogs and drove them to the drop area so they could do their business. She was so lazy she couldn't even walk the dogs— she gave them a ride.

Don't follow the crowd because you will end up with heart disease or cancer like the rest of them. I hate to put things so bluntly, but it is true. Most of my friends and co-workers are carrying extra weight around the midsection, thighs, and everywhere else. Most of them do not exercise regularly and their bodies are showing it. If you go to our county pool during the summer time you will see a lot of overweight people- kids and parents. If you get stuck behind a middle school bus emptying kids out after school, you will see some teenagers that wear bigger clothes than you.

My wife and I are trying to make a positive influence in our community and among our friends. We have seen several friends and couples begin running again after a break of about 10 years. We consider ourselves as ambassadors of Christ and ambassadors of fitness. We encourage everyone by example and by word to become more physically fit. My wife started a free aerobics class at our church and it has spread like wildfire. She has had more than 80 ladies show up and pack into our relatively small fellowship hall to change their bodies and change their lives. It brings tears to my eyes when she tells me testimonies of the ladies who have lost weight, gained self esteem, and have become hooked on getting in shape.

Before PE class I usually give my students a fitness tip. One tip I have given them goes something like this: 'Boys and girls, you have to be responsible for your own health. You have to make a decision that you are going to take care of your body by exercising and eating right. You are not your parents. If they have not taken care of themselves or smoke or do drugs, that doesn't mean you have to. I know most of you have good parents that are encouraging you to do the right thing, but some people don't have it so lucky. But the bottom line is you can make a decision to take care of yourself by doing the things you need to, to have a healthy body. It is your choice.' I am no way trying to undermine the parents when I tell the boys and girls this. I am simply trying to give them hope and make them realize that they do not have to be a product of their environment if it is a negative one.

It is a message we all need to here. We do not have to be a product of the environment around us. We can go against the flow and take care of our bodies. We can exercise every day and eat right. America has produced a toxic environment of fast food, sedentary lifestyle, and laziness. We ride our cars everywhere, sit in our air conditioning, eat our junk food, drink our sodas, watch our televisions way too much, play our video games, and spend hours on the Internet. We even computer date instead of going out and meeting someone. We have created an environment that does not promote health. All of the research points to the fact that our nation is going in the wrong direction in terms of health. The only way out is to take the narrow road.

The great news is that we can overcome negative environmental factors by adopting positive personal health behaviors. We can begin and stick to a daily exercise schedule. We can join a gym or purchase some exercise equipment. We can turn off the television,

Leading Health Indicators

Physical Activity: only 15% of adults engage in recommended amount of physical activity

Overweight and Obesity: nearly 60% of the adult population is overweight with 22.5% being obese.

Tobacco Use: 35% of adolescents and 25% of adults smoke cigarettes

Substance abuse: 23% of adolescents report alcohol or drug use, 32% of adults age 18-25 report binge drinking

Responsible sexual behavior: only 23% of sexually active 18-44 year olds reported using condoms to prevent STD's

Mental Health: 1 in 5 Americans face mental illness including depression. Only 23% receive treatment.

Injury and Violence: Injuries are the leading cause of death for ages 1-44 with motor vehicle crashes being the most prevalent cause.

Environmental Quality: 25% of all preventable illness is a result of poor environmental factors such as outdoor air quality, water quality, toxic waste, or poor home or work environment.

Immunization: while vaccination rates continue to climb the combination of pneumonia, influenza, and HIV represent the fifth leading cause of death in the US.

Access to health care: There is a societal disparity in health care coverage with some minority groups reporting 40% of its population having no health care coverage.

From Healthy People 2010

video games, and computer and make our children go outside and exercise for at least one hour everyday. We can buy and prepare healthy meals at home. When we are on the road we can order the salad option or healthy fast food choices, instead of the grease and fat food choices. We can reduce or eliminate the sodas and drink more water. We can throw out the chips and sweets and start eating the fruits and vegetables that are so readily available in our super-markets (unlike the rest of the world). We can walk or bike more and drive less. We can cut back on the amount of food we eat and establish a healthy diet.

These are all healthy options that are well within the reach of almost everyone. The elimination of television and computer alone would probably give most people an extra 2-4 hours a day. Imagine what you could do to change your life and your family with that kind of time. The wide road leads to destruction. The narrow road leads to life. Adopting these healthy habits will add years to your life. You will feel better, look better, and live longer and healthier. You can rise up and change things by exercising your faith, your choice, and your body. Don't be a product of your environment any longer. Don't follow the wide road that leads to destruction. Turn, with the Lord's help, and follow the path that leads to life.

Faith in Action: Drive the speed limit for one full week. (Accidents are one of the leading causes of death for most of your life. Don't be one by following the crowd.)

14.

Persistence

—⁓—

Faith

Luke 11:9-10 "So I say to you, ask, and it will be given to you; seek, and you will find; knock, and it will be opened to you. For everyone who asks, receives; and he who seeks, finds; and to him who knocks, it will be opened."

To persist means "to go on resolutely or stubbornly in spite of opposition, importunity, or warning" (Merriam-Webster). Jesus taught His disciples to be persistent in prayer. In the passage above a more accurate translation would be 'ask, and keep on asking, seek, and keep on seeking, and knock, and keep on knocking.' Jesus said if you ask, and keep on asking, it will be given to you. Just prior to telling His disciples these words, Jesus told them a parable about persistence. He said in **Luke 11:5-8 "Suppose one of you has a friend, and goes to him at midnight and says to him, 'Friend, lend me three loaves; for a friend of mine has come to me from a journey, and I have nothing to set before him'; and from inside he answers and says, 'Do not bother me; the door has already been shut and my children and I are in bed; I cannot get up and give you anything.' I tell you, even though he will not get up and give him anything because he is his friend, yet because of his persistence he will get up and give him as much as he needs."** I believe Jesus was telling us to be persistent in prayer. In fact both of these passages follow the spot in the Bible where Jesus taught His disciples the Lord's Prayer. I think He was sending a clear message that if we go on resolutely in prayer, we will find the answers.

There is a way to lay hold of God. There is a way to get answers to your prayers. There is a way to get healed from the Lord. There is a way to be blessed from the Lord. The way is through persistent faith. If you believe that He is able to do exceedingly, abundantly beyond what you ask or think, and if you believe that God is a loving Father who wants to bless you, all you have to do is get His attention, and you will receive what you are seeking. I know from the Word and from personal experience that He loves me and that He is available. I also know that through faith and patience I have received His promises. He has blessed me, He has healed me, He has opened doors for me, He has directed me, and He has protected me. Once in the midst of a great trial, He spoke to my heart and told me "I will never leave you nor forsake you." Doesn't that sound like a good Father? If you think you love your children, how much more do you think God loves you? He is love.

Sometimes the answers tarry. Sometimes the blessing or the healing doesn't come immediately. But the Lord is faithful if you are persistent. If you determine in your heart that He is willing and able, He will show up strong on your behalf.

I believe sometimes the Lord tests our faith and commitment to Him. He tested Abraham to see if he would sacrifice his own son to the Lord. Abraham passed the test and the Lord spared his son. I believe the Lord wants to know if we are serious about what we want, and if we truly believe. When the children of Israel were tested in the desert, they cowered and turned back in their hearts. They died in the wilderness and did not receive the promise because they were not persistent in their faith. Only the two who believed, Joshua and Caleb, men of a different spirit, entered into the Promised Land. The unbelievers did not receive the promise but our merciful Father did allow their children to enter in.

If you want something from the Lord you are going to have to ask Him and continue to ask Him until you receive from Him. If you continue on asking Him persistently, He will reward you.

If you are not serious about what you want from the Lord, you will quickly turn to other things and the Lord will know you were not serious. Jesus Himself said in **Matthew 7:6 "Do not give what is holy to dogs and do not throw your pearls before swine...."** The Lord is not going to bless you with something precious if you are not sincere and purposeful in what you desire. There is a price to pay in getting something from the Lord. The price is persistence.

Have your children ever asked you for something? Have they ever begged you (or Santa Claus) for a specific gift? I don't know how yours are, but mine don't let up. One year my son was dead set on getting a dirt bike for Christmas. I tried to persuade him to ask Santa Claus for something else like a remote control car, a Chopper bicycle, a portable DVD player...anything but a dirt bike. He wouldn't give in. He was persistent in his humble request for a dirt bike. I tried every parenting trick in the book, including many visits to the toy store to see what he wanted for Christmas. The answer was always the same, a dirt bike. Guess what he got for Christmas—a dirt bike. (FYI: We live on a farm and he had a small dirt bike that was destroyed with the rest of our belongings when our home burned to the ground. I tell you this so you don't think I give my kids crazy gifts that would be nonsensical.)

Our heavenly Father is similar to us in the way we deal with our children. Of course He would not give us something that didn't make sense, like a replacement for your wife or husband. He may delay your request for awhile (like when your kid asks for an ice cream...you say "later"). But when the Lord sees your persistence, He goes to the freezer and brings you two scoops of mint chocolate chip. If you will be persistent in your asking, seeking, and knocking, the Lord will reward you.

Fitness

You will never reach your fitness goals if you don't pursue them with a fervent passion. Losing weight and getting in shape are achieved through persistent work. A haphazard approach to your workout regime will not yield the results you are looking for. If you want it, I mean really want it, it will cost you something.

You will have to develop a militant approach to your eating habits and workout schedule. It is absolutely inevitable that you will lose weight if you consume less calories and burn more calories than what you are normally used to doing.

If you were to eat 250 less calories a day, and burn 250 more calories a day due to exercise, you would have a net loss of 500 calories a day. If you persistently did this for seven days straight, one week, you would have a net loss of 3500 calories which is equal to one pound of fat. If you lose one pound a week for an entire year, you would lose 52 pounds. Most people don't need to lose this much, but you get the picture.

A deliberate and persistent approach to weight loss and getting in shape will produce life-long results that far outlast fad diets, pills, or starvation techniques. If you change your lifestyle and make exercise and eating right a part of your life, you will make a permanent change. You have to want it bad enough and you have to show you want it by your actions. Talk is cheap. To persist is a verb. It requires action.

When I set my goal of running the Big Sur Marathon, I was resolute in my training. I didn't want to run in the race, I wanted to finish. I knew that running 26.2 miles was not going to be something that I could just go out and 'wing it'. I heard stories of people cramping up and locking down and not being able to finish. I wasn't going to fly 3000 miles and invest a lot of money to run in a marathon that I wasn't able to finish. So I gathered some good information on marathon training and plotted my course. The race was in April so I would have to train during some cold months in Georgia. To say the least, it wasn't easy. I ran in cold, in rain, and even snow. I ran when I was tired and I ran when I was sore. But I was persistent in pursuing my dream. During one 21-mile run I turned the corner into my driveway and my legs locked up. I was in excruciating pain, the kind where you have to cry out. I hadn't eaten during my run and learned that I must not only drink, but also eat while running the long ones. I was back out there a few days later keeping to my schedule. I was persistent in pursuing my dream and it paid off. The marathon was one of the most rewarding experiences of my life.

The Persistence of Walter Elias Disney

The legendary animator and company founder Walt Disney was not an instant success in the film and animation industry. Consider some of the highlights of his professional career:

- In 1920 his first company, Iwerks-Disney went out of business.
- In 1922 his second company, Laugh-O-gram went bankrupt.
- In the mid twenties he developed a successful cartoon character named Oswald the Rabbit but later lost the rights to him as well as his cartoonists to Universal Pictures.
- Mickey Mouse was created and gave Disney success along with some other animations called Symphonies.
- In 1929 his best animator Ub Iwerks left him for another offer.
- He developed color animation and later "Snow White", the first feature length animated film.
- During the Wartime of the 1940's he lost his foreign market and had several slow moving projects on the table, 1500 employees, and $4.5 million in debt.
- In 1941 his cartoonists went on strike.
- After the war he developed several True Life adventure films and opened a theme park named Disneyland.
- In 1961 his company experienced the first time of being out of debt.
- He founded Cal Arts, a college for all aspects of the arts.
- In 1964 he produced "Mary Poppins" which received 13 Academy Awards.
- His ability to follow his dream eventually led to 48 Academy Awards, 7 Emmys, and a company that is worth $30 billion. His pioneer spirit and persistence paid off.

Persistent pursuit of your fitness goals will bring results. A sign in my gym reads "Winners never quit, and quitters never win." When I talk with my students about this sign I make sure they understand that they can win in life if they just don't give up. If they continue to press on, they can achieve their goals. The only thing that can keep them back is their self, by quitting.

A real way my students learn about persistence is in their pursuit of the national and presidential award in our President's Challenge fitness testing. Students who achieve the 50th percentile or better in all five fitness categories can achieve the national award. Students who achieve the 85th percentile or better in all five categories can achieve the Presidential award. When we test in the fall, inevitably some students fall short in one or more categories. It is then that we talk about hard work and determination. I explain to them that if they practice their push-up, crunches, running, and stretching, THEY WILL GET STRONGER. It is absolutely inevitable. However, if they don't practice, they won't get any stronger. By spring time, during our second testing, the true heroes are evident. I see who bought into the dream, caught the vision, and ran with it. They tell me they have been practicing at home and when I see the results, I congratulate them for a job well done. When I hang the medal around a Presidential Award winner's neck, one thing is for sure, they earned it through persistence.

If you show persistence in your diet and exercise routines you will see lasting results. Don't quit, see it through!

Faith in Action: Lose five pounds the right way. Eat 250 calories less and burn 250 calories more everyday until you permanently lose the weight. It should take five weeks if you are persistent.

15.

Sowing and Reaping

—ന—

Faith

Galatians 6:7-8 "Do not be deceived, God is not mocked; for whatever a man sows, this he will also reap. For the one who sows to his own flesh shall from the flesh reap corruption, but the one who sows to the Spirit shall from the Spirit reap eternal life."

One of the most powerful laws operating on earth is the law of sowing and reaping. In very simple terms it states that whatever you sow, you will also reap. If you sow good seed, you will reap a good crop. If you sow bad seed or seed filled with weeds, your crop will be a mess. The act of sowing involves placing a seed in some fertile, prepared soil that will produce some fruit when it grows to full measure. The law of sowing and reaping can be seen in many, many things.

If you read the Bible, speak to the Lord in prayer, worship and praise Him, and love and bless others you will sow spiritual seed. In time you will reap the spiritual benefits of stronger faith, peace, love, joy, patience, kindness, goodness, faithfulness, self-control, and eternal life. The more you sow in the Spirit, the more you will reap spiritual things.

The Bible talks about giving as a means of sowing and promises that the more you give, the more it will come back to you. In fact **2 Corinthians 9:6** says **"he who sows sparingly will also reap sparingly, and he who sows bountifully will also reap bountifully."** Have you ever known anyone who seems to constantly give to those around them and they seem to be filled with joy as they continue to give? There aren't too many people with giving hearts that just overflow with love. But if you ever find someone who has a giving heart it is a great joy to be around them and they have lots of friends because they are so wonderful.

A cool bumper sticker came out awhile ago. It said "Practice random acts of kindness." What a great concept. Live your life being kind to others. Sow seeds of joy into other people's lives by blessing them everyday. How? Start by smiling and being nice to others. Greet them, bless them and show interest in them. Help your coworkers. Bring in a special homemade treat for the Sunday school class. Pick up the check when you and a friend have dinner. Edge the neighbor's lawn and blow off the leaves for them. Jesus said feed the hungry, clothe the naked, visit the sick, visit those in prison, and give the thirsty something to drink. He said when you do it to the least of people you do it to Him. What would the world be like if everyone sowed acts of kindness? What would your life be like if you changed and began to do something special for someone every day?

One year during teacher appreciation week my principle asked PTA if they would be willing to wash the teachers' cars for them as a token of appreciation. Somehow "Coach" got roped into the job of securing everyone's keys and driving their vehicle around to the wash area for the parents to wash the cars and then driving the cars back to their spots. I valet parked about sixty cars in two hours. I had sweat pouring down my body. During the adventure I learned which teachers were head bangers (hard rockers), how loud they listened, what they ate for breakfast that morning (and some dinner last night), how clean or messy they were, and what else they did while driving their car to school. I had a blast with the other parents that were washing the cars and I was able to make a more personal connection with some of the teachers, as I teased them about my discoveries. We had a great time doing something good for some nice people.

Jesus said in **Matthew 6:20** that we could "........**store up for yourselves treasures in heaven...**" We have a heavenly bank account and I am convinced that we can make daily deposits into it. We can add a little treasure to our heavenly account by sowing nice things here on earth. You can be rich in heaven if you start making deposits now. Give one tenth of your money to the Lord. Give to the poor. Help your family members and friends that need a boost. Help people that you know will never be able to repay you. Help the elderly. Go on a mission trip. Find a worthy organization and volunteer your time. Witness every day for the Lord by showing and telling others what He has done in your life. Forgive those who have wronged you. Love your neighbor as yourself. Every kind deed that you sow will be a deposit into your heavenly bank account. Your heavenly bank account will yield blessings in this life and in eternal life.

If you sow abundantly into God's kingdom and sow spiritual things into the lives of others you will reap an abundant harvest. I am totally convinced by the magnificent and faithful blessings of the Lord that have overtaken my family that God is faithful to those who give to Him. It is a spiritual law that He has set forth that cannot be broken. When we sow by giving to others or doing nice things to others, blessings and nice things happen back to us. It is not karma. It is the law of sowing and reaping.

Unfortunately the converse is also true. If you are a miser, a scrooge, or a mean and hateful person, you will reap what you sow.... nothing. People will return to you what you have given to them.

Those who sow to a greedy or immoral lifestyle will reap bondage, corruption, and an empty life that lacks meaning, purpose, and genuine fulfillment. **Galatians 5:19-21** has some bad news for those who sow to the flesh: "**Now the deeds of the flesh are evident, which are: immorality, impurity, sensuality, idolatry, sorcery, enmities, strife, jealousy, outbursts of anger, disputes, dissensions, factions, envying, drunkenness, carousing, and things like these, of which I forewarn you, just as I have forewarned you, that those who practice such things will not inherit the kingdom**

of God." If you sow to the flesh, and neglect the spirit, you will not inherit eternal life.

We all have choices in life. We have a choice every day to sow to the Spirit or sow to the flesh. I hope you will chose life and chose to sow to the Spirit. Sowing to the Spirit will bring an abundant harvest of blessings that you will never regret.

Fitness

Our physical body is very responsive to the environment in which we subject it. If we subject our body to healthy stimulus we will develop a healthy body. If we subject our body to an unhealthy climate our body will deteriorate more rapidly. The law of sowing and reaping is very evident in the health of our human body. Our health is determined by what we do with and to our body. If we sow good things into our body, we will reap a healthy return. If we sow unhealthy things in our body, we will destroy our health.

Most of the things that affect our health are things that we as individuals have the ability to control. We control the amount of exercise we get. We can control our weight by the amount of food we eat. We can control whether or not we use tobacco and drugs. We can control our sexual behavior. We can control our driving habits and seat belt use. Most of us can control whether or not we go to see the doctor for annual check ups and recommended diagnosis. We are in the driver's seat in regards to our health. We can sow healthy habits so that we can reap some health benefits.

The U.S. Department of Health and Human Services believes that 70% of the premature deaths due to the leading causes of death in America (heart disease, cancer, stroke, respiratory diseases, accidents, and diabetes) are preventable. If they are preventable that means that there are things we can do to make a difference in our health and how long we live. We must sow healthy seed.

Every little healthy thing you do for your body can add minutes, hours, days, months, or years to your life. Not only can you add time, but you can add healthy time to your life. What if you decided you were going to eat the recommended servings of 5-7 fruits and vegetables every day? What could it do for your life? It would do

---

Cancer Facts

Being overweight or obese is clearly linked with an increased risk of developing several types of cancer:
      breast (among postmenopausal women)   esophagus
      colon   kidney
      endometrium (uterus)

Obesity also likely raises the risk of other cancers:
      cervix   gallbladder
      Hodgkin lymphoma   multiple myeloma
      ovary   pancreas
      thyroid   aggressive forms of prostate cancer

Estimated new cases of cancer in U.S. in 2005: 1,372,910

Estimated deaths from cancer in US in 2005: 570,280

Estimate of current Americans with previous diagnosis of cancer: 10.1 million

5 year survival rate of all types of cancer from 1997-2002: 65%

Lifetime risk of developing cancer: 41%

Probability of developing cancer between 50-70 years of age:
Men 21%   Women: 16%

Average years of life lost due to cancer: 15.4 years

Most prevalent cancers:

Men-Prostate (33%), Lung (13%), Colon/rectum (10%), Urinary (7%), Skin (5%)

Women- Breast (32%), Lung (12%), Colon/rectum (11%), Uterine (6%), Skin (4%)

From American Cancer Society, National Cancer Institute, CDC

---

several things. First you would greatly increase your fiber intake which is a good thing. You would be a lot less likely to get colon or rectal cancer. You would also probably fill up on healthy food and eat a lot less junk food because you would be stuffed with healthy snacks. This would reduce your risk of heart disease and stroke because you are eating less French fries, Dorritos, potato chips, cookies, candy, and other junk because you are eating carrots, apples, oranges, and bananas. You would be at less risk for hypertension and high cholesterol because you are eating right. If you ate your 5-a-day you would also be getting a lot more vitamins, minerals, and enzymes that your body desperately needs. Fruits and vegetables contain antioxidants which help absorb free radicals in your body. Free radicals break down cells which can lead to cancer. So, eating more fruits and veggies can reduce your risk of other types of cancer as well. Isn't it amazing what you will reap by just sowing 5-7 fruits and vegetables into your life each day?

Now let's talk about exercise. If you were to continue eating the same amount of calories that you are eating now, but you began to exercise for one hour per day, you would begin to lose weight. Exercise burns calories. The more intense you exercise the more you would lose. The more you exercise the healthier your heart, lungs, and arteries will become. Daily physical exercise will reduce your risk of heart disease and stroke. If you continue to lose weight until you reach your ideal weight you will reduce your risk of diabetes. Exercise will relieve the effects of stress in your life which will help reduce high blood pressure. Exercise can boost your immune system and make you less susceptible to sickness. Exercise will increase your circulation and make you less likely to suffer the pains of arthritis. Exercise will strengthen your muscles and skeletal frame making you less likely to experience premature osteoporosis as well as decrease your chances of falling and breaking hips or other bones. Wow, sowing daily exercise has some awesome rewards!

There are other healthy habits you can also sow that will make a difference in your health. Little things like drinking enough water, washing your hands frequently, getting enough rest, practicing stress relief techniques, driving the speed limit, limiting your alcohol intake, practicing abstinence before marriage, and getting routine checkups can greatly promote your health. Every little bit that you sow can add a little more health to your life. And the more you sow the more health conscious you become. Pretty soon your life will become a health garden where you sow, water, and weed with the meticulous skill of a master gardener.

Please remember that whatever you sow, you will reap. There is no magic formula. If you use tobacco, you are sowing the WORST thing possible for your health. There is nothing more harmful than smoking. You attack your heart and lungs. The second worst thing you can sow is inactivity (you thought I was going to say junk food…it's third). You must get out and exercise everyday. If you are inactive all the junk you eat is going to cake on the walls of your arteries, the valves of your heart, and your intestinal tract and you are going to be a clogged up mess. You will greatly increase your risk of heart disease, stroke, several types of cancer, and diabetes by sowing inactivity.

The use of illicit drugs and sex before marriage are also bad seeds to sow. Illicit drugs have profound effects on the brain, nervous system, and body organs. The commercial that features an egg in the frying pan and the saying 'this is your brain on drugs' is no lie. The truth is the egg represents your whole body. You can fry your brain, nervous system, heart, lungs, and organs by drug addiction. Sex outside of marriage is also very risky business. As a PE teacher that has taught sex education to middle school students I have found it very helpful to show the students some pictures of the damaging results of sexually transmitted diseases. Besides the risk of losing your life to AIDS, you can seriously mess up your sexual organs by having sex outside of marriage. When you have sex with someone it is like having sex with everyone they were with for the last ten years….not a good idea. Use your head and take care of your body.

The best way to promote your own health is to understand and embrace the law of sowing and reaping. Sow well and sow often into your life. Sow healthy habits that will produce a wonderful, healthy body that you will enjoy well into your eighties. Whatever you sow, you will reap.

Faith in Action: Go find someone to help and help them. Clean their house, rake their leaves, cut their grass, wash their car, or help them with a project. When they ask why just tell them "I like you and I want to bless you, it's what neighbors do."

16.

Iron Sharpens Iron

—ᴍ—

Faith

Proverbs 27:17 Iron sharpens iron, so one man sharpens another.

Have you ever had a very close friend who was able to spiritually and mentally stimulate you and provoke you to greater depths of the Spirit? I have been blessed to find a few over my years of walking with the Lord. It is a rare and precious thing to find someone who will get in the trenches with you and stir you up to 'fight the good fight' of faith. I am not talking about a preacher or motivational speaker but rather a trusted friend who you interact with on a personal level. You speak into their life and they speak into your life. You pray together about things and you stir up God's calling on one another's life. **1 Thessalonians 5:11** says **"Therefore encourage one another and build up one another, just as you also are doing."** God's plan for His saints is for them to be in unity and work together for His kingdom.

It is important that we seek out a spiritual friend that can sharpen us. This is easier said than done. It has been my observation that women in general have a much easier time of finding spiritual friends than men. Men seem to be more reserved about opening up to each other and relying on others. They also don't call to chat with a friend. If a guy calls his friend, it is for a purpose and not just to talk or pray. But spiritual relationships are vitally important and we all need them. Jesus often pulled His disciples away to talk. He poured His life into them and they often challenged (or argued with) each other. This was all part of the sharpening process.

No man is a rock or an island. We all need somebody to lean on. **Ecclesiastes 4:9-10** says **"Two are better than one because they have a good return for their labor. For if either of them falls, the one will lift up his companion. But woe to the one who falls when there is not another to lift him up."** It is good to have a close friend who can help you through the storms and trials of life. A good friend is more valuable than a lot of the things we pursue. A friend is an investment in time, but one that is well worth it. A good friend can shoot it straight to you when you have messed up or gotten off track. A good friend can kick you in the pants when you need it. A good friend can celebrate the victories of life with you.

When two people join forces there is a power of agreement that transcends normal bounds. Jesus Himself said in **Matthew 18:19 "Again I say to you, that if two of you agree on earth about anything that they may ask, it shall be done for them by My Father who is in heaven."** God blesses two that are in agreement. Moses and Aaron led the captives to freedom. David and Jonathon had a special bond that enabled a godly king to rule over Israel. Paul and Barnabas brought salvation to thousands and thousands of Gentiles. Martha and Mary were able to get Jesus to raise their brother Lazarus from the dead. The Lord provides a special faith bond and blessing upon Christian brothers and sisters who gather together in His name.

So what do you look for in a friend that will sharpen you? You are looking for a spiritual sparing partner. One who will step in the ring with you and go at it to make you a better boxer. They will help you develop that jab and upper cut. They will buff you around a little so you can learn how to put up your defense. This kind of person is not an elder mentor. We need those too. This person is your equal but brings different gifts and talents to your relationship. You share common interests. You are around the same age and are on the same journey in life. Of course, if your goal is to grow spiritually, they need to be a Christian pursuing the Lord.

I think there are two other qualities that are necessary as well. I think your friend needs to love you unconditionally no matter whether you win or lose, fall or even backslide. They should be there for you, to pick you up and point you in the right direction. I think this kind of love is best seen by the father in the story of the prodigal son. When his son came within view he ran to him and threw his arms around him and received him back. He did not judge him or condemn him or disown him. A true friend will always love you like the Lord loves you. A true friend may not agree with you, but that does not change your relationship or bond one bit.

I also think a true friend needs to be able to 'speak the truth in love.' Nobody wants a 'yes man.' Your friend ought to be able to say it like it is with the comfort of knowing you will both continue to love each other and be there for each other (just like marriage). **Proverbs 27:6** says **"Faithful are the wounds of a friend, but deceitful are the kisses of an enemy."** Once I was riding with a friend in his brother's truck to move some furniture. We pulled into a gas station and were easing towards the pump. I looked over and thought he was coming close to one of those poles that stick up to protect the pump, but I didn't say anything because I didn't want to hurt his feelings by telling him how to drive. He made contact with the pole and made a nice wrinkle down his brother's rear quarter panel. As we surveyed the damage I mentioned that I thought he was getting awful close. His response in disbelief was "And you didn't say anything? Why didn't you speak up?" I learned then that it was better to say something to point your friend in the right direction and risk hurting their ego, rather than being quiet and letting them suffer real damage.

If you could describe a really good coaching partnership it would be similar to the relationship I have with my friend Leon. He is the manager of our boys' baseball team and I am his assistant coach. We share many commonalities and yet we are different in our personalities and the gifts we bring to our friendship and coaching roles. We both have sons the same age who are very good athletes. We have young families. We both share a strong faith in the Lord, we work in occupations serving our community, we believe in taking care of our body by exercising regularly, and we enjoy developing boys into responsible young men. Leon serves as a Marine in the reserves. He is very structured, organized, and disciplined. I am emotional, passionate, and nurturing. There are plenty of times during coaching where one of us will take the lead and the other will think 'I wouldn't have done it that way or said it that way.' But we respect each other's gifts and are both focused and committed to making better ball players and developing character in our players. Last year, when some our players' parents decided to split off and form another team, Leon and I stuck together. We had developed a bond that enabled us to not only speak truthfully to one another but also support one another through mistakes and adversity.

Open up your life to someone who can stir you up in your faith. Pray that the Lord will help you find a friend who can sharpen you as you do the same for them. Be a good friend to others and they will be there for you.

Fitness

My wife, Susan, is the perfect workout partner. She has inspired 'tons' of ladies to get back in shape. Her favorite saying to her ladies is "Make up your mind and your body will do the rest." She started a free aerobics class at our church a few years ago and now she has a following of 80 to 100 ladies. They regularly email each other, talk about spiritual things, and of course inspire each other to get in better shape. She has dragged several ladies out onto the local track to teach them how to run. Sometimes they would meet at 7am to run before the husbands took off for work. As the wives started getting in shape, the husbands began to show interest as well. What an awesome trickle down effect!

My wife has a unique gift of seeing the absolute best in people and inspiring them to believe that there are no limits to what they can achieve in their level of fitness. She talks with her friends about running 10K races and even a marathon. She talks with them about losing dress sizes and experiencing tranquility through spirit, mind, and body. She has inspired a 50 year old gal named Donna to the point that she now confesses that she has never been in better shape in all of her life. Susan used to walk or run with Donna a few times a week. This happened for several months. But now Donna doesn't need Susan anymore. Now she hits the track regularly each week and is in the process of establishing a strength training program, besides aerobics twice a week. When Susan is not available to teach aerobics, Donna takes over the class and leads at a fervent pace. Susan was able to sow a seed in Donna that has now produced an awesome tree of wellness.

Finding a fitness partner is a great strategy to develop lifelong fitness habits. Some people hook up in the gym, others make a commitment with a friend to begin working out; some hire a personal trainer, and still others meet through clubs or teams. Finding a fitness partner is great for a couple of reasons. First, you are more accountable when you have to meet someone to workout. **Proverbs 12:27** says **"the precious possession of a man is diligence."** If you don't have diligence, then maybe you can ride on your friend's diligence for a while. When you don't feel like getting up in the morning to head to the gym to workout, but you know your friend will be there waiting, you sometimes feel that extra tug to get out of bed. Your own guilt complex will not allow you to let your friend down.

Another good reason to find a partner is so that you can share the pain with someone. There is nothing like getting together for a little torture and then having a pity party afterward. 'Whew, that was a hard workout. I am dead.' Truthfully, you can build great relationships with friends as you exercise together. I began road biking with my neighbor Steve a few years ago. We hardly knew each other and he saw me riding a couple of times and took the chance of asking me if I would be interested in riding together sometime. I said "Sure", and after a few botched time conflicts we were able to schedule our first ride together. I was a medium grade rider who was pretty fit and Steve was an expert. Our first ride together was pretty comical but now we have some great ones. I have learned a lot from him with respect to riding and we have developed a good friendship as a result of our times together on the bike. 'Iron sharpens iron and one man sharpens another.' Exercising with someone is a great way to do two important things: take care of your body and maintain a friendship.

Fitness Partner Considerations

Accountability-a fitness partner can help keep you motivated and accountable to your workout routine.

Safety-a fitness partner can spot you while lifting and keep an eye on you when you are pushing it on a hard run or bike. They can critique your form and style.

Similarities-you should pick a partner that has similar fitness goals and is at a similar fitness level as yourself.

Common interests-choose a partner that has common interests and values so you will have something to talk about. Meeting a partner should be fun and productive.

Time and Place-find a partner with a similar schedule to yours and someone that lives or works reasonably close to you. Workouts should be scheduled at convenient times and places.

Professional etiquette-if you have to miss a workout give your partner a call as soon as possible so they can make adjustments.

From various sources

Make one the greatest investment in life—close friends. A close friend can inspire you, motivate you, keep you on the straight and narrow, and help you become a better person. The time you invest with them can change their life and make it worth living.

Faith in Action: Find a workout partner who will hold you account-able to press on in your fitness. Invite someone to join you for a workout and see if you can develop a fitness relationship. If your first choice doesn't work out keep looking until you find someone.

17.

It's Never Too Late to Start

—ɯ—

Faith

Romans 4:18-21 "In hope against hope he believed, so that he might become a father of many nations according to that which had been spoken, 'So shall your descendants be.' Without becoming weak in faith he contemplated his own body, now as good as dead since he was about a hundred years old, and the deadness of Sarah's womb; yet, with respect to the promise of God, he did not waver in unbelief but grew strong in faith, giving glory to God, and being fully assured that what God had promised, He was able also to perform."

A braham received the promise of God at 101 years of age. He and his wife Sarah became parents in their late years of life. So did Zacharias and Elizabeth, the parents of John the Baptist. Can you imagine them changing diapers and playing ball with their son at that age? Can you imagine how many times they were called grandma or grandpa instead of mother or father? Yet these men and women pressed on in God and fulfilled their divine calling when they were advanced in years. Father Abraham became famous and the 'father of many nations.' Jesus said of John the Baptist 'among those born of women there is no one greater than John.' His parents must have been instrumental in raising him to serve the Lord.

Moses did not answer the call of the Lord until he was eighty years old. The Lord sent a strong message through these fathers and mothers of the faith that you can serve Him throughout your entire life. It is never too late to answer the call of God and make a difference. Moses led God's people for forty years in the wilderness. **Deuteronomy 34:7** reports that **"Although Moses was one hundred and twenty years old when he died, his eye was not dim, nor his vigor abated."**

When some people retire from work they sit around the house and quit doing things and quit living. Others just begin to live and see the world. Retirement is really not a Biblical principle as you can see from the examples above. One thing our young generation needs today is good examples to follow. They need a little 'old school.' The folks in their seventies, eighties, and nineties now are the ones who have seen great distress and have had character built into their lives. They are of great value to our society. It isn't time for them to pass away quietly, it is time for them to speak up and show the next generation the way.

I don't know where my family would be without my parents continuing to play an active role in our lives. I have four brothers and two sisters. Those of us with children would be lost without mom and dad. Although my dad is 'retired' and he and mom are in their mid sixties, they continue to minister to their family in a very active role. We all love them and dearly cherish their guidance, friendship, fellowship, support, and help. When I began to build a new home after a devastating house fire my dad was there every day sweeping, nailing, cutting, painting, running wire, or moving dirt. He was employee of the year and I tripled his salary several times ($3 \times 0 = 0$).

No matter how old a person gets, he or she still has a vital role in their call from God. Whether it is being a grandparent, a parent, a mentor for young children, a volunteer at the library, a voter's registrar, or a Sunday school teacher the Lord needs all of us to accomplish His business. It's never too late to serve Him.

Fitness

It's never too late to change your lifestyle and begin to live healthy. The decision to begin an exercise program and eat right will benefit you the moment you begin.

After surgery, heart surgeons used to tell their patients to take it easy for three months before beginning to move around. Now they realize that getting the patient up the next day to walk the halls will provide immediate benefit and strength for the heart. The patient is usually not too happy about it because it is painful and physically draining, but the heart is a muscle and strengthens quickly.

Our bodies are the same way. They will receive immediate benefit from exercise, and IT IS NEVER TOO LATE TO START. If you are older or heavier, the battle will be more challenging, but not impossible or unfruitful. **Isaiah 43:18-19** says **"Do not call to mind the former things, or ponder things of the past. Behold, I will do something new, now it will spring forth; will you not be aware of it? I will even make a roadway in the wilderness, rivers in the desert."**

Just because you are older or heavier is no excuse to keep you from stepping forward to a new life that is healthy and fit.

When I was studying physical education at Kennesaw State University I saw a video in my Kinesiology class that greatly impacted my view concerning this subject. A team of health professionals were doing a study on the aged. They went to a nursing home and did some testing on a good mix of older people. They tested mobility, strength, bone density, and some other indicators. After the initial testing they placed the participants on a daily workout program. I remember a charming, older gentleman who was using a cane to move around. He had reached a place in his life where his legs would not move him along sufficiently. Part of his workout program was strapping a weight attached to a cable around his waist and making him walk forward about eight steps with his cane and then walk backwards to slowly release the resistance. Others had similar resistance and cardio programs. After six weeks the older gentleman was off his cane and moving better than he had in years. Besides the increase in mobility, every participant measured an increase in muscle mass and bone density. The study proved several things to me. First, it showed me that it is never too late to begin working out and seeing a benefit. It also showed me that the apparent aging process of muscle atrophy and osteoporosis is more an effect of inactivity than it is an effect of getting older. Seeing the older gentleman walk around without his cane and dance a little shuffle of joy left an imprint on me.....IT'S NEVER TOO LATE TO START.

In June 2006 my family and I camped at St. Andrews Park in Panama City Beach, Florida. We spent most of the day on the sugar white beach and in the clear ocean. While enjoying the sun one day I saw an older man jogging down the beach in his bare feet. It was at least 80 degrees and he was moving along at a fast pace. I watched him run to the end of the jetty and back down the beach. He was really moving and I was impressed. About two days later I saw him cruising effortlessly down the sand again and I could not resist the urge to run after him and get his story. As we jogged along I found out that he was sixty years old and ran four miles a day on the sand in his bare feet. Every other weekend he would run a 5K race (3.1 miles) in less than 21 minutes. He usually won his age group. His name was Ed and he was a former NFL kicker whose career ended in the seventies. After chasing women and drinking too much beer Ed found himself overweight and in need of a life change. At the age of fifty he took up running and now, 10 years later, he looks great and will probably be going strong for at least another 10 years. I was encouraged and hoped I would be able to match his accomplishments when I reach that milestone. After all, sixty is relatively young if you take care of yourself.

When I was in my mid-twenties I was a lifeguard at the YMCA. I had the 6:30 am shift and sat in the chair and watched all the diehard swimmers come and go before work every morning. Around 9:00am on most mornings an older man named Dave would come in. He was a good Christian man and must have been in his late seventies. We had many engaging conversations. He would come to the pool to aqua jog. He would strap a flotation device around his waist and jump in the deep end and jog in the water. It was a low impact way of getting his exercise. Dave was by no means a physical specimen. He had a healthy gut and the aging process had taken its toll with wrinkles and sagging. But Dave told me something profound that I will never forget. He said, "Patrick, most people my age wake up and feel the aches and pains of old age and never get past them. They go sit in the chair and hurt all day. I have found that if I get up and start exercising I can work the soreness out of my body and feel pretty good the rest of the day. The arthritis pain goes away as well as the other nagging aches. You just have to get your blood flowing and loosen up your joints." Through my studies I found out years later, that Dave was exactly right.

My closest friend in high school got the revelation at about age 38. He was a hard worker and devoted a lot of time to his job. We would see each other every 5 or so years after high school and his physical shape grew in the wrong direction. Too much eating out on the road and lack of exercise created a mess. Finally he decided that he would hire a personal trainer to help him and his wife get back into shape. They met with her regularly until they had established a good routine. They fell in love with their trainer and when she moved on they were heartbroken. They hooked up with another trainer and found a new love that even proved more promising. When he and I spoke about his newfound love for fitness he said something I won't forget: "Pat, I haven't felt this good in a long, long time. I just wish I would have gotten a hold of this back in high school. I could have kicked some serious butt back then and I wouldn't have had such a hard road to climb."

Take a good look at your parents and grandparents. Genetically speaking, you will probably look a lot like them when you get older. You will also probably have similar health problems and take similar medications if you take care of yourself the same way they took care of themselves. It doesn't have to be that way, but it could if you follow in the same footsteps of exercise, eating, and other health habits as them.

It is never too late to start taking care of yourself. Please don't let age, an injury, or a setback keep you from continuing to practice lifelong fitness. I plan on exercising every day until the day I go home to be with the Lord. Age is only a number. I have seen people well advanced in their years continuing to exercise vigorously. One year while running the Peachtree Road Race I saw a man in his

---

Healthy Aging Facts

- By the year 2030 the number of older Americans will have doubled to 70 million, or about one in every five Americans.
- 88% of those over 65 years of age have at least one chronic health condition which is brought on by tobacco use, lack of physical activity, and poor eating habits.
- Nearly 20% of the population over age 55 experience specific mental disorders that are **not** part of normal aging including depression, anxiety disorders, and dementia (including Alzheimer's disease).
- More than 60% of older adults are inactive.
- Regular physical activity has shown to greatly reduce a person's risk of dying from heart disease, decrease the risk of colon cancer, diabetes, and high blood pressure, help control weight, strengthen muscles and bones, relieve arthritis pain, increase mobility and flexibility, and reduce anxiety and depression.
- Research has proven that strength training 2-3 days per week has produced the following benefits in older adults: 43% reduction in pain caused by osteoarthritis of the knee (over 16 weeks), 40% reduction in falls of women 80 years or older, 15% increase in metabolic rate, and a 12 month study showed 1% increase in bone density, 75% increase in strength, and 13% increase in dynamic balance.

From the CDC

---

late seventies moving along at a good pace. The crazy thing was he was wearing long polyester pants with a belt, and old grandpa-style walking shoes. (I hope to be more stylish.) He wasn't the coolest dressed, but he was definitely in the best shape of anyone his age.

There are countless folks who defy aging and live healthy lives. At age 45, George Foreman regained the heavyweight boxing title. Tina Turner continues to defy age and throw down some serious dance moves while performing during concerts in her late sixties. At age 89, the fitness guru Jack LaLanne continued to wake up at 5am and lift weights and swim for two hours. Joshua, who led the nation of Israel into the promised land at age 85 had this to say in **Joshua 14:7,10-11, "I was forty years old when Moses the servant of the Lord sent me from Kadesh-barnea to spy out the land, and I brought word back to him as it was in my heart".…… "Now behold, the Lord has let me live, just as He spoke, these forty-five years, from the time that the Lord spoke this word to Moses, when Israel walked in the wilderness; and now behold, I am eighty-five years old today. I am still as strong today as I was in the day Moses sent me; as my strength was then, so my strength is now, for war and for going out and coming in."** Joshua was as strong at 85 as he was at 40 years of age. It is amazing what a positive outlook on life will do for your health and strength.

You, too, are as old as you feel. Attitude and faith will far outweigh age. It is never too late to start an exercise program. And when you start, don't ever quit. Your body will thank you and you will be blessed in many ways.

Faith in Action: Take the 31 day challenge. Set a start date and make a plan to exercise for 31 days straight taking only one day off per week. Write down what you will do and when. Incorporate aerobic exercise and strength training into your routine. Make back up plans in case it rains. Reward yourself at the end of 31 days.

18.

I don't feel like…..

—ᴍ—

Faith

Mark 14:38 "Watch and pray, lest you enter into temptation. The spirit indeed is willing, but the flesh is weak."

As children of God we are called to be led by His Spirit and walk in the Spirit. However, sometimes, maybe even many times, our flesh is in objection to following the Spirit. The nature of the flesh is to take it easy, pamper itself, indulge itself, and basically relax or even become complacent and lazy. The Spirit on the other hand is filled with self-control, discipline, diligence, and an unquenchable desire to do the will of the Lord. When the two are in opposition, we must make a choice which one we will follow.

Sometimes I don't feel like going to church. Sometimes I don't feel like reading my Bible or praying. Sometimes I feel like sitting in front of the television for far more hours than I should. Many times I am too tired to make my son do his homework, get his shower, and send him to get ready for bed at his scheduled time. I rarely feel like helping my wife with the household chores of dishes, laundry, or cleaning and vacuuming. Cutting the grass, weed eating, and taking out the trash aren't that appealing sometimes either. If I lived by my feelings my home and family would be a wreck and I wouldn't be very strong in the Spirit.

Galatians 5:16 says **"But I say, walk by the Spirit, and you will not carry out the desire of the flesh."** As followers of Christ we must be filled every day with His Spirit so we can become empowered to overcome the flesh. Jesus prayed "lead us not into temptation but deliver us from evil." Every day there are barriers to overcome. We must be prepared to face tough choices and make the right decisions. We will face temptations, weakness, fatigue, and monotony. When these times come we must know the right direction and continue to press on in it. We cannot rely on fickle feelings to guide us. Noah had a word from God to build an ark. He spent many days and a lot of ridicule getting the ark ready. I'm sure he faced doubt, fatigue, resistance, and attacks from the enemy. But he knew what he was supposed to do and he kept on going. I'm sure there were times of loneliness as well as times of refreshing and encouragement from the Lord. Like Noah, we must continue to head in the right direction and follow what we believe to be God's will for our lives.

Part of being a believer is showing some backbone. **James 1:6-8** says **"for the one who doubts is like the surf of the sea, driven and tossed by the wind. For that man ought not to expect that he will receive anything from the Lord, being a double-minded man, unstable in all his ways."** We shouldn't take too much time to contemplate certain things in life. We have to put on our clothes, go to work or school, and perform the every day tasks. Some spiritual things should be the same way. We should spend some time in the word, prayer, and worship everyday. As we develop these fundamental practices of walking in the Spirit, every thing else will fall into place. Believers must follow God's Spirit and not our weak, fleshly feelings.

Fitness

I wake up at 5:45am to shower, shave, dress, and head off to work. After the usual 45-minute commute I punch the clock and start my daily grind at work. Dealing with a new set of 40 to 90 kids every 50 minutes is fast paced and fun, but requires a lot of energy. I see four sets in the morning, have an hour for combined lunch and planning, and see two more sets before dismissal. After teaching about seventy kindergarteners (ages 5-6), and tying five pairs of shoes, and answering 75 questions, I am about spent. When I wrap things up, I head to the car for my usual 40-minute commute home (less traffic). About twenty minutes into the ride, I have to fight to stay awake. The mental fatigue of the day, the constant bombardment of personal interaction, and the sugar low of having eaten two hours ago, cause my energy level to crash. After many prayers of "Jesus, help me to stay awake," and a few high choruses of "Hallelujah!" I make it down the last 100 yards of my gravel driveway to the carport.

As I exit my cyber green Volkswagen Beetle, I look through the glass French doors to see my one-year-old daughter with her hands on her knees, pacifier in mouth, grinning ear to ear, and squealing with delight because daddy is home. I climb the three steps into the kitchen and kiss my wife hello, while my daughter grabs my leg and then runs into the family room. AAAHHHH, home at last! Peace, love, my sanctuary! I get down on my hands and knees and crawl into the family room and chase my daughter until she turns and tackles me. I end up on my back on the carpet and she ends up sitting on my chest. My wife fills me with stories of the day. Then those fatal, awful, heavy words infiltrate my mind, heart, and body: "I don't feel like working out today."

I have every reason under the sun as to why I shouldn't work out today. I am exhausted. I stayed up too late last night, and rest would be better for my body. Work was so stressful I need to unwind and relax. I worked out yesterday. I need to spend time with the kids. My body is sore. It is too cold outside. Blah, blah, blah, blah, blah.

My flesh often does not want to exercise. **But Galatians 5:24 says "And those who are Christ's have crucified the flesh with its passions and desires."** This is right where the rubber meets the road in my fitness journey. I have to make a decision whether I will listen to the flesh or rise up in my spirit and crucify the flesh. Sometimes it is almost a comical debate between my flesh and my spirit as to whether or not I should workout. The flesh is like the devil sitting on one shoulder telling me every excuse under the sun as to why I should remain on the couch and not get up. The Spirit is on my other shoulder whispering scriptures into my ear: "The hand of the diligent will prosper." "Those who belong to Christ Jesus have crucified the flesh." "I can do all things through Christ who strengthens me." As my inner self debates, I am forced to make a choice. Thankfully, the Spirit usually wins. **Romans 8:13** takes on new meaning for me, **"for if you are living according to the flesh, you must die; but if by the Spirit you are putting to death the deeds of the body, you will live."** I sometimes feel as if my spirit is actually putting a shepherd's staff around the neck of my stubborn flesh and dragging it to the door (and you thought you had it rough).

This scenario has unfolded hundreds of times for me. The weight of the world is usually on my shoulders as I stumble up the stairs, get dressed to workout, and head towards the door. Here is the key to victory: the hardest two steps are the two out the door. If you make it out the door each step gets easier. Once I get my momentum going in the right direction, the Spirit will take over and bless me. As I make it down the driveway, my blood starts pumping, my adrenaline will elevate, and I will begin to soar. I return refreshed, replenished, and reinvigorated for the rest of the evening.

As Christians, we need to put our fleshly nature on the cross, we need to crucify it. And once it is crucified we need to walk in the Spirit. The fruit of the Spirit includes longsuffering, faithfulness, and self-control. The Spirit will direct us to get up, be faithful, put on those running shoes, and hit the pavement and give your flesh a good workout. If we follow the Spirit we can be blessed with renewed energy, vigor, and release of stress. Following the flesh will result in a two-inch love handle before you know it.

The problem with giving yourself a break is, once you do it the first time, it is much easier the next time. Each workout you miss doesn't seem like a big deal, until you don't have a routine anymore. Suddenly, the last time you worked out was a week ago, and then suddenly it is impossible to get over the hurdle and get out the door.

Cal Ripken knew how to overcome pain and excuses to play the game and fulfill his calling. The apostle Paul also understood the necessity of taking control of the flesh. In **1Corinthians 9:27** he said **"But I discipline my body and bring it into subjection, lest, when I have preached to others, I myself should become**

The Legendary Cal Ripkin Jr.

Cal Ripken Jr. played shortstop and third base for the Baltimore Orioles from 1981-2001. He made the All Star team 19 times. His lifetime batting average was .276 and he had 3,184 hits and 431 homeruns. He is known as baseball's Iron Man because he played in 2,632 consecutive games. He started every one of those games and spent 99.8% of the game on the field. He has played with a swollen ankle, a twisted knee, and a broken nose.

From Wikipedia

---

disqualified." Don't think you will ever be exempt from the fight. You might find great seasons of joy in exercising but watch out for the days when your flesh puts up a fight. The struggle is just like raising kids, sometimes they are a joy and it's a piece of cake. Other times they fight you to the bitter end.

I remember one afternoon I went through the usual circus act of fighting excuses. As I stepped out onto the driveway, the clouds loomed gray. I fought off the excuse of rain and started down the driveway and onto the road. A light drizzle started, followed by a steady downpour and then some thunder and brief lightening. In the 50-degree weather, the cold rain did not feel so refreshing. By the time I hit the second mile the rain lightened up and then subsided. I looked over my right shoulder to see a neighbor wave and give me the thumbs up. I glanced above him and in the sky appeared a beautiful rainbow as the sun broke through the clouds. My remaining miles were, needless to say, in glorious fellowship with the Lord. I was glad I pressed through the excuses. I felt like Noah seeing the rainbow and knowing good things were just ahead.

Faith in Action: Create a collection of faith filled songs that you can play to overcome the flesh and get you motivated to exercise. Burn your songs onto a CD or download them into your MP3 player. Crank up your selection before your next workout.

19.

Fathers of the Faith

—૧૦૦—

Faith

Philippians 4:9 "The things you have learned and received and heard and seen in me, practice these things, and the God of peace will be with you."

We all need inspiring leaders or fathers of the faith who will challenge us to do great things for God. The apostles had Jesus, Timothy had Paul, Elisha had Elijah. These fathers of the faith mentored their pupils and pushed them to be all they could be for God. They instructed them in the way of righteousness and set an example for them to follow. They imparted spiritual gifts and wisdom to their disciples.

God raises up mighty men and women to serve Him and be lights and examples of the Christian faith. He raises up people to lead the way and break new ground for His kingdom. He sends prophetic messengers to point out the evil and unrighteousness of the day, and direct humanity in the way to go. God provides mentors and Fathers of the faith from whom we can learn.

Do you have a particular pastor, preacher, or evangelist who gets you fired up to serve God? Have they sown spiritual things into your life that have gotten you on the right track to a deeper understanding of life and a deeper relationship with the Father? Are there men of God you admire for their bold stance and outstanding achievements for Christ? We all need someone who can give us a little wisdom or show us that there are stars out there that we can actually reach.

The Bible lists the hall of fame in **Hebrews 11.** In verses 33-38 Paul describes those heroes **"who by faith conquered kingdoms, performed acts of righteousness, obtained promises, shut the mouths of lions, quenched the power of fire, escaped the edge of the sword, from weakness were made strong, became mighty in war, put foreign armies to flight. Women received back their dead by resurrection; and others were tortured, not accepting their release, so that they might obtain a better resurrection; and others experienced mockings and scourgings, yes, also chains and imprisonment. They were stoned, they were sawn in two, they were tempted, they were put to death with the sword; they went about in sheepskins, in goatskins, being destitute, afflicted, ill-treated (men of whom the world was not worthy), wandering in deserts and mountains and caves and holes in the ground."**

I have drawn great inspiration from the lives of many Biblical heroes. I can see in my spirit Noah building the arc, Moses telling Pharoah off, David fighting Goliath, Peter getting out of the boat, Jesus raising Lazarus from the dead, Stephen looking into heaven and seeing Jesus as he was being stoned, Paul preaching the good news to the Gentiles, and many more wonderful things. We are blessed in the fact that we not only have those Biblical heroes who have gone before us, but we also have modern-day heroes who have made great strides in teaching us about the Father, faith, love, healing, service, and life. The works of many modern-day preachers and teachers have changed our lives and inspired us to follow Jesus.

Not only have we been blessed with wonderful preachers but also there have been godly statesmen and our founding fathers have made a tremendous impact on the destiny of our country. Every founding father that signed the Declaration of Independence and the Constitution proclaimed their faith in God. They challenged future generations to trust in Him and take a stand for what is right. They made powerful statements and backed up their words with their blood and actions. Their words and deeds are nothing short of awesome.

We have also had many presidents that changed the course of history by establishing righteousness, beating down evil and spreading freedom. I would hate to drop names and forget some-body that was pivotal, so I won't. The great thing is we have plenty of examples to draw inspiration from.

Let me finish these thoughts with the words of **Hebrews 12:1 "Therefore, since we have so great a cloud of witnesses surrounding us, let us also lay aside every encumbrance and the sin which so easily entangles us, and let us run with endurance the race that is set before us..."** Be inspired by the great men and women who have gone before us and rise up and meet the challenges of this generation. Find inspiration, be inspired, and go for it.

Fitness

There have been several people who have inspired me in my pursuit of fitness. When I first began working out in college, friends inspired me by their persistent workout habits. As I became grounded in a workout program of lifting and running, I began to seek profes-sional advice from experts and trade publications that offered diet and training techniques. Now I look for inspiration from others who have either run the fitness race with endurance or have made great achievements in their sport.

We all need someone to get us started. If you have never started a workout program, chances are you never will, unless someone shows you the way. We all need someone to introduce us to the fitness way of life. We need someone to open the door to a whole different way of living. This other way of living involves people voluntarily torturing their bodies on a regular basis to keep it in shape. Not really. But the concept of working out is new and foreign to those who have never been introduced to it. Beginning a workout program is kind of like a parent who takes a baby by the fingers and helps him or her walk across the floor. If you are new to fitness, you need a parent to help you begin to walk across the fitness floor. If you are looking for someone to introduce you to fitness, find someone who looks as if they are pretty fit, find out what they do, and see if they are passionate enough about it to help you get started. Most people who love what they do don't mind helping you get started. They might be able to take you to the track and point you in the right direction with a pacing plan. They might be able to take you to the gym and introduce you to a circuit strength training routine. Or they might be able to bring you to an aerobics class or kick boxing class that will literally kick your backside with a good workout. Listen to what they have to say, follow their advice for at least a month, and then dig deeper.

When I first started strength training in the gym, my college roommate dragged me through his workout routine. I was pathetic. He was throwing some serious weight around and all I could bench press was the bar (45 lbs.). I had no idea what I was doing and I even dropped the bar on my head one time, giving me a nice little lump. I did stick with it however and worked my way up to 25 pounds on each side of the bench press bar. I was making progress and could feel the difference. I was thankful for his patience and guidance in helping me. Soon I was heading to the gym whether he was going to make it or not.

After I had invested enough time into my fitness routine to make it a priority in life I began to seek professional advice on running, lifting, and eating right. The most profound impact on my life and philosophy of fitness came from Dr. Kenneth Cooper. Dr. Cooper is the man who termed the phrase "aerobics." If anyone knows about exercise and the body, he does. He has done more research on exercise and the body than probably anyone alive today. He has written numerous books and his advice is sound because he has the research to back it up. Dr. Cooper taught me the importance of exercise and strength training and how to eat right. I had the chance to meet him at a PE conference in Georgia and at 80 years of age he was as sharp as a tack and was still physically fit.

Besides Dr. Cooper I also began to read fitness magazines. Fitness magazines can help give you techniques and suggestions to get better work outs, overcome injuries, find cool places to train, and give you small blips on the latest research. But beware fitness magazines are not peer reviewed journals. There is some advice that is not based on research and may not be sound. However, if you know your stuff you will be able to find some good and discard the bad.

The more you read, the more grounded you become in your beliefs. After awhile some of those magazines become very repetitive. I have now become a research junkie and would much rather read research-related articles and brush up on statistics than get workout advice. I have now focused my attention on this and on finding inspirational stories from every day people and athletes who have overcome tremendous odds to either get in shape or achieve something great. Recently I came across the powerful story of Dick and Rick Hoyt, a father and son team who have competed in the following events:

Team Hoyt Accomplishments

Total Events	Personal Bests
• 206 Triathlons, 6 Iron man distances	* 2:40:47 Marathon
• 20 Duathlons	* 56:21 15K
• 64 Marathons, 24 straight Boston Marathons	* 1:21:12 Half Marathon
• 7 18.6 Milers	* 40:27 7.1 Miler
• 78 Half Marathons	* 13:43:37 Iron man Triathlon
• 1 20K	* 35:48 10K
• 34 10 Milers	* 2:01:54 18.6 Miler
• 27 Falmouth 7.1 Milers, 1 Falmouth in the Fall	* 27:17 5 Miler
• 8 15K	* 59:01 10 Miler
• 204 10K	* 17:40 5K
• 143 5 Milers	* 2:10:45 20 Miler
• 4 8K	
• 15 4 Milers	
• 92 5K	
• 6 20 Milers	
• 2 11K	

Total 911 Events

Biked and ran across the USA in 1992- 3,735 miles in 45 consecutive days
Biked the states of Connecticut, Rhode Island, Massachusetts, with "Axa World Ride '95"
Biked from Pittsburgh, PA to Washington, DC with "Axa World Ride 95"
www.teamhoyt.com

There is one catch to this father and son team. Rick has cerebral palsy and cannot walk or talk. Dick pushes or pulls him the entire distance. The reason he does it is simple and moving. Dick Hoyt says, "Rick told us he just didn't feel handicapped when we were competing." Dick, who is now 65 years old, has been competing with his son for 25 years. He pushes Rick in a modified jogger, puts him on his handle bars in a rigged up basket, or pulls him in a bike-type trailer. Can you imagine pushing a 125 pound man for 26.2 miles? How about at an elite pace of under 3 hours? Rick and Dick have a book about their adventures and go on speaking engagements sharing their powerful story. And you and I have excuses about working out...ha! It is stories like Team Hoyt that inspire me to press on in fitness and help others see the light.

I hope you will make some steps to find some inspiration in your life in regards to fitness. Don't fall into the trap of thinking you know everything. Dig deeper and be inspired. If you do know a few things, find someone to share it with, and change their life forever by giving them the gift of fitness.

Faith in Action: Go to the bookstore or library and find one good book written by a father or mother of fitness that will give you deeper understanding and inspiration into a healthy lifestyle. Get the book and begin reading it.

20.

No Condemnation

—⁓—

Faith

**Romans 8:1-2 "Therefore there is now no condemna-
tion for those who are in Christ Jesus. For the law of the
Spirit of life in Christ Jesus has set you free from the law
of sin and of death."**

When we give our lives to Christ and receive His forgiveness,
we are free from our sins. Our sins are removed from us as
far as the east is from the west. We are no longer a sinner but rather a
saint. Our slate is wiped clean and we become a totally new creature
in Christ. We become part of the family of God and are literally His
sons and daughters. The power of His work in us makes us born of
His Spirit. When we are born of His Spirit we are no longer born of
a sin nature but rather a new nature that seeks to do the will of God
and glorify Him. The more we begin to walk with Him in our new
life the more power and grace we receive to be children of God.

The enemy—the devil—doesn't like it when we begin to understand who we are in Christ. The devil doesn't like it when we begin
to realize that we are free from the sins of the past. He wants us to
be in bondage to sin. He wants us to live in a defeated mentality and
life. If the devil can get us to continue to think about our sins of the
past then he can convince us that we are sinners instead of saints

who are forgiven and cleansed. In **Revelations 12:10** the devil is called the **"accuser of the brethren."** He is always ready to accuse us and remind us of the past. He is always ready to use his weapon of discouragement to bring us back down into the gutter. He will be glad to whisper in your mind all the terrible things you have done in the past. He will be glad to remind you of what a loser you were.

If the devil can't bring you down because of mistakes in the past, he will magnify your mistakes in the present. If you sin or fall down he will be glad to let you know that you are a loser and you will never be a winner. He will condemn you for your mistake and let you know that you are a sinner and that you will continue to sin and you might as well give up on trying. God is the God of hope and the devil is the king of discouragement. Everything negative, ill-willed, demoralizing, despairing, disheartening, defeating, gloomy, depressing, and pessimistic comes from the devil. The devil would like to condemn us to a life of misery and defeat. He would like to condemn us to failure and eternal damnation.

But **Proverbs 24:16** says **"For the righteous man falls seven times and rises again but the wicked stumble in time of calamity."** In life the righteous will fall—the Bible says so. We will fall down and make mistakes. But the glory of the righteous is that we will rise again. We have the right as believers in Christ to get back up from our mistakes, ask God to forgive us, dust ourselves off, and move on. The righteous have a winning attitude that says "I will not quit, I will give myself another chance."

Abraham made a few mistakes before receiving the promise of Isaac. Jonah tried to kill himself before he turned and did the will of God. Samson made a mistake. David made quite a few mistakes. Peter denied Christ three times. Paul persecuted the Christians. All of these men got back up, received forgiveness, and went on to serve the Lord in His calling and did mighty things for Him. **Hebrews 10:39** says **"But we are not of those who shrink back to destruction, but of those who have faith to the preserving of the soul."** We must not shrink back into sin, but rather keep on believing that we are able to overcome.

1John 4:8 tells us that **"God is love."** It is in His loving nature to forgive us and restore us when we fall down. The God of all love, encouragement, perseverance, and forgiveness wants us to be over-comers. He does not want us to be defeated by sin or by a mistake but rather to be forgiven and cleansed so that we can move on. As the ultimate loving Father, it is not His desire to strike His child down for making a mistake. He will lift us up and encourage us to keep going.

Any good parent will not destroy their own child when the child makes a mistake. They will not constantly remind their child of how he messed up and what a loser he is. They will discipline the child for doing wrong, point him in the right direction, forgive him, and encourage him to move on. Any parent who loves their child and wants him or her to succeed in life will teach their child how to over-come obstacles, mistakes, and set backs. Life is full of them and no child is immune to them. The key is adopting a winning attitude.

Condemnation is a losing attitude. Forgiveness and repentance are winning attitudes. When we fall down we must rise again. We must get back up, ask God for His forgiveness, turn in the right direction, and move on. God is willing and waiting for us to get the victory. There is no sin more powerful than the blood of His Son. Jesus' blood will wash away all mistakes and give us new life in God. When we are forgiven we must learn from our mistake and move on in victory in the Lord.

Fitness

Changing your habits to live a healthy lifestyle is an incred-ible step. Some of our habits have been ingrained in us since youth. Some of our environments make change difficult and the temptation to relapse easy. Change takes time, discipline, and determination. Most people, like 99.2% of people, don't radically change their diet and exercise habits over night. Forest Gump took off running one day and ran across the United States, but that was a movie.

Most people will begin an exercise routine or healthy diet with good intentions. Like a New Year's resolution they will start with enthusiasm and passion. The first few weeks will go great and then an obstacle will beset them. A bump in the road disguised as a party with lots of good food or an injury of some sort will try to set them off course.

Sometimes words of discouragement from others or even criticism from ourselves will deter us from pressing on. Sometimes family or friends will laugh and say we are crazy or ridiculous for trying to run a mile. They will make fun of our appearance or point out the fact that we haven't lost any weight. Sometimes we get on ourselves for lack of apparent progress or for mistakes. We feel discouraged because we have tried hard and see no results or we miss a few workouts or eat a few deserts and feel this new lifestyle is impossible.

Most people who pack on the weight did not do it overnight. Most people spend a lifetime or at least a few years growing to their present size. To think you can lose it in a few weeks or months is not very smart thinking.

Losing weight, eating healthy, and exercising regularly are all things that take time to develop. Setbacks will occur. No one is perfect in their discipline and mistakes will happen. Bad habits are hard to break. If you don't think so, ask a smoker. They will tell you it is the hardest thing they have ever done. (Thanks to the tobacco makers for creating such a great product.) But progress is inevitable if you adopt a winning attitude.

'Winners never quit, and quitters never win!' If you want to be successful in your lifestyle change you will need to deal with negative attitudes, negative words from others, and mistakes.

Thinking of yourself as a loser is not a winning attitude. Thinking of yourself as weak or incapable of success is not the way to win. To make a change you have to think different. You have to embrace your power in Christ to overcome all obstacles, including physical ones. **Philippians 4:13** says **"I can do all things through Him who strengthens me."** This is a winning attitude that draws on divine power within to succeed. God is a winner. If He lives on the inside of you, then you are a winner too. He can give you power to achieve your goals and live a healthy life.

Negative words can also be harmful when trying to change. People will say the most discouraging things inadvertently. Sometimes others will discourage you from change because they feel guilty or convicted and they don't like that feeling. They see the changes you are trying to make and realize they should be doing the same thing, but don't feel they can. So they try to discourage you so you will quit and rejoin them in a miserable lifestyle. 'Misery loves company.' Don't listen to the negative words. Use them as a fuel to change. Adopt an attitude of 'I'll show them.' Beat them at the game and not at the mouth. Show them by your actions that you are determined and will change. Arguing or cutting people to the quick is not the correct way to deal with negative words. A humble attitude and response of "I'm going to keep on trying" may even win some people to your side. If the negative words don't stop, just try to avoid them. **Proverbs 21:19** says **"It is better to live in a desert land than with a contentious and vexing woman."**

My sister is a perfect example of someone who did not let negative words, attitudes, or perceptions influence her life. She was the youngest girl in an athletic family of seven children. If you were in our family you played sports and she followed along with the tradition by playing soccer. Her youth league soccer coach told her she couldn't play offense because she liked to play with the flowers and grass more than pay attention to the game. In high school she was disappointed when she was cut from the soccer team for her senior year after making the team the three previous years. During family vacations at the beach she refused to play volleyball with family members who would knock her out of the way to make a play on the ball to "help" her. Her experiences with sports left her feeling like she was not an athlete. In college however, she took up mountain biking and quickly developed a love for the outdoors, camping, and cycling. Mountain biking developed her endurance, strength, and provided an opportunity for her to see some beautiful places. She found a niche in fitness that opened up many more doors. Upon graduating she moved to Aspen, Colorado to explore some more beautiful trails. We thought it would be a winter expedition but she never came back. She took up snowboarding and now has the highest level of certification an instructor can achieve. She manages the snowboard lessons for Snowmass Mountain. She was featured on ESPN during four segments of Ski World—giving snowboard tips. Her love of cycling continued to grow and she was the women's overall winner for two years in the Aspen Cycling Club Town Series—a total of ten mountain bike races and ten road races. She also won each of the individual categories on different years. She has now taken up a new passion in rock climbing. She is rated a five point ten climber and is able to lead climbs. She has climbed in Colorado, Utah, Wyoming, and even Thailand. The runt of the family who was cut from the soccer team continues to climb to new heights in her fitness and athletic passions. She did not let negative words, attitudes, or perceptions determine her life.

Relapse Prevention

Relapse-an extended setback, returning to a negative behavior

Factors that contribute to a relapse- negative emotional or physiological states, limited coping skills, social pressure, interpersonal conflict, limited social support, low motivation, high risk situations, stress

Principles of Relapse Prevention
*Identify high risk situations (i.e. change of seasons, fast food)
*Develop appropriate solutions (walk on treadmill, bring lunch)
*Distinguish between lapse (missing exercise for a few days) and a relapse (an extended period of non-participation)

Additional strategies- set boundaries, learn coping skills, learn stress reduction techniques, develop support group

A popular behavioral theory developed by Marlatt and Gordon 1985

Besides negativity, mistakes are another obstacle that can prevent you from achieving your goals. If you break your diet with a weekend of partying, don't throw your diet out the window. If you fall into a week of fast food and gain back five pounds don't give up. If you miss the gym or the walking track for a week because the family schedule is hectic, don't quit. Don't beat yourself up because of setbacks. Identify them for what they are and move on. If you condemn yourself for a mistake, you will never succeed. Defeatism, negativism, and condemnation are from the devil. Don't allow them to run your life, your diet, or your exercise program. If you fall down, get up, forgive yourself, and move on. Don't quit and you will be a winner.

In graduate school I learned an interesting strategy called relapse prevention. Check out the textbox on page 158.

To prevent a relapse we need to set up some boundaries. To overcome a relapse we need to learn some coping skills. If you fall down, get back up and keep plugging. Lifestyle changes take time. Identify the pitfalls of condemnation and overcome them. Draw on God's forgiveness and strength to be a winner.

Faith in Action: Create a list of ten positive faith affirmations that you can speak aloud every morning. You can use ten scriptures from this book or some other favorites. Type them up and tape them to your mirror or place them in your car. Speak them aloud every morning. After a month create a new list.

21.

Setting Goals

—ᴍ—

Faith

Philippians 3:14 "I press on toward the goal for the prize of the upward call of God in Christ Jesus."

Paul the Apostle was focused on his goal from the Lord. His life was totally committed to preaching the gospel to the Gentiles. Do you have any goals or dreams? Oftentimes the goals or dreams we have in life are put in us from the Lord. He plants a seed in us to do something great or achieve a certain destiny. When I was a child I had a dream of being close to the Lord and being His "main man" like Moses or Abraham. When I was in high school I had a dream of being a writer. I wanted to study journalism in college. Later I had a dream of becoming a teacher and working with young people. With a little planning and effort our dream (somewhat farfetched ideas) can become our goal (calculated objective). When God gives us a dream (or goal) He also gives us the talent and abilities to achieve it. When we press on and achieve our goal He is glorified and others are blessed or inspired, and society is a better place.

There are many Biblical heroes who received a dream or goal from the Lord and set out to achieve that dream. Abraham set out to find a city whose architect was the Lord. Jacob set out to find a good wife. Joseph dreamed of being a ruler. Moses was called to set

God's people free. Joshua led God's people into the Promised Land. David had a goal of defeating Goliath. Solomon built a temple for the Lord. Esther became queen and saved the Jews. Nehemiah rebuilt the walls of Jerusalem. Jonah turned back the city of Nineveh. Mary had a son by the Holy Spirit who became Savior of the world. Paul preached the good news to the Gentiles. All of these individuals and many others had dreams and goals from the Lord. They earnestly pursued their goals with help from the Lord and they made a difference in their lifetimes.

When I was in college I shared a five bedroom house with nine other guys. We were all Christians and called our place the House of Faith. One of my roommates was a big, country-boy from South Georgia. He had broad shoulders, a wide grin, and a rolling laugh. He was a lot of fun to be around but struck you as a somewhat goofy, happy-go-lucky guy. He struggled through his studies, worked at Taco Bell to pay his way through school, jammed to heavy metal Christian music, and told us some crazy stories of his days before he gave his life to Christ. He always shared with us that he would like to be a Baptist preacher some day in a rural church setting but those of us who knew him thought it was a pretty big leap of faith. After college he joined the Army reserves and we lost touch for awhile. The next time we heard from him he was in Bible College and was engaged to a preacher's daughter. After a few years we heard he was married and was preaching in a little church in the country just as he dreamed of doing. Later we heard he was in seminary getting his doctorate. When "the Doctor" finished we heard he was preaching in a bigger church. Recently I saw a picture of him in a newsletter. He was a Chaplain in the Army and was baptizing soldiers in the Iraqi desert. My humble, redneck roommate (who I love dearly) kept his eye on his dream from the Lord and went way beyond what I ever would have suspected. Dreams can become goals which can become reality. I am sure he has touched many lives in his ministry.

Goals can come in all shapes and sizes. Your goal can be occupational like becoming a spouse, a parent, a teacher, a preacher, a public servant, a soldier, a musician, a singer, an artist, a president, or a business owner. Or your goal may be more subtle such as reading the Bible in a year or spending more time with your children. The Lord will place heavenly dreams and goals in you. They will come as a small inkling that says "I really would like to......" Whatever the Lord calls you to do, pursue it with passion. Use all your resources, talents, and brains to achieve the goal He has placed in you. To achieve it will require great focus and effort. It may require a commitment of your entire life. Don't think it will fall into your lap. Press on toward your goal so you will realize an incredible satisfaction in accomplishing it and make this world a better place.

Fitness

Setting fitness goals can help you make progress to a healthier life. Your goals may include losing weight, fitting into a certain dress or pant size, running a certain distance, or overcoming a certain chronic illness. Everyone's goals are a little different because they are personal. Achieving your goals will give you a great sense of accomplishment and will enable you to set more goals, maybe even higher ones. As you achieve your goals you may inspire those around you to set similar ones. Setting fitness goals is a great way to stay focused and become healthier.

Before each sports season I set goals for the team I coach. Whether the sport is soccer, baseball, or basketball we set out to achieve three goals. Our first goal is to increase our personal skills related to the sport—shooting, dribbling, hitting, throwing, catching, etc... Our next goal is to learn more about the sport and the strategy involved in playing it. Our final goal is to enjoy the sport and enjoy making new friends and working together as a team. Every single thing we do on the field or court is related to achieving one of these three goals. We don't focus or set our goal on winning but rather becoming better players. Because this is our focus we develop our skills to a point where we usually have successful teams. Besides winning, which is fun, we enjoy our time together. We enjoy the sport and when our season is over we have fond memories and most of my players want to play again and would prefer it if I was their coach. Setting goals helps us stay focused on what is important and what we are trying to achieve. Your personal fitness goals should do the same.

One of my fitness goals was to run a marathon. It was a lofty goal but I think every serious runner wants to know if they have what it takes to run the ultimate race. I wanted to run the most beautiful marathon in the world so I chose the Big Sur International Marathon which runs along the California shoreline from Big Sur to Carmel. My goal was to run and finish the race. I savored every moment of the race and wrote my experience down in a little story so I could remember it years later. I emailed it to several friends with the hopes of sharing the thrill of my experience and inspiring them to aim high. I hope you enjoy it and if you decide to run a marathon, I won't hold it against you.

ODE TO BIG SUR
(My Marathon Story)

Little did I know, as the wake-up call rang the room at 3:30am on April 25, 2004, that I would embark on one of the most incredible experiences of my life.

I stumbled to the shower to wake up, slid in to my running shorts and dry-fit shirt (with number attached from last night), slipped my shoes on and laced them tighter (time chip attached), clipped my radio around my waist, packed my Cliff bar into my radio pouch, grabbed an 8 oz (12oz less than my normal dose) coffee and bagel in one hand, a water bottle in the other and headed for the door (all within 12 minutes).

My mind was hazy from jetlag, lack of sleep, and bewilderment about the task before me, as my wife spent three minutes backing the car out of the spot we were in. She drove me the six minutes to the bus pickup area, the Monterey Marriott. Hundreds of runners quietly lined up at 3:50am to head single file into the school buses that would take us 26.2 miles to the start of the Big Sur Marathon.

My seatmate was Christoph, a Polish anesthesiologist, hailing from Michigan. We exchanged stories while sipping on water as the bus slowly wound backwards through the course, which was too dark to see. We were both first-time marathoners, and silence stimulated by nerves, dominated our 40-plus minute drive. Flashbacks of my months of training worked through my conscience... the threshold of pain that moved further up the road each week first eight miles then ten miles, then 12, 15, 17, 17 again, 18, and finally 21 miles... the bad 21-mile run that put me on the ground in front of my house, and then the good one...losing 6 pounds after a run...Gatorade or water every two miles...blistered feet...snow, rain, sunshine, and even a rainbow.

I gnawed on my whole-wheat bagel occasionally, and although it tasted like cardboard, I knew I needed the energy and stomach settling qualities. As the bus made a wide u-turn in the gravel and pulled up to the curb, heading north, we shook hands, wished each other good luck, and stepped from the bus into the staging area at Pfeiffer State Park in Big Sur.

The beauty of the backdrop of the staging area was masked by the darkness of the morning. Runners slowly unloaded and formed lines for water, bagels, coffee, and the porta-potties. After taking care of business, I found a place on the ground amongst the other runners.

The public address announcer directed the masses to comfort stations, introduced famed Olympian Jeff Galloway for words of advice, commended the VIP Grizzled Vets (who have run the past 18 Big Surs) and played us a little inspirational music.

Over the next two hours the sun slowly rose in the backdrop and revealed a gorgeous mountain range behind us. First the glimmer of a halo silhouetted the mountain range, followed by beams of light, and then illumination of the beautiful canopy of redwoods and evergreens that surrounded us.

At about 30 minutes prior to race time, runners lined up to turn in race bags for claiming at the other end. Extra long porta-potty lines forced me and others to stream into the tree line for one last relief. The announcer warned us to let it hang out but not too low because we were standing in a bed of poison oak. "That's one itch you don't want to scratch."

As nearly 3000 runners piled onto Highway 1 for the start of the 19th Big Sur International Marathon the announcer reported that the weather this year would be the nicest in history. He even predicted an abnormal tail wind that might help us along.

A word of thanksgiving and prayer was followed by the "Star Spangled Banner" and the releasing of a flock of doves that circled twice and soared heavenward. The elite runners stepped into the reserved front spot and with a shout of "good luck," the honorary starter, running legend, Galloway, fired the starting pistol.

The first two to three miles were downhill under a canopy of redwoods and evergreens. I reached out and tagged a gentle giant that had somehow survived a few hundred years without getting nailed by a car. The beginning run was cool and quick. The shade of the trees and mountain range to the right shaded us from the sun ahead.

Eventually we spilled out onto the flats with meadows on one side and rolling hills on the other. The evidence of the beautiful "warm" weather became very apparent. I made a decision before the start to go with my newfound strategy handed down from my brother's friend, Art. He picked it up from the master himself, Galloway. Run a mile and walk a minute. Well I tweaked it a little and made it, run a mile, walk 30 seconds. By the end of five miles I was under an eight minute/mile pace and felt great.

My strategy also included three sips of water or Gatorade every 2nd mile with food at miles seven, 14, and 21. This plan was immediately shot down when I realized the water stations were more sporadically spaced than every two miles. I would make improvisations as I went.

My running strategy worked like a charm and kept me fresh for nearly 18 miles. Much of the marathon I played cat and mouse with the same group of runners. I would pass them, walk, they would pass me, and then we would start over. The glory of it was that they were looking beat, and I felt great.

The surroundings of the run were so breathtaking that they are nearly indescribable. We had miles of ocean and beaches on the left side and cliffs and mountains on the right side. Sometimes we ran beside rails with a sheer drop off to the surf hundreds of feet below. The ocean rolled in and smashed against jutting rocks spraying water 15 feet into the air.

As we wound around the curves of Highway 1 we passed over many bridges including the spectacular Bixby Bridge, which was an arched expanse bridge that gave me chills when I looked back at its beauty and surroundings.

My race was truly blessed by God. It seemed that every time I would begin to feel the heat of the sun, we would turn a corner and go into the shade of some huge rock formation and feel a nice ocean breeze. It was literally like running into an air-conditioned room for a few minutes.

At mile ten we climbed toward the summit of Hurricane Point. The two mile uphill grade was not as difficult as I had imagined, mainly due to my hill training and my run/walk strategy. At the top was a sign that said, "Look back and see what you have accomplished!" The view was exquisite. I have a picture from the previous day where we were above the clouds, looking down on them and the beach and ocean. On this race day it was clear and sunshiny and the view revealed miles of runners.

What goes up does come down. The descent of Hurricane Point was fast and in the shade. Half way down the other side was the beautiful Bixby Bridge. Upon crossing the bridge, a perfect photo moment, there was a gentleman playing on a grand piano. Next to him, sitting in a lawn chair and waving to the runners, was the artist who painted the Big Sur poster, Ric Masten. The pianist was one of many musicians we encountered along the way, who came out to inspire the runners. There were several school bands, jazz players, drummers/dancers, rock bands, a flutist, a bagpipe, and others.

Besides the musicians there were about 11 aid stations, filled with volunteers who cheered us on while refueling us with water, Gatorade, Gu, bananas, oranges, and even wet sponges. The volunteers, some under the age of 10, were a godsend.

Since there were other races going at the same time, we marathoners also got a boost from the race/walkers and the teammates of the marathon relay teams. Literally ten people per mile would praise you or encourage you to 'keep going, you're almost there.' At one relay exchange around mile 15, I ran through a gauntlet about 200 feet long of relayers on each side clapping and cheering. I had to kick it in to give them a little bang for their efforts. That group was a great lift.

Around mile 18 my legs began to tighten up. I thought it might be a good idea to stretch for a few seconds during my 30-second walk. Big wrong! When I pulled my right foot behind me to stretch my right quad, it locked up as well as my left hamstring (which was supporting all weight and balance for too long). I winced in pain and quickly lowered my leg and prayed they would unlock. I hit the reset button and slowly began walking and then jogging forward. Whew! I made it out of a near fatal lockdown.

The gravity of finishing my first marathon began to set in as I began, too often, counting down the remaining mileage—eight, seven, six, five… I got confused for a while and was counting 26 as another whole mile to run and begged myself to quit thinking about it. At 20 miles I walked a few extra seconds and had to plead with my body to give me another good eight minutes of running. At 21 miles we hit the last serious hill and it almost broke me. I was on pace according to the split callers to finish at about 3:30 until I hit this last hill. The previous winner of the last two years reached this point about an hour earlier than me and dropped to a walk surrendering his three-peat. Between the hill, my legs beginning to cramp, and the heat setting in, somehow I missed a mile marker and kept going and going and going. It took me a whopping 17:49 to hit the next marker. I was a bit delusional at this point, thinking it had taken me that long to run one mile. I lost track of my countdown and added in an extra mile until I would hit the finish line.

I prayed earnestly during these difficult miles that the Lord would carry me through. "I can do all things through Christ who strengthens me. Greater is He that is in me, than he that is in the world."

I began to reason and make deals with myself. 'Come on Pat, you can do it. You didn't come this far to quit now. There are a lot of people counting on you to be a hero in this thing. If it were easy everyone would do it. Just give me seven more minutes and you can walk again.'

On the last two miles, each time either foot hit the ground, my calf would wince in pain. At any minute I felt it could lock down in some serious pain. At my last two walk points I could only hope, pray, and bargain with myself that my body would restart on the jog.

When I hit the 25-mile marker, because I had missed the split, I actually thought that I had to finish 2 more miles—25 and 26. When I hit twenty-six and saw the finish line, my body, soul, and mind were flushed with thanksgiving. I shouted "Glory to God" as my calves tightened in pain.

The last 2/10 of a mile I half jogged and half shuffled my spent legs across the pavement towards my goal. I scanned the crowd of frenzied, cheering fans at the right for my wife. Finally, I caught her wave only a few steps from the finish line. I smiled at her for the photo finish and trudged over the timing pad to look up and see my finish time: 3hours 40minutes 37seconds. It was better than I had expected.

A girl at the finish line hung a medallion around my neck. They were offering solar blankets but I declined, I was hot enough. In the next few steps I fought back the tears of gratitude and triumph. I was grateful to the Lord for getting me through those last few painful miles. I also felt a unique sense of triumph...I had just accomplished a lifetime goal of running a marathon, and had finished it in not too shabby of a time.

At the start of the race Galloway said less than 1% of the population has ever run a marathon. Now I was a member of the club. I had finished 26.2 miles. The gravity brought me to tears several times in the ensuing hour.

As I painfully walked through the refreshment tent gulping Gatorade and water, I loaded a cardboard tray with fruit and other carbs. My legs were screaming in cramping pain and all I wanted to do was sit or lie down and rest. I met my beautiful, beaming wife on the other side of the tent and she helped me hobble towards a grassy spot near our car.

I'll spare you the details of the pain. I'll just say I made the mistake of sitting down after about five minutes and my calves locked up tight. I screamed in pain and had to be lifted to my feet to walk off the cramps. I literally had to walk and drink for an hour before the cramps subsided.

The euphoria of my Big Sur experience is something I will never forget. The beauty of this course, the challenge of pushing my body to its physical limit, and the reward of crossing the finish line are nothing short of exhilarating.

Will I run another marathon? I don't know. I do have some other bridges to cross. But you know how people can talk you into things...

Hey, I heard Maui has a beautiful course. If you think you might be interested in running one I put a beginner's marathon training schedule at the end of this chapter...you know, just in case.

As you contemplate your fitness goals, choose some that are challenging but attainable. Set some small goals that you can achieve so that you can build your confidence to set and achieve some bigger ones. When you achieve them you will notice a difference in your body and strength and will be able to press on to bigger goals. Reward yourself for your achievements a new outfit, a trip to the beach, or a new piece of exercise equipment (no food rewards).

Setting goals will keep you focused in the right direction and promote your health. When you reach your goals you will glorify God with a healthier body and you will inspire others to make a change for the better.

My First Time Marathon Training Schedule

Week	Mon	Tues	Weds	Thurs	Fri	Sat	Sun	Total
1	3 miles	Rest	3 miles	Rest	3 miles	Rest	3 miles	12miles
2	Rest	4 miles	Rest	4 miles	Rest	4 miles	Rest	12miles
3	4 miles	Rest	4 miles	Rest	4 miles	Rest	5 miles	17miles
4	Rest	4 miles	Rest	6 miles	Rest	7 miles	Rest	17miles
5	4 miles	Rest	7 miles	Rest	4 miles	Rest	7 miles	22miles
6	Rest	4 miles	Rest	8 miles	Rest	10miles	Rest	22miles
7	4 miles	Rest	7 miles	Rest	4 miles	Rest	12miles	27miles
8	Rest	4 miles	Rest	8 miles	Rest	14miles	Rest	28miles
9	4 miles	Rest	7 miles	Rest	4 miles	Rest	16miles	31miles
10	Rest	4 miles	Rest	8 miles	Rest	17miles	Rest	29miles
11	4 miles	Rest	7 miles	Rest	4 miles	Rest	18miles	33miles
12	Rest	4 miles	Rest	8 miles	Rest	20miles	Rest	32miles
13	4 miles	Rest	7 miles	Rest	4 miles	Rest	21miles	36miles
14	Rest	4 miles	Rest	8 miles	Rest	21miles	Rest	33miles
15	4 miles	Rest	7 miles	Rest	4 miles	Rest	23miles	38miles
16	Rest	4 miles	Rest	8 miles	Rest	15miles	Rest	27miles
17	4 miles	Rest	4 miles	Rest	4 miles	Rest	M-Day	38miles

This schedule is for experienced runners who are preparing for their first marathon.
Hydrate properly and carbohydrate load the day before long runs.
Store on your person or roadside and consume ample fluids and food during the long runs.
Bring a cell phone or make plans in case you cramp up during long runs.
Rest and stretch.
Vary speed and terrain (include hills).
Experiment with run/walk method (run a mile/walk for 30-60 seconds, resume run).

Faith in Action: Set a fitness goal and develop a plan to achieve it. It may be to run a 10K race, a half-marathon, or a marathon. It may be to ride your bike a certain distance, climb a mountain, or learn a new sport or activity. Create a concrete plan and follow through.

22.

Bondage

—ᴍ—

Faith

John 8:34 "Jesus answered them, "Truly, truly, I say to you, everyone who commits sin is the slave of sin.""

Slavery is submission to a dominating influence. Slaves lack freedom and control of their life. It doesn't take long to become a slave to sin. The first time we disobey our parents or lie or take a drink of alcohol (underage) or try drugs or check out some pornography or do something else that our conscience tells us not to do, we feel bad about it. But when we don't get caught and nobody seems to get hurt, we continue on. Pretty soon it becomes our mode of operation. Our conscience is seared and it doesn't bother us to do something illegal, immoral, harmful, or disrespectful. After awhile we become a ring leader, recruiting others to our bad behavior. Misery loves company. The Bible outlines the progression of sin in **Romans 1:28-32: "And just as they did not see fit to acknowledge God any longer, God gave them over to a depraved mind, to do those things which are not proper, being filled with all unrighteousness, wickedness, greed, evil; full of envy, murder, strife, deceit, malice; they are gossips, slanderers, haters of God, insolent, arrogant, boastful, inventors of evil, disobedient to parents, without understanding, untrustworthy, unloving, unmerciful;**

and although they know the ordinance of God, that those who practice such things are worthy of death, they not only do the same, but also give hearty approval to those who practice them." In the end we become a slave to sin. We can't live our life with out our evil habit. We have no control over changing.

I consider myself somewhat of an expert on addictive behaviors. My high school days and first two years of college were filled with many enslaving behaviors. Since I have been there and done that and now I'm free, I feel as if I was a prisoner of war. I have seen the enemy's camp, I have learned how he operates, and I have escaped with my life to warn others. Now that I know how the devil works I will be on guard for my children and friends. I will be on the lookout for signs of destructive habits in my loved ones.

Since I have been freed from enslavement to sin for more than twenty years I have come to recognize three stages of sin that result in bondage. The first cord that entangles the sinner is deception from the devil. The deceiver makes sin look good. The deceiver promises that sin won't hurt us. The deceiver promises that we will get some benefit or satisfaction from the sin. Sometimes the deceiver presents himself in the form of peer pressure from friends. Deception is the start of a corrupted life. Ask Adam and Eve. They were deceived into eating the fruit. Take smoking pot for example. Plenty of movies have portrayed smoking pot as no big deal. They make it look like it is a barrel of laughs with no consequences. The circle of friends that smokes pot is the same way. "It's fun… it's a good high… it won't hurt you... you can be our friend and have a good time." Once your friends deceive you into taking your first hit, you have bought the lie and started down the road to bondage.

The second stage of bondage to sin is surrendering of the will. When we align our will to sin we become further entangled with a self-destructive life. When sin becomes pleasurable, we want more of it. Our mind and our heart become consumed with the desire to practice the enslaving behavior. We wholeheartedly give ourselves to the behavior without regard to our conscience, the command of God, or any consequences. Our life and identity become wrapped up in the sin that we frequently practice. If you started smoking pot on a regular basis you would be labeled a pothead. You would hang out with the druggies and every recreational moment would revolve around getting high. You would look forward to lighting up before the football game or during a party. You would crave the feeling of getting high. Your discussions would not be about grades or school or college plans or parenting strategies but rather who got wasted last night and what foolish thing they did.

The final stage of enslavement to sin is bondage. When we reach bondage, we are no longer in control. The sin has possessed our soul and we can't quit. We may recognize the emptiness of the sin or its damaging effects on our life, but we just can't do anything about it. We are a slave. Being a slave to sin is a dangerous place to be. More destructive behaviors surface like deeper engagement in other sins or even thoughts of suicide. **James 1:14-15** says **"But each one is tempted when he is carried away and enticed by his own lust. Then when lust has conceived, it gives birth to sin; and when sin is accomplished, it brings forth death."** If you became a pothead you would reach a place in your drug-abused life where you needed to get high to function socially. You would want to escape to an alternate state so you could enjoy life and tolerate others. You become dependent on pot much like an alcoholic craves alcohol. You would not only continue your pot use but also look for and experiment with other drugs that give you an easier or quicker and deeper fix. Pot is called a gateway drug for that very reason. Smoking pot is a sin because it alters and destroys the normal function of your mind and body. It takes a person to another state of consciousness that often leads them to engage in other sins. Escaping from your problems and the life that God created for you by doing drugs is sin.

Throughout high school and college I had a friend that was my drinking partner. When I gave my life to Christ and was set free from alcohol he had a hard time with my conversion because I would not drink with him. He came from a religious background but had some misconceptions about the nature of God. He reasoned that God was in heaven smiling and chuckling at him when he was getting drunk and doing crazy things and didn't see any problems with his behavior. He did not understand that God does not condone the sin that His Son had to die for on the cross.

Sin is nothing to play around with. Sin should not be justified or rationalized. Sin has dire consequences. When we sin we must be quick to recognize it, confess it, and repent. Christians should not be in bondage to sin. Jesus has set us free and we should walk in that freedom. **Romans 6:12-14 says "Therefore do not let sin reign in your mortal body so that you obey its lusts, and do not go on presenting the members of your body to sin as instruments of unrighteousness; but present yourselves to God as those alive from the dead, and your members as instruments of righteousness to God. For sin shall not be master over you, for you are not under law but under grace."**

As a former slave who was in bondage to sin I can honestly testify that Jesus set me free. When I heard the truth of the gospel and fell under the conviction of the Holy Spirit I knew my life was a wreck and I surrendered to the Lord. I asked for His forgiveness. I asked Jesus to come into my life and change me. He and I both knew my sins and I acknowledged to Him that I had no power to change. I had tried in the past and failed. He heard my heartfelt plea and surrender and He came and delivered me. The Lord rescued me from bondage to many sins. He changed my life and gave me a new heart, a new conscience, and a desire to please Him. He is willing to forgive and deliver all who call on His name with a repentant heart. He is the only true way out of bondage to sin.

Fitness

There are many addictive behaviors that are damaging to the body. All the popular sins can really destroy one's health. Smoking, drinking, drugs, and illicit sex, to name a few, can have some pretty negative effects on the body. Frequent practice of these habits can destroy the lungs, brain cells, nervous system, liver, and sex organs.

Besides the 'big sins' there are other addictive behaviors that are less talked about but are equally damaging to your heath. Specifically food addiction and laziness are two habits that can wreak havoc on your health.

Food is very addictive. Eating too much food or living off the wrong kinds of foods will pack on the pounds and create chronic

Drug Abuse and Addiction Facts

- Smoking, drug abuse, and alcohol cost our nation $484 billion per year
- Drug abuse is the most commonly viewed 'Very serious problem' in our country by 82% of Americans (followed by cancer, drunk driving, and heart disease)
- Tobacco contributes to 11-30% of cancer deaths and 30% of heart disease deaths.
- One third of AIDS/HIV cases are associated with drug injection.
- Between 10-22% of highway crashes were a result of drug and alcohol combinations.
- At least fifty percent of those arrested for homicide, theft, and assault were under the influence of illicit drugs at the time of the arrest.
- 2/3 of those seeking treatment for drug abuse were physically or sexually abused as a child
- Each year 40 million debilitating illnesses or injuries result from tobacco, alcohol, or addictive drug use
- In 2000, 460,000 deaths were attributable to smoking and drug abuse
- 50-80% of child abuse and neglect cases involve parents who have substance abuse problems
- There may be as many as 45,000 cocaine exposed babies born each year
- 31% of America's homeless suffer from alcohol and drug abuse
- 60% of adults in Federal prison are there for drug related crimes

From National Institute on Drug Abuse
National Institutes of Health

health problems. Do you know anyone who can really put away some food? I know some folks who can eat pretty steady for a couple of hours. How about someone who is a sugar-aholic (a sweets lover)? Diabetes, heart disease and some cancers are brought on by what and how much we eat. It is easy to get hooked on unhealthy foods like chocolate, ice cream, fried foods, sodas, candy, and chips. The food companies go to great length to manufacture the right taste and look so that their foods are irresistible.

When I worked in landscaping I became addicted to fast food. I was on a busy schedule and going through the drive-thru was a great way to get a quick bite and keep moving. On many occasions I had fast food for breakfast, lunch, and dinner. I'm sure there were times when I went several days without a fruit or vegetable, unless you count French fries as a vegetable. It didn't take long until I craved the smell, the taste, and the effects of fast food in my body. The fries, the grease, the juicy burgers, the crispy yet tender chicken, and the big thirst buster Coke to chase it down seemed to be rewarding and filling. I was burning a lot of calories so I could eat anything I wanted, but I was getting very little in the way of nutritional value. The addiction to fast food lasted well past my landscaping days. Oftentimes I would convince my wife to blow off a family meal and grab a quick bite to eat. Breaking the addiction to fast food was a difficult one.

Laziness is another addiction that can be dangerous to our health. Being a couch potato is addictive. Life is hectic and sometimes we need to chill out and relax. But some people take a break too long and it becomes a habit, a bad habit. I am pretty regimented about my workouts. I will not blow off too many because I know I can get too lazy really quickly and not want to work out anymore. We can find many things to do around the house that will fill in the time and take the place of our exercise routine. The World Wide Web is endless and there is always something to watch when you have 150 channels. But those things will enslave us to the house and the couch. It will be hard to break the easy lifestyle habit and get back on an exercise routine. A while ago there was a story on the news about a man who was stuck in his bedroom. He weighed over five hundred pounds and could not get up or out of his room.

They had to cut open the door frame to literally haul him to the hospital. His bondage to laziness and food addiction put himself at serious health risk not to mention the fact that he didn't have a very high quality of life.

Fortunately there is a road to freedom. There is a way to break the bondage to unhealthy habits. Once we taste the freedom, we will not want to go back to our destructive ways. The bondage of our former habit will even become repulsive to us.

The first step in getting free from bondage is hearing the truth about our habit. If we don't realize the damage we are doing to our life, our body, our health, and the lives of others, we may never have the desire to change. The truth must bring some conviction into our mind and heart that we need and want to change. The truth may not just be in the form of what we are doing to destroy our own body. It is sad to say that most people don't respect their own body and health enough to change. The truth may be the alarming reality that our bondage to a bad habit is destroying the life of others. Sometimes the people that love us the most hurt inside tremendously because they see us destroying our lives by engaging in unhealthy behaviors. Destroying your own life is one thing, but destroying the lives of your loved one's by drinking, smoking, or becoming obese is another. If your bondage to sin hurts others, you need to change.

My wife and I have a very dear friend that is married to a man that is obese. Although she has gently reminded him that he needs to stop eating junk and drinking sodas he continues on. He has had numerous health problems and must take his pills several times during the day to keep his blood pressure in check. Our friend has been brought to tears on several occasions because she believes that she will end up having to take care of him for the rest of his life because of his neglect. She is distraught by the thought that she may have to spend many of her senior days in the hospital by his bedside or waiting on him hand and foot at home because his health has deteriorated to the point where he can't get up any more. Her painstaking remark to us was "It's just not fair!" If her husband only knew the truth about how she felt, he might be willing to change because of his love for her.

The next step in breaking the bondage to unhealthy habits is admitting our enslavement and getting help. I believe the greatest helper is the Lord. In **2Corinthians 12:9** the apostle Paul said **"And He has said to me, "My grace is sufficient for you, for power is perfected in weakness. ""** Confessing our sin to the Lord and others allows us to humble ourselves and get the help we need. Addiction is very difficult to break by ourselves. The Lord Jesus went to the cross to pay the price for our sins and His resurrection gave us the power to overcome sins. When we confess our sin to Him and ask for His forgiveness and help, we join in the Spirit with Him and we receive His strength to overcome. Sometimes His help will come in the form of other people that we can confide in and get help from. Recovering alcoholics for example find strength in joining together to overcome their addiction.

The next step to freedom from bondage is making a clean break. We must turn our back on the sin and walk away. We must not go back. **2 Corinthians 6:17** says **"Therefore, COME OUT FROM THEIR MIDST AND BE SEPARATE," says the Lord." AND DO NOT TOUCH WHAT IS UNCLEAN; And I will welcome you."** If we want to break free from an addictive habit we are going to have to turn and walk the other way.

When I became a Christian in college I was involved with a fraternity. We had regularly participated in heavy drinking and some other unhealthy habits. When I came across the above scripture during some of my first Bible studies I knew it was time to part ways with my fraternity friends. I went to the fraternity treasurer and told him to 'calculate my bill, I was serving the Lord and it was time for me to get out of here.' He didn't quite understand and neither did I. But I knew that if I wanted to serve the Lord and be free from some bondage, I was going to have to get out of my current surroundings. The Lord set me free from drinking as I made a step in the right direction.

The final step in freedom is practicing healthy habits. When we begin to practice healthy habits we will feel great and we will wonder why we ever did the things that were destructive to our health. We will develop new passions in life and will experience a desire to help those who are in bondage to our former way of living.

Freedom from bondage is a great place to reside. Don't be a slave to any bad habit. Live free. There is nothing more rewarding than living healthy and feeling great. Make steps today to break your addictions and practice healthy habits.

Faith in Action: Television, internet, fast food, soda, sweets, or alcohol. Choose one of the following vices and eliminate it from your life for thirty one days. Replace it with something health or faith enhancing.

23.

Train Up a Child

—·ʌ·—

Faith

Proverbs 22:6 "Train up a child in the way he should go, even when he is old he will not depart from it."

It is vitally important that parents take responsibility for teaching their children about the Lord. It is your God given right and heavenly mandate to pass on your love for the Lord to the next generation. The importance of honoring the Lord, obeying His commandments, and doing what is right are things that are most often learned from parents. Your child's Sunday school teacher and vacation Bible school teacher can point your child in the right direction. But the nuts and bolts of faith in action need to come from you.

To that end I have taken time over the years to teach my son about the Lord. I have looked for teachable moments where I could share my faith and the Word of God. As a family, we have gone to church on most Sundays and we pray before each meal and at bedtime. We mostly listen to Christian music, and he knows why we don't listen to some of the pop culture music. Mom and I have made it very clear to our son that this life is a journey on which he must walk every day and every moment with the Lord. His direction and guidance comes into every decision we make. We have told Sam that the Lord has a plan for his life and something special for him to do. He realizes that a God given destiny awaits him. As our daughter grows older we will teach her the same things.

There is a saying that is used often: The family that prays together stays together. I think it is true. Praying together as a family teaches your children some very important things. First it lets them know that "I care about you." Next, it allows the family to agree together and unite their faith about important issues. There is great power in agreement. And finally it allows your family to humble themselves before the Lord which will bring His exaltation. Prayer makes a statement that 'We are not alone on this, but now have turned it over to God, and He is on our side.'

Teaching your children about the Bible is also paramount to the development of their faith. When I was a child my mom would read us stories from the children's Bible. I remember reading about Noah, Abraham, and Moses. I knew as a child that these men were close to God, and a seed was planted in my heart, for the desire to be like them. There are countless materials available to promote the faith of your children, from books to tapes, CD's, videos, and DVD's. Use them, but also speak the Word with your children.

Since I am a teacher, Sam and I ride to school every day; we have for nearly six years. When Sam turned ten we began confessing the word together. I developed two pages of about twenty verses of scripture that we speak out loud together. As we confess the word we put on our spiritual armor for the day. They are positive verses that set our steps in the right direction. The first scripture we confess is from **Psalm 118:24 "This is the day the Lord has made, let us rejoice and be glad in it."** From there we take off into the spiritual realm. Sam has memorized two sets of scriptures and we will continue to add new sets.

I once read about a father who challenged his kids to memorize a scripture verse each day. At the end of the week, if they could recite them all they received a reward. What a great plan for learning the Word. **Proverbs 20:15** says **"There is gold, and an abundance of jewels; but the lips of knowledge are a more precious thing."**

My wife has been instrumental in developing the faith of our three-year-old daughter Molly. They have school on most weekday mornings, and one of the stations is worship. They spend time singing and dancing before the Lord. My daughter probably knows more words to more songs than I do. It is a great blessing to hear her sing to the Lord at the top of her voice.

When we go to church together my son will often ask, "Do we have to go to church today?" Imagine that. My answer is "Yes." His reply is "Why?" Ever heard it? Instead of just saying "Because I said so" I take the time to explain to him why it is important to go to church. First, I explain that it is good to honor the Lord on the Sabbath by spending time in His house. Then I explain that it is important to join together with other believers in fellowship. I tell him that we are a part of the living church and we must bring our gifts to serve others and be served by others. Finally, I explain that we don't know everything there is to know about God and it is good to go to church and learn some things. By this time he is in the car and quiet without protest. It is important that we as parents take the time to explain to kids why we do the things we do and what we believe and why we believe it. Communicating our faith, values, and wisdom are vital tools in training up our children.

Besides taking purposeful steps in training our children to follow the Lord, there is another, maybe even more important tool, that we must use—our example. We must set a godly example before our children. Our words and deeds will speak volumes to them. If they hear us cursing all the time, they will pick it up. If they observe you reading your Bible every morning or calling the family together for prayer, they will pick it up. Children are very observant, and don't miss a lick. One scripture that puts the fear of the Lord in me is found in **Mark 9:42.** It says **"Whoever causes one of these little ones who believe to stumble, it would be better for him if, with a heavy millstone hung around his neck, he had been cast into the sea."** In other words, if we were to purposefully lead a child into sin, or maybe even set a bad example that would cause them to stumble...well, you know the rest. It is our job to be a light to our children. Watching filth on television, laughing at inappropriate stuff, getting drunk, talking inappropriately about the opposite sex, and not living a godly life are all stumbling blocks that our children can pick up. We must be diligent to set a good example for our children to follow.

During my nearly 17 years of working with children (14 years as a teacher) I have noticed one particularly important thing about children. The ones who behave the best and seem to have a solid emotional foundation have parents that are active in their life. Their parents are interested in them and it is obvious that they spend time with them. On the other hand, the students who have displayed the worst behavior and who have been emotionally unstable are the ones whose parents showed very little interest in them. These students are often hungry for attention and approval because they aren't getting enough at home.

We, as parents, need to be resolute in taking careful, calculated steps to train our children, and set a good example for them to follow.

Fitness

There are many aspects to fitness and wellness. What have you taught your children? What example have you set for them to follow? If those two questions don't slap you broadside and wake you up, I don't know what will.

The number one reason why people get sick is because they don't wash their hands. Their hands pick up germs and then they are transferred into the mouth or eye ducts and they get sick. Have you taught your child to wash their hands frequently, especially before eating? Have you taught them to take a bath or shower every day so they don't stink? Have you taught them how to brush their teeth so they don't rot out? Have you taught them and enforced that they need to eat their fruits and vegetables? Have you limited their sugar intake? Have you made them turn off the television or computer or video game and MADE THEM go outside and play or get some exercise?

Did you know that the number of children overweight has tripled in the last twenty years? There are serious health and emotional hazards associated with being overweight and obese.

We must train our children in the way they are to take care of their body and manage their health. We must teach them that they must go outside every day and exercise for 60 minutes. And if they don't want to, we must make them. I was one of seven children and I can remember my mom running us out of the house. We were not allowed to stay inside and get under her skin or mess up the house or play rough inside. We played in the backyard, in the cul-de-sac with the neighbors, or down at the creek.

We were also involved in youth sports. Getting your kids to play soccer, baseball, basketball, football, hockey, swimming, gymnastics, dance, tennis, cheerleading, karate, or whatever your community offers is a great way for kids to have fun while being active, and make friends. It's never too late to learn a sport and a good coach can help anyone learn the basics. Personal practice and discipline can help any kid make up ground and excel in any sport.

If your child isn't into team sports, then they are going to have to develop a fitness routine of walking, running, biking, roller-blading, hiking, or something else that will get them out and get them moving at a brisk pace. This is where you can make it a family affair. You can all go for a bike ride or go to a state park and hike up to the waterfall or rent a canoe and paddle till your arms fall off. Family fitness is a great way to stress the importance of physical fitness.

Kids are hungry to learn the right things, to take care of their bodies, and to get in shape. Each physical education class I give my students a fitness tip. I can't tell you the number of hundreds of parents who have said, "Coach, my kid said you told them to ... and you should see them go at it." I might have told them to do pushups and crunches during commercials, or take a bath every night, or wear deodorant, or watch their calories. They listen and they learn. Once I told a kindergarten class that I noticed that some kids were eating an ice cream every day at school and that this was too much. I told them they should only give themselves a treat once a week. A week later their teacher came to me and reported that over half her 'regulars' quit getting ice cream every day because Coach told them they can't have ice cream every day because it is not good for them. Kids want to do the right thing.

At age 10, my son was invited to a boy/girl swim party. He was hesitant about going because he had a little jelly around his belly. He stays active and I explained to him that it is natural for the body to add a little weight before going through a growth spurt, but he

187

wanted to lose some of the jiggle. He and mom set out some strict dietary guidelines and he, by his own internal motivation, changed his eating habits. He watched his portion sizes, laid off the sugar, ate more fruits, and drank more water. He was satisfied with his results and swam with his shirt off at the pool. He learned a valuable lesson on paying attention to what you eat and how much you eat.

Health Facts About Young People

* The prevalence of overweight children ages 6-11 has more than doubled in the past 20 years. The rate of adolescents age 12-19 has more than tripled.
* Less than 40% of children and adolescents in the U.S. meet the U.S. dietary guidelines for saturated fats.
*14% of students have lifetime asthma

High school students report the following:
* 80% do not eat 5 helpings of fruits and vegetables per day.
* 64% do not meet currently recommended levels of physical education.
* 23% smoked cigarettes in the past 30 days
* 28% rode with a drunk driver
* 10% rarely or never wore a seat belt
* 18% carried a weapon in the last month
* 43% drank alcohol in the last month
* 20% used marijuana in the last month
* 26% had episodic heavy drinking during the past month
* 47% ever had sexual intercourse
* 14% had sexual intercourse with 4 or more people
* 34% had sexual intercourse in the past 3 months
* 37% did not use a condom during last sexual intercourse
* 82% did not use birth control pills during last sexual intercourse
* 21% used the computer for 3 or more hours on an average school day
* 37% watched 3 or more hours of television on an average school day

From Department of Health and Human Services
2005 Youth Risk Behavior Survey

"Do as I say, and not as I do?' Ever heard that one? Sorry, it just doesn't float. You have to set an example for your kids. If you are overweight, eat a bunch of junk, smoke or chew tobacco, get drunk, or practice other bad habits, IT IS TIME TO CHANGE. Remember the scripture above about causing one of these little ones to stumble? Your example will speak volumes to your children. Jesus attacked the religious hypocrites. He called them "brood of vipers and white-washed tombs." Nobody likes a hypocrite. Your children need to see you exercising and eating right every day.

My kids see me take off for a run or bike ride every other day. They see me lifting weights or doing pushups and crunches. My three-year-old daughter joins in and will crank out a few pushups or crunches herself. We are always encouraging our kids about taking their vitamins and eating fruits and vegetables. They see us doing it and we gently encourage them along the way to do the same. My wife and I have run the Peachtree Road Race 10K for the last 15 or so years and my son has announced his intention to run next year. He already runs the Peachtree Junior 3K. He also has announced his intention to run a marathon one day. Hopefully we will run it together. I have announced my intention to ride a bike across the U.S. in 30 days with him but he has not bought into my vision yet. We will see.

By setting an example you can build a value into your child's life without even saying a word. They can see that taking care of your body is just a part of every day life, and they will adopt that philosophy. Teach your children what to do and lead them by example.

I saw a great movie about a boy in a wheelchair who was feeling sorry for himself. An older gentleman, also in a wheelchair, was giving him some advice on setting a date of when he would quit feeling sorry for himself. The boy said "Why is everyone telling me what to do?" He replied, "I am not telling you what to do, I am telling you how to think." Teach your children how to think about life and their health.

Faith in Action: Set aside a block of time each week for family fitness. Get active with your children for a minimum of thirty minutes. Play ball, take a hike, or ride bikes. If you don't have kids, find a niece or nephew or a kid in the neighborhood. Make it a habit and build relationships.

24.

Truly Good Things

—∿∿—

Faith

Genesis 1:31 "God saw all that He had made, and behold, it was very good."

The truly good things in life are free. They are free and they come from God. The colors in the morning sky as the sun rises, the infinite view of the ocean from a sugar white beach, the sound of the waves crashing, a cool breeze, the first snowfall of the year, the view of the Rockies from the top of Snowmass Mountain, a clear summer night with a really big and bright moon and a million stars, a thunder and lightening storm, a good hard rain, a brilliant rainbow, a deer bounding away into the woods, the smell of fresh flowers, the taste of a sweet, juicy piece of fruit, and the sound of a grand cricket orchestra are all wonderful works of God. God has made the world's most spectacular things for us to enjoy. The million dollar question is…how do you get some people to STOP and enjoy them? Do you enjoy all the wonderful things that God has created? Do you seize every view and every moment as if it may be your last? Or are you oblivious to them because you can't see past the problems and challenges of life? Are you focused on the petty details of life or the beautiful masterpieces of the Lord?

One of the greatest pets we ever had the pleasure of owning was a German Shepherd named Queen. She was the happiest most playful dog I have ever known. She was up at the crack of dawn to greet us when we went to school in the morning and I would hear her bark well into the night or see her lay in the grass enjoying the silver moonlight. When we washed the cars or watered the plants she was right there snapping at the water and getting soaked. When I went for a run I would have to send her back home several times because she was always up for an adventure. When we road off into the woods on the four wheeler she would follow us for miles. She would eventually find a mud puddle in the woods and get caked in brown mud-to her delight. If we shot the bb-guns she would hunt in the grass or near the trees and yelp with glee while she tried to find them. She would relentlessly chase and wrestle with our other two dogs until we would scold her to leave them alone. When we pulled into the driveway and opened the door to the car her nose and then two paws were in the door before we could get a foot on the ground. She loved the water, the snow, the sunshine, chasing anything, and affectionate petting. She was always up for something and she loved life even in her later years when she suffered from hip pain. If we humans had even half of her zest for life we would have an extraordinary life.

I greatly enjoy the sound of my daughter's laughter. If I could put it in a jar and listen to it at different times during the day it would be like sunshine breaking through the clouds. To see her run after our little dog and play chase is truly one of the great wonders of the world. Her little feet are the cutest feet in the world. Her gentle blue eyes and angelic grin would melt the coldest heart. She asks the most amazing questions and remembers the funniest things. I adore every moment with her and treasure them in my heart. I realize time is swift and I have only NOW to enjoy the present, and then it will be gone. I don't want to miss out on any time with my family. My son and daughter are growing fast. They will be in our life for a moment and then they will be off to start their own. I know one day they won't want dad 'hanging around' so much. It will break my heart but I will understand. I must make time now in my busy schedule to enjoy them, because they will be grown before I know it. They are a gift from God to my wife and me. They are a wonderful gift.

You really don't have to look very far to find a wonderful gift of God. However, it may take a lifetime before you realize it is right in front of you. Someone once said that 'Beauty is in the eye of the beholder.' Pray that you will find and appreciate beauty every day. Cutting the grass can be a pain, but where can you ever find the smell of freshly mowed grass. Raking the leaves may seem endless but where else can you find the beautiful change of tree colors. Winters may get awfully cold but there is nothing like enjoying a cup of hot cocoa while viewing the first blanket of snow. Everything is so white and shiny and beautiful. The summer sun can burn you real bad, but there is nothing more gentle and comforting than the warm sun on your back as you lay on your towel after a dip in the cool ocean. God's blessings surround us and all we need is our eyes and heart opened so that we may enjoy them.

Paul the apostle said in **Ephesians 1:18-19 "I pray that the eyes of your heart may be enlightened, so that you will know what is the hope of His calling, what are the riches of the glory of His inheritance in the saints, and what is the surpassing greatness of His power toward us who believe."** If our spiritual eyes can be opened we will see a great big world out there that the Lord has created for our enjoyment. We won't see the negative world view portrayed on the news every night. We won't focus on angry, hateful, murderous, crooked, adulterous, dishonest people. We will see the good things of God. We will see the beauty of His creation and beauty of the spirit of the every day folks who follow Him. My frequent prayer is "Lord, give me eyes to see, ears to hear, a hearing heart, and a receptive spirit." I want to truly see and hear Him and enjoy His creation.

Fitness

The truly good food is straight from God. You will never find anything that tastes better or is better for you than the food that God created at the beginning. He made apples, bananas, cherries, dates, eggplant, figs, grapes, honeydew melon, kiwi, lemons, mangos, nectarine, oranges, peas, quince, radishes, strawberries, tomatoes, walnuts, xigua, yellow squash, and zucchini for us to eat. The fruits and vegetables that God created for us to eat are nutrient-dense foods. Bite for bite you won't find anything that will satisfy the needs of your body more than fruits and vegetables. His original design for mankind was to eat the fruit of the ground and trees. **Genesis 1:29-31** says **"Then God said, "Behold, I have given you every plant yielding seed that is on the surface of all the earth, and every tree which has fruit yielding seed; it shall be food for you; and to every beast of the earth and to every bird of the sky and to every thing that moves on the earth which has life, I have given every green plant for food"; and it was so. God saw all that He had made, and behold, it was very good."**

If He designed us, it only makes sense that He knows what is best for us. A consistent variety of fruits and vegetables will provide your body with all the vitamins, minerals, carbohydrates, proteins, fats and fiber that your body needs.

Dr. George Malkmus wrote an excellent book entitled "God's Way to Ultimate Health." In it he describes in detail the natural diet that we are intended to eat. He also provides plenty of research and testimonies of people who have adopted an all-natural diet and have dropped lots of weight and were even cured from various illnesses, including cancer.

I have taken two vegetarian sabbaticals in my life where I have excluded meat from my diet for a prolonged period of time. The difference in how I felt was amazing. I experienced a clean feeling that is hard to describe unless you have actually done it. By eliminating all the meat that has to be filtered down your intestines, your digestive system is free to absorb more nutrients. Acid levels return to normal and your body experiences a state of homeostasis. I found that upon returning to a diet that included meat I experienced nausea, diarrhea, and stomach pains for a few days.

God's good diet is a natural one that involves consuming foods that are as close to their natural form as possible. Raw fruits and vegetables provide the best nutrients. When they are cooked much of the vitamin content is leeched out. Foods that are processed and prepared are often manipulated so much that they are a fraction of their original food value and are often loaded with preservatives, artificial flavors and colors, and sodium. One can of hearty chicken

Eat the Colors of the Rainbow

Blue and purple fruits and vegetables contain varying amounts of health-promoting *phytochemicals* such as *anthocyanins* and *phenolics,* currently being studied for their antioxidant and anti-aging benefits. These colors lower the risk of some cancers, promote urinary tract health, increase memory function, and promote healthy aging. Get blue/purple every day with foods such as: blackberries, blueberries, black currants, dried plums, elderberries, purple figs, purple grapes, plums, raisins, purple asparagus, purple cabbage, purple carrots, eggplant, purple belgian endive, purple peppers, potatoes (purple fleshed), and black salsify.

Green fruits and vegetables contain varying amounts of potent *phytochemicals* such as *lutein and indoles* which interest researches because of their potential antioxidant, health promoting benefits. These green foods lower the risk of some cancers, support vision health, and develop strong bones and teeth: avocados, green apples, green grapes, honeydew, kiwifruit, limes, green pears, artichokes, arugula, asparagus, broccoflower, broccoli, broccoli rabe, brussels sprouts, chinese cabbage, green beans, green cabbage, celery, chayote, squash, cucumbers, endive, leafy greens, leeks, lettuce, green onion, okra, peas, green pepper, sno peas, sugar snap peas, spinach, watercress, and zucchini.

White, tan, and **brown** fruits and vegetables contain varying amounts of *phytochemicals* such as *allicin,* found in the onion family. White foods like the following help heart health, maintain cholesterol levels, and lower risk of some cancers: bananas, brown pears, dates, white nectarines, white peaches, cauliflower, garlic, ginger, Jerusalem artichoke, jicama, kohlrabi, mushrooms, onions, parsnips, potatoes (white fleshed), shallots, turnips, and white Corn.

Orange and **yellow** fruits and vegetables contain varying amounts of antioxidants such as *vitamin C* as well as *carotenoids* and *bioflavonoids,* two classes of *phytochemicals* that scientists are studying for their health-promoting potential. Orange and yellow foods like these promote heart health, vision health, a healthy immune system and lower the risk of some cancers: yellow apples, apricots, cantaloupe,, cape gooseberries, yellow figs, grapefruit, golden kiwifruit, lemon, mangoes, nectarines, oranges, papayas, peaches, yellow pears, persimmons, pineapples, tangerines, yellow watermelon, yellow beets, butternut squash, carrots, yellow peppers, yellow potatoes, pumpkin, rutabagas, yellow summer squash, sweet corn, sweet potatoes, yellow tomatoes, and yellow winter squash.

Red fruits and vegetables are rich in health promoting *phytochemicals* such as *lycopene* and *anthocyanins*. These red foods promote heart health, memory function, urinary tract health, and lower the risk of some cancers: red apples, blood oranges, cherries, cranberries, red grapes, pink/red grapefruit, red pears, pomegranates, raspberries, strawberries, watermelon, beets, red peppers, radishes, radicchio, red onions, red potatoes, rhubarb, and tomatoes.

From Produce for Better Health Foundation, www.5aday.org

soup, for example, contains as much as 1100 mg of sodium which is almost half of the daily recommended amount. If you read the label of anything bought in a box or can you will find a lot of chemicals and ingredients that are not grown in a garden. Chemicals are toxins and toxins are bad for your body. As your immune system fights off all the toxins that are introduced to your body at every feeding and every breath, it has less time to do its job in maintaining healthy cell growth. Cancer is more apt to strike someone who has an immune system that is overloaded with toxins.

Jesus declared all foods clean. If we receive and eat our food with thankfulness then we are not sinning before the Lord. However, if we want the best, we will drive our grocery cart down the first two aisles of the supermarket where we find the produce department and load it up with fruit and vegetables. We are so blessed to live in a country where we don't have to grow any food if we don't want to. We can simply go to the market and purchase some of the best and most exotic natural foods ever grown on planet Earth. Every color of fruit and vegetable is right at our fingertips. We don't have to plow, sow, water, weed, or reap. We don't have to toil in the sun with the bugs. All we have to do is pick it up and put it in our cart. God couldn't have made it any easier for our generation to live healthy. Everything we need is right there in our air conditioned supermarket. All we have to do is skip the fried chicken, donuts, potato chips, Twinkies, cookies, and other junk and fill up on the truly good stuff.

My biking friend relayed a story to me that opened my eyes to the abundance of blessings we have in America. He had some biking friends who biked across part of Russia with some Russian bikers. When his friends returned to the U.S. the Russians came to visit about a year later. Before their first ride they brought the Russians to a Harris Teeter supermarket to stock up on food supplies for a long trip. Upon entering the store the Russians were blown away by the magnitude and vast selection of the foods in the store. They ran out into the parking lot weeping. They explained to their American biking friends that in Russia food is in very short supply, often the stores don't have bread, and they had a hard time grasping the abundance of the American store. We are truly blessed in America to have the very best food at our fingertips.

God has blessed us with many good things. Feed your body the way He designed it to be fed and you and your body will be truly thankful that you did.

Faith in Action: Plan your daily meal schedule for one week including five helpings of fruits and vegetables each day. Go to the store and purchase your supplies so that you can follow through with your plan of healthy eating. Make it a habit for life.

25.

We are judged by our deeds

—⁓—

Faith

2 Corinthians 5:10 "For we must all appear before the judgment seat of Christ, so that each one may be recompensed for his deeds in the body, according to what he has done, whether good or bad."

Do you ever think about eternity? Do you ever ponder the question of whether or not you will go to heaven and what it will be like? I am totally convinced that there is a day of reckoning. I also believe we will give an account for our lives. The Bible teaches that we will be judged by our faith, our words and our deeds.

I have come to see in life that many Christians in particular discount the fact that they will be judged by their deeds. Christians feel that since they have faith in Christ, and that they are forgiven for their sins, they don't have too much to worry about. In fact, many act as though it doesn't really matter what they do, as long as they have confessed Jesus as their Savior.

There are several scriptures that are in direct conflict with this laissez faire (whatever will be will be) thinking. Jesus Himself said in **Luke 6:46 "Why do you call me Lord, Lord and do not do what I say?"** The apostle James warned in **James 2:14-18 "What use is it, my brethren, if someone says he has faith but he has no** works? Can that faith save him? If a brother or sister is without clothing and in need of daily food, and one of you says to them, "Go in peace, be warmed and be filled," and yet you do not give them what is necessary for their body, what use is that? Even so faith, if it has no works, is dead, being by itself. But someone may well say, "You have faith and I have works; show me your faith without the works, and I will show you my faith by my works."" James pointed out that there should be a connection between faith and works. He stressed that if you have faith then your works will testify of your faith.

In **Revelations chapters 2&3** John is transcribing a letter from Jesus. As Jesus speaks to the churches five times He says **"I know your deeds..."** It is interesting to note that the Lord first told the churches that He noticed their deeds. He was paying particular attention to what they were doing. Their actions were a clear indication of what their life was all about. Their deeds were a declaration of what they believed, how passionately they believed it, and how much they really loved the Lord. Christians and others must not discount the importance of their actions. As the scriptures above have revealed, the Lord is watching our deeds, and they will have an eternal significance.

Like most parents, I believe the Father is proud of us when He sees us doing something good. Jesus was proud of Peter when he got out of the boat and walked on water. When the disciples returned to Jesus with great joy after going on a mission to the surrounding areas to preach and heal the sick, Jesus was so proud of them that He wanted to take them aside and hear their stories of the great deeds they had done. When Stephen was preaching the gospel to the Jewish council and high priest while he was on trial, **Acts 7:56** says that Stephen said **"Behold, I see the heavens opened up and the Son of Man standing at the right hand of God."** Jesus, who is usually seated at the right hand of God, stood up to get a better look and to cheer on His disciple whom he was proud of. The Lord is proud of the good deeds we do in much the same way that we are proud of good things our children do.

What we do in life is a clear reflection of who we are. Our deeds tell what we think and what we believe. There are plenty of people who can talk a good game. They go on and on about this or that. Some people can tell some great stories. Some people can sound very convincing when they are talking about their faith, their love for their family, their hard work, etc. But the bottom line must always be.....what do their actions prove?

Someone who says one thing but does another is a hypocrite. If your deeds don't match up with what you say or believe, you are a hypocrite. Most of us need to act more and talk less. James said in **James 1:22 "But prove yourselves doers of the word, and not merely hearers who delude themselves."** I have met some people who are totally convinced in their mind about something, but their actions are in direct conflict with what they say they believe. They deceive themselves.

Society has produced too many politicians and preachers who turn out to be hypocrites. Their deeds don't match their words. Politicians make grand promises to the people when they are running for office and then once they are elected they are bought out by the highest contributor. Public servants turn into prostitutes. They give favors in return for money. They make decisions and policies based on how they and their friends can prosper instead of what they promised the people they represent.

Even a few preachers have taken the pulpit to rant and rave and speak with great boldness and conviction about the Lord while their deeds in secret speak something else that is not representative of God and His word.

Our deeds need to speak volumes about who we are and what we believe. People need to know that they were touched by the kingdom of God when they see what we do. Every moment of time is absorbed with our deeds. Whether we are serving others or serving ourselves we are taking some action. Our actions can be a declaration before the Lord of our faith in Him, or our actions can be filthy rags of sin. We will clothe ourselves in eternity with deeds done in righteousness or these rags of sin. We will be judged by our deeds.

Jesus told us to feed the hungry, give to the poor, clothe the naked, visit the sick and those in prison, and give the thirsty something to drink. He told us to be His witnesses and confess Him before others. He told us to love our neighbor and help him out if it was within our power to do so. He said the world will know His disciples by their love for one another. Love is a verb.

Make a decision that when the video of your life is replayed on judgment day, there will be many clips of you helping others. You cannot earn your way into heaven by doing enough good deeds. But our deeds are a reflection of our faith that is on the inside. The Lord and the world should know what we are all about by the things we do every day.

Fitness

What do your actions speak about the value you have placed on your fitness and health? Do people describe you as an outdoorsy or active person? Do your friends think of you as a health nut because of your healthy eating habits?

What are your health habits? What deeds do you practice every day that are observed by others? How do these deeds affect your health? Do you exercise every day for 60 minutes? Do you perform resistance training or weight lifting to strengthen your frame? Do you eat moderate portion sizes? Do you eat a variety of healthy foods? Do you eat five helpings of fruits and vegetables every day? Do you eat a lot of junk food and fried foods? Do you drink 64 ounces of water everyday? Do you drink too many sodas? Do you brush and floss your teeth? Do you get 7-8 hours of sleep every night? Do you take drugs? Do you drink too much alcohol? Do you smoke or use other forms of tobacco? Do you visit the doctor for regular checkups? Do you drive too fast or reckless? Do you drink and drive? Do you wear sunscreen? Do you deal with stress well? The answers to these questions describe your health actions or deeds. Your particular responses greatly determine your health.

What we practice on a daily basis describes our beliefs and thoughts about our health. Our exercise habits, our shopping habits, and our eating habits are all testimonies of our wellness. These deeds will determine our health.

Routines are the greatest things in the world. I am a creature of habit and have no problems developing routines that I habitually practice. I don't totally lose it when my routine is broken but if things are running according to plan, I am a pretty happy man. My routines provide the framework for me to practice what is important. I usually fall asleep at 10:30 pm. and get up at 6:20am. After my morning shower I either shave or floss (I alternate days). I get dressed, get my coffee and vitamins, pack my breakfast (yogurt, banana, and instant oatmeal) and lunch (sandwich, chips, carrots and grapes or apple), and get in the car to head to work at the same time each weekday. After an active day of teaching I usually leave around 3:45pm. I come home and rest for 15 minutes and then begin my workout. My daily workout routine rotates each day from running 5 miles to lifting weights to biking 15 miles to lifting weights back to running 5 miles. I take one day per week off of my fitness routine. During the course of the day I drink two or three bottled waters along with some juice and tea. Around 7pm I eat a moderately healthy dinner with a salad. Evening activities may include my daily Bible reading along with coaching, playing with my children, or watching a little television. Then I shower, and go to bed. This is my normal routine. Of course things vary and I become flexible when other things challenge the schedule, but I do have a solid fitness routine and pretty healthy eating habits focused on eating five helpings of fruits and vegetables every day. Everybody needs to set some healthy habits in motion that are practiced regularly, but may be changed occasionally.

When I worked at the YMCA as a lifeguard, I had the opening shift at 6am. The same fitness nuts would come in everyday before work to swim laps. They would show up at the same time, wear the same suit, swim in the same lane, and leave at the same time. As I walked around the pool and looked through the huge glass windows I could see the same people working out in the adjoining weight room. I never had to look at the clock because I knew what time it was by the arrival and departure of the fitness "freaks." What an inspiration! These people practiced the same habits every day. If the pool was ever closed due to chemical problems, power outage, or a lightening storm, they were a little disgruntled. They valued their fitness and made an appointment everyday to practice it.

My dad is an expert at establishing routines. He diets frequently after the holidays and has developed a simple formula that has proven successful. He sets his goal at one week. His philosophy is

Regular physical activity can improve health and reduce the risk of premature death in the following ways:

Reduces the risk of developing coronary heart disease (CHD) and the risk of dying from CHD

Reduces the risk of stroke

Reduces the risk of having a second heart attack in people who have already had one heart attack

Lowers both total blood cholesterol and triglycerides and increases high-density lipoproteins (HDL or the "good" cholesterol)

Lowers the risk of developing high blood pressure

Helps reduce blood pressure in people who already have hypertension

Lowers the risk of developing non-insulin-dependent (type 2) diabetes mellitus

Reduces the risk of developing colon cancer

Helps people achieve and maintain a healthy body weight

Reduces feelings of depression and anxiety

Promotes psychological well-being and reduces feelings of stress

Helps build and maintain healthy bones, muscles, and joints

Helps older adults become stronger and better able to move about without falling or becoming excessively fatigued

Centers for Disease Control (CDC)

"Anybody can do anything for a week. Once you have changed your habit for a week, then you realize it didn't kill you and you go for two, and then continue on from there." Routines can be established by setting small, attainable goals.

Our deeds of fitness not only tell who we are and what we believe but also act as the actual force behind our wellness. Our deeds act as the official log of wellness. The more we participate, the healthier we become. The more we exercise, the stronger our bodies become.

The healthier we eat, the more nourished our bodies become. We will be recompensed for the deeds of wellness we perform.

Let your life be saturated with healthy deeds.

Faith in Action: Besides walking or jogging choose one other aerobic activity and begin to work it into your fitness routine. Try biking, rollerblading, aerobics, stair master, elliptical trainer, rowing machine, or a sport. Alternate aerobic days with your new activity.

26.

Appearances

—ᴍ—

Faith

1Samuel 16:7 "for God sees not as man sees, for man looks at the outward appearance, but the LORD looks at the heart."

Our main focus in life should be to develop a heart that is filled with the good things of God. A person filled with a heart of love, faith, hope, peace, patience, goodness, kindness, and gentleness is a rare and beautiful thing. God looks for this inner beauty in each one of His creations. His eyes search the earth for those who want to completely serve Him. We all have the potential to be filled with His grace. The Lord promised in **2 Chronicles 16:9 "For the eyes of the Lord move to and fro throughout the earth that He may strongly support those whose heart is completely His."** The Lord is looking for pure hearts that are completely His.

I am a blessed man because I have found a wife who is beautiful on the inside and on the outside. My wife loves the Lord. She fears the Lord and desires to serve Him in holiness and devotion. She is not ashamed of Him or His word and shares the good news at every opportunity. My wife loves people and can talk to anyone. She is loved by many and has many friends that seek her counsel and support. She always sees the best in people and is able to bring that out in many. My wife loves me. As we follow the Lord in His calling she supports me greatly even leaving her dream home in the city to follow me to a "fixer upper" farmhouse in the country (with well water and a septic tank). My wife loves our children and wants the very best for them. She showers them with affection and does many special things for them to make life spiritual, educational, and fun. As I mentioned, she is a hottie. But over time, I suspect her outward beauty will age gracefully (as will mine). But the most wonderful part of her will continue to shine on ever stronger until she goes on to be with the Lord.

Susan and I plan on growing stronger in the Lord every day. We plan on influencing our family, friends, and community in a positive way. We want our lights to shine so that people will see the goodness of God and glorify Him. We have a wonderful partnership based on the most important thing—our faith and love in Jesus Christ. Our life together has been a ministry for Him. We have taken on many adventures where our heart has always been to glorify Him and serve others. Each time we were faithful to the Lord, He moved us on to bigger challenges and blessings. We can't wait to see what is next!

Unfortunately many young dating couples today are not looking at the heart. They are looking at the outward appearance. I have a good friend who is 35 years old. He has dated many girls but can't seem to find the right one. Many times he is very picky about their appearance. Once I introduced him to a teacher friend of mine. She has a wonderful heart and is very sweet to the children she teaches. She is strong, independent and cute. After a few emails my friend made an unannounced visit to my school to peek in on this girl before he asked her out. I guess she didn't have her make up in place perfectly that day so he turned his nose up at her and told me—and I assume her as well—that he didn't think it would work out. She, of course, was mad at me for bringing him by unannounced. That would be my last attempt at matchmaking. I was sad that my friend judged her merely by appearance. I told him that he must want to marry an angel instead of a human and I reminded him that there weren't any around. As the clock continues to tick I hope he will come to a more realistic and biblical approach to finding a wife. The inside is what counts. The outside is going to fade away slowly. **Isaiah 40:7-8** says **"The grass withers, the flower fades, when the breath of the LORD blows upon it; surely the people are grass. The grass withers, the flower fades, but the word of our God stands forever."**

Good looks will only get you so far. After marriage, most people find comfortable bliss, and settle down and gain weight. They don't have to look good to "catch" anyone, so why bother? If they don't gain weight after marriage, many women will gain weight during pregnancy. Sometimes this weight is hard to get off. I thank God that I am a man and don't have to deal with the repercussions of carrying a child, but I am empathetic. If two people marry based on appearance and physical attraction, what will happen when they start to gain weight or get wrinkles or lose hair or turn gray? Is the marriage over because there is less attraction and that was the basis of the relationship? Since the divorce rate is around 50%, maybe that is the case.

People looking for a spouse should be looking for someone who is beautiful on the inside. Faith, hope, and love can go a long, long way. A kind and gentle person won't be too difficult to find. Their deeds and words will give them away. Someone who is faithful and responsible will probably have a decent job and will probably still be in close contact with their parents and siblings. Someone filled with hope will have dreams and aspirations of a bright future.

Find someone who loves the Lord and has some excellent qualities that remind you of what the Lord is like. You will marry a winner and have an excellent life together doing some things that are truly important.

Fitness

The pursuit of physical fitness should be about one thing, a healthy body. The goal of exercising and eating right should be to increase your health and healthy life span. A healthy body will enable you and empower you to be highly efficient in everything God has called you to do. You will be able to go harder and longer if you are physically fit. You will be free from the complications of chronic health problems. A healthy body will enable you to live well into your senior years without becoming a burden to your children or others. You will be able to live an active and vibrant life into your eighties and nineties if you take care of yourself.

Physical fitness is not about appearance. A byproduct of becoming physically fit is that you will trim down and maintain a healthy body composition. However, this is not the goal or motive. Exercise should be about health, not looks.

Our society has gone crazy trying to propagate looks and physical attraction. The extreme makeover craze took off at an out-of-control pace. Women now subject their bodies to all kinds of unhealthy things for appearance sakes: face lifts, breast implants, liposuction, diet pills, fad diets, starvation diets, tummy tucks, and even stapling their stomach together. Some of these desperate measures have very high risks and side effects. Societal pressures from advertising, magazines, television, and other media have caused women to make poor choices in an effort to appear a certain way.

A friend of mine decided to get breast implants. She was very charming and very attractive. I didn't really understand why she was doing it but I guess she bought into the lie that she had to have really big breasts to be complete. After her surgery she couldn't wear a seatbelt because she was so sore. She was pulled over for not wearing one. She offered to show the police officer her breasts as "proof" that she just had surgery and couldn't wear a belt. He declined and she got off with a warning. It was alarming and intriguing to me that my friend was so willing to show her breasts to another man that was not her husband. It seems that society's pressure to look a certain way may have messed up her values to the point that she was anxious to show something off that was inappropriate.

Men too have turned to extreme measures for appearances sake. They have tried everything from steroids, to excessive supplements, to hair implants, to surgeries. Some guys will go to great risks and pains to appear a certain way. Serious body builders, for example, usually end up at a point where if they want to continue to improve they will need to either use steroids or continue to blast their liver with high doses of protein. I read a study once that indicated that a high percentage of highly competitive body builders would be willing to sacrifice their health to win in their sport. Any "sport" that is strictly based on appearance and encourages unhealthy means of attainment should be examined closely for its merit.

I have a very good friend who is totally into appearances. He shops at Neiman Marcus, wears the fanciest clothes and shoes, drives a really nice car, and likes to eat at trendy places. He spent the entire year before his fortieth birthday eating right and working out religiously. He trimmed way down and looked the best he had since college. On his fortieth birthday he sent himself a birthday card at his office. It was a life-size poster of himself in his bikini bathing suit with the caption "Look who's forty but has the body of an 18-year-old." He hung the card up for all his coworkers to see. You would have to know him to realize that only he could get away with such a feat because he is so strikingly vain. His pursuit of a fit body was only to make a show and his workout habits and healthy diet tapered off considerably after his birthday extravaganza. He was pursuing the wrong motive.

The focus on "looks" has even caused many young women to engage in unhealthy behaviors like starving themselves or binging and purging as a means of maintaining a thin figure. When my wife and I worked at the YMCA we met a wonderful girl who had survived a battle with anorexia. During dinner one night she described her journey in detail. She told us of the power she felt when she would purge or when she would order a plate of food or a dessert, and only eat a few bites and send it back at the end of the meal. She mentioned how she was thirty pounds underweight and showing bones everywhere yet she still felt fat. Her misconceptions about the importance of appearance and society's pressures put her in the hospital fighting for her life. Thankfully she got the help she needed and made a full recovery. The night we ate together we shared a "death by chocolate" desert and finished the whole thing.

Our society has deemed that skinny, muscular, big-breasted, and hair on your head is in. Any way to achieve these objectives has been considered permissible. Often the pursuit of societal norms has led to many men and women taking unhealthy approaches to unhealthy objectives.

2005 Cosmetic Procedures Facts

- 11.5 million people spent approximately $12.4 billion on cosmetic procedures.
- Since 1997 there has been a 444% increase in total number of procedures.
- The top surgical procedures were:
  Liposuction (455,489 at $2,697 avg. cost)
  Breast Augmentation (364,610 at $3,582 avg. cost)
  Cosmetic eyelid surgery (231,467 at $2,813 avg. cost)
  Rhinoplasty (Nose reshaping) (200,924 at $4,188 avg. cost)
  Abdominoplasty (Tummy tucks) (169,314 at $5,232 avg. cost).
- The top non-surgical procedures were:
  Botox injections (3.2 million at $382 avg. cost)
  Laser hair removal (1.5million at $347 avg. cost)
  Hyaluronic acid injections (1.2 million at $527 avg. cost)
  Microdermabrasions (1million at $149 avg. cost)
  Chemical peels (1/2 million at $848 avg. cost).

From The American Society for Aesthetic Plastic Surgery

Cosmetic Procedure Risks/Complications

Liposuction complications- The FDA reports that most people are pleased with the results however the non-necessary surgical procedure carries the following risks: infections, embolism, visceral perforations (puncture of organs), seroma, nerve compression and changes in sensation, swelling, skin necrosis, burns, fluid imbalance, toxicity from anesthesia, and death.

Breast augmentation-will not last a lifetime. The following complications have occurred frequent enough to present a concern to the FDA: asymmetry, breast pain, breast tissue atrophy, calcification, capsular contracture, chest wall deformity, delayed wound healing, extrusion, galactorrhea, granuloma, hematoma, Iatrogenic injury/damage, infection including Toxic Shock Syndrome, inflammation/irritation, malposition/displacement, necrosis, nipple/breast sensation changes, palpability/visibility, ptosis, redness/bruising, rupture/deflation, scarring, seroma, unsatisfactory style/size, and wrinkling/rippling.

Botox injections- A clinical trial found that 50% of the participants had symptoms ranging from headache, respiratory infection, flu syndrome, pain in the face, redness, blepharoptosis (droopy eyelids), and nausea.

Other surgeries- Surgery always presents the risk of nerve damage, scarring, infections, bleeding, unnatural look, asymmetry, as well as the discomforts of swelling, pain, bruising, stiffness, and loss of motion.
From the Food & Drug Administration

For appearances sake, many men and women have greatly damaged their health and have put themselves at risk for lifelong health complications. They have done this to create an image that isn't really them. They have adjusted their natural appearance through unnatural means to create an illusion to attract someone. That doesn't sound too healthy.

Don't be caught in society's trap of abusing your body for appearance's sake. Value your health and exercise so that you can achieve and maintain a healthy body that will serve you your entire life. There is nothing more beautiful than a natural, healthy, vibrant body. It is the most beautiful thing because it is the real you in optimum form. May God bless you as you pursue Him and a healthy life.

Faith in Action: Train yourself to have a godly perspective-look on the inside. Write three positive notes or give three positive remarks to people complimenting them on their inner beauty.

27.

Keeping Things in Perspective

Faith

Philippians 4:11-13 "Not that I speak from want, for I have learned to be content in whatever circumstances I am. I know how to get along with humble means, and I also know how to live in prosperity; in any and every circumstance I have learned the secret of being filled and going hungry, both of having abundance and suffering need. I can do all things through Him who strengthens me."

Life is sometimes a rat race. The more society progresses, the more frazzled things get. Life has become increasingly fast-paced and agitated. Instead of progress making things easier, life has become more stressful. In America, especially, we have all bought into the falsehood of the technological age (except for maybe the Amish). Everybody thinks they need the best camera cell phone, an mp3 player, high-speed Internet, a fast computer, an SUV, a 52-inch plasma screen TV, 180 channels plus HBO, onSTAR, surround sound, and....need I go on? What did previous generations do without all these luxuries? Honestly, they probably had a more peaceful life. There are still a few folks alive today that were here on earth BEFORE the automobile. Can you imagine the changes that they have seen in their lifetime? It is mind-boggling.

The problem with rapid development is that we, as a society, have lost perspective of what is important. We have gotten trapped in a cycle of striving to achieve and receive the latest and greatest inventions. Instead of allowing the inventions to make our life easier and less stressful, we have developed an instantaneous mentality where we must get faster, faster, faster. Have you ever stood at the microwave and tapped your foot and said "hurry up"? This is a sign that you are stressing.

Being content in life has become a lost art. Can you think of anybody that you know who is happy where they are and with what they have? There are very few people who live within their means and are content. TV (the one-eyed devil) has shown us what everybody else has and has tricked us into thinking that we need it too. **1 John 2:15-17** says **"Do not love the world nor the things in the world. If anyone loves the world, the love of the Father is not in him. For all that is in the world, the lust of the flesh and the lust of the eyes and the boastful pride of life, is not from the Father, but is from the world. The world is passing away, and also its lusts; but the one who does the will of God lives forever."** Lusting after the things of the world is an enslavement that can never be filled. There will always be nicer things and faster cars that will be developed. The key to being satisfied is to pray for contentment.

Paul the apostle stated in the scripture above that he learned to be content in whatever circumstance he found himself. The reason he could do this is because he realized that true contentment was based on knowing the Lord and walking with Him, and not on what material possessions you have. He set his treasure in heaven and counted all things but loss for the surpassing greatness of knowing Christ Jesus. Paul knew that the 'one with the most toys' does not win. He also knew he couldn't take them with him. In fact, being rich on earth usually means being poor in heaven—if you make it.

Being rich on earth often means that you have set a priority in your life to make money so you can have an excellent lifestyle. There is NOTHING WRONG with having nice stuff. But when you pursue the best of the best, there is usually a price to pay. To be able to afford the best you have to be a 'player'. And if you are a player, you have to devote a lot of your soul to playing the game. This means you have to possess (or really be possessed by) a high stress job. You also have to devote a lot of your time to that high stress job to make it a success. You often have to travel or be away from your family. You spend a lot of your life on the job or thinking about the job, but hey, you are making good money. And you can buy those toys you want, although you really don't get to enjoy them as much as you want. In fact you are so tired from the job that you can't enjoy life or your family. What a shame! Where is the contentment?

I wonder if people who win the lottery end up enjoying life more. I wonder if they become content. I have noticed that people who get more stuff end up worrying about their stuff more. Getting stuff becomes an appetite that you can't fill. And then it becomes your focus in life. And then, you lose perspective.

How do you regain perspective in life? One word—downsize. If you are stuck in the rat race and you know it, you have to downsize. Downsize your mortgage, downsize your autos, downsize your lifestyle, and downsize your job. When you downsize these, you can downsize the stress in your life and find some contentment. Life should be about enjoying the Lord, family, and friends. Life is a gift from the Lord. It should be filled with good times and memories, not stress. I have begged friends and relatives to take less stressful jobs. Making the big money is just not worth it. Stress can kill you and is one of the most harmful things to your health.

1 Timothy 6:7-9 says **"For we have brought nothing into the world, so we cannot take anything out of it either. If we have food and covering, with these we shall be content. But those who want to get rich fall into temptation and a snare and many foolish and harmful desires which plunge men into ruin and destruction."** I hope you will take some time to examine your life and job situation. Have you kept things in perspective? Remember that all you really need is food, shelter, and clothing. With these you can survive and serve the Lord. The world pursues the riches of this life. The followers of Jesus left everything and followed Him. Find some ways to free up your life so that you can enjoy the Lord, your family, your friends, and life itself.

Fitness

It is very important that we keep our fitness pursuits in perspective. I am very committed to working out and keeping in shape. It is a priority in my life and I practice it everyday. I have a rotating workout where I go from aerobic exercise one day to strength training the next day. My typical workout runs between an hour to 1 ½ hours. If the average day has 16 waking hours then I spend about 12% of the day (roughly 2 hours) devoted to my workout, preparation, and clean up. IT IS ENOUGH!

Exercise is important and needs to be part of everyday life, but it should be kept in perspective. Some people go way overboard in their devotion to fitness and their pursuit of athletics and competition. Some people over train and are actually damaging their body instead of promoting its health.

How much is enough? It really depends on your family status, your job status, and your other commitments. If your extended workout is stressing out your family and throwing a big wrench in the family schedule resulting in excessive burden on your spouse, then you probably need to reevaluate your workout time. If you are single, or don't have any children, my advice is....enjoy your freedom while you can because when you have kids, things must change for harmony's sake.

When I was single and newly married I was able to participate in more races and team sports. I ran 10Ks, did mountain bike races, played amateur soccer, and played on a softball team. I was able to do this until my first child was about two. My wife was supportive of my endeavors and life was fun. Eventually our family schedules changed, our jobs changed and I had to cut back on my athletic commitments. Things became too stressful and we knew it was time to change. As my son grew and became old enough to play sports it was time for dad to hang up his career and allow my son to develop some love for activities and sports. We realized that we can't do everything. I had to cut back on my sports so that our schedule had time for my son's sports. My time was up. I still exercise every day, but that is all I get for now. I don't play on any teams, I don't play 4-5 hours of golf on the weekend, and I don't go hunting or fishing with my buddies all the time. I realized that I had to keep things in perspective and limit my activities so that my wife and kids would have time to exercise. There are only so many hours in a day, and so many days in a week. You can't do everything.

One of my lifelong goals was to run a marathon. In 2003 I set the date for the April 2004 Big Sur International Marathon the most scenic marathon in the U.S. I thought if I was going to run 26.2 miles, it might as well be the most beautiful run available. To train for a marathon is a daunting task. You can't just wing it. With my wife's support I was able to block off long runs on weekends to train for the Big Sur. I would run for up to three hours on some Saturdays in order to train for the event. Other runs would be well over an hour. On the long ones I would basically be useless for the rest of the day (too tired to do much of anything). I made it through more than three months of training and enjoyed an awesome marathon.

I survived the marathon, but will probably not do it again until I can run one with my son. Why? Running a marathon puts a huge tax on your body and your schedule. Your fitness pursuits and exercise habits get out of perspective. Once was okay, but I have married (with children) friends that run these races all the time. I have other friends who lift weights for a couple of hours each day. They go to the gym daily and work out a different body part each day. They are body building instead of strength training. My friends will never win a race and won't be featured on a body building magazine. I don't know what they are pursuing. They have gone way beyond trying to stay healthy and in shape. I honestly don't know how the family life survives with all the training time and the events. There is probably some bitterness and resentment welling up in the spouse and children because of the excess. When large amounts of time are spent on individual fitness pursuits a spouse may think that they are being taken advantage of and the children may think mom or dad doesn't love me because they never spend any time with me. Harmony and contentment are found when people keep their fitness pursuits in perspective.

Physical Activity Recommendations

Adults should engage in <u>moderate-intensity</u> physical activity for at least 30 minutes on 5 or more days of the week.

OR

Adults should engage in <u>vigorous-intensity</u> physical activity 3 or more days per week for 20 or more minutes per occasion.

Light -Intensity Activities: walking slowly, golf in powered cart, swimming or slow treading, gardening or pruning, bicycling very lightly, dusting or vacuuming, conditioning exercise (light stretching or warm up).

Moderate -Intensity Activities: walking briskly, golf while pulling or carrying clubs, swimming recreational, mowing lawn with power mower, tennis (doubles), bicycling 5-9 mph, scrubbing floors or washing windows, weight lifting (Nautilus or free weights)

Vigorous Intensity Activities: race-walking, jogging or running, swimming laps, mowing lawn with push mower, tennis singles, bicycling 10mph or more, moving or pushing furniture, circuit training.

From Centers for Disease Control and Prevention

Even something great like exercise can be taken to the extreme. A certain amount of exercise will definitely benefit the body. Extreme, chronic exercise however can abuse the body and cause a breakdown in muscle as well as cell structure. Many long distance runners and competitive bike riders end up on the surgery table because they have over-abused their muscles, tendons, ligaments, bones, and joints. Knee or ankle surgery is not uncommon. Besides surgery there are other dangers of extreme exercise. The more you exercise, the more nutrients and oxygen are filtered through your body. The more processing your body does, the more free radicals are released in your body. Free radicals are known to break down the body and cause cancer. An exercise routine and schedule is important. However the goal of a healthy body should be the sole focus and not the intense desire to look a certain way or go to exercise extremes. The body needs a moderate amount of exercise and some rest time to recuperate.

Daily exercise is important. It is a must. But please remember to keep things in perspective. The goal of any fitness program should be to maintain a healthy body for life. The pursuits of a faster time, bigger muscles, or buns of steel are vain pursuits that can pull people out of perspective. Make sure you are working out for the right reasons. You should be training to live a long and healthy life. Don't stress out your family and abuse your body. Find the appropriate exercise commitment for your health, and the harmony of your family. Keep things in perspective.

Faith in Action: Take a good look at your life and identify one thing that creates a time or financial commitment that is stressful. Adjust it or eliminate it and make life a little easier.

28.

First Love

—⦚⦚—

Faith

**Revelations 2:4-5 "But I have this against you, that you
have left your first love. Therefore remember from where
you have fallen, and repent and do the deeds you did at
first; or else I am coming to you and will remove your
lamp stand out of its place—unless you repent."**

On November 6, 1986 I came forward during a Bible study at
Georgia Tech to receive Jesus Christ as my Savior and Lord.
A heavy burden of sin was lifted off of my soul and I entered into
a glorious state of joy that lasted for years. Everything in the Lord
was exciting and fresh. I learned things in the Bible that made so
much sense, things I had never seen or heard before. During times
of worship and praise I danced before the Lord. His Spirit was
so alive and fresh I felt as if my faith could move any mountain.
My friends and I had many adventures in our faith as we prayed
together, witnessed on the campus, and held Bible studies in dorms.
We attended conferences and went on missions trips. We were on
fire for the Lord.

After graduation and a seven month job in my major of construction, I went into full time ministry as a campus evangelist. My full

time job was witnessing for the Lord. My passion for the kingdom was strong. I lived and breathed to do the will of the Lord.

As time progressed my ministry approach changed. I began to mature in the Lord and understand more of God's big picture. As I worked more in youth ministry I developed a desire to become a teacher so I resigned from campus ministry and went back to school for an education degree. While pursuing my second degree and working two jobs to pay the bills, my relationship with the Lord simmered a bit. I had to get certain things done-schoolwork, attend classes, and make money to live. I did not forsake my faith, but the amount of time I spent seeking the Lord and witnessing for Him changed dramatically. I was growing up and my calling was changing. This period of growth was long, spanning years.

When I married and had children, there was more growth and more change. Fighting to make a living, pay the bills, raise a family, and increase our standard of living took time and effort, LOTS of time and effort. I would say that more than once I had to pull back and re-evaluate my relationship with the Lord. Sometimes I had to repent and renew my love and devotion to Him. I never turned my back on the Lord, but there were definitely times that were cold and dry. I remember crying out to the Lord and saying "Lord, in **Isaiah 42:3** you said **'A bruised reed He will not break and a dimly burning wick He will not extinguish.'** Please don't break me off Lord. And please don't snuff me out. Blow your fire on me again and help me to burn for you." The Lord is faithful, even when we are not. He has never left me or forsaken me. He brought me back under His wing many times. He would renew a fire in me and a sense of His calling and destiny.

Jesus taught His disciples the parable of the sower. In it He described the fruitful life and the wasted life. He said of the wasted life in **Mark 4: 18-19 "And others are the ones on whom seed was sown among the thorns; these are the ones who have heard the word, but the worries of the world, and the deceitfulness of riches, and the desires for other things enter in and choke the word, and it becomes unfruitful."** Sometimes the cares of life slowly surround us and overtake us. We become choked out of the life giving rays of the Son. We forget our first love. We forget the true source of life, love, peace, and joy which is Jesus.

It is sad when married couples separate and then get divorced. The stresses of life overtake them, they forget their deep love for one another and what attracted them to each other in the first place, and they part ways. It is even sadder when people leave their first love of the Lord. Something powerful happens when you become born again, when you turn from sin and receive Christ's forgiveness and salvation. You enter into oneness with God in the spirit. He fills your heart with His precious Spirit. The Bible calls it **"Christ in you, the hope of glory"** in **Colossians 1:27**. When the cares of life cause you to lose this first love it is the greatest tragedy of all. Turning your back on the Lord or walking out of a relationship with Him is like pulling the plug on the true source of life itself.

The good news is He never leaves. He is faithful when we are not. As long as you still have breath left in your body you can turn to Him, ask forgiveness and be accepted back into His loving arms. All He wants is you, all of you. He won't be second fiddle or a standby God. If you want to make Him your number one first love, He will accept the position. Just like in the story of the prodigal son, He will see you coming from a distance. He will run to you, scoop you up, put the family ring on your finger, a robe on your back, and celebrate your safe return home. God is waiting anxiously for your return. He wants to be your first love.

Fitness

When I talk to people about fitness, running, biking, lifting, playing sports, or health related matters one of the most common things I hear is "I USED TO..." I used to play football in high school. I used to be a gymnast. I used to run a race every weekend. I used to be a size 6. I used to weigh____. I used to work out at Gold's Gym every day. Unfortunately for these folks, you can't live in the past. Otherwise I bet they would look great and feel great. My question is—why did you quit? The answer is usually an injury, kids, marriage, a job, or a move that resulted in the loss of a fitness partner. Regardless of the answer, there is no real excuse to leave your love of a healthy lifestyle. How can you experience the benefits of feeling healthy and looking healthy and just walk away from it? It just doesn't make sense. What are you willing to trade in for your health? Do you want to be a slave to your corporation or job so you can make a few extra bucks? Is it really worth the cost of your health?

I once read an interview with a tennis player who offered some fitness advice to the readers. He said "…find something you like doing and do it for a life time." If you like to play tennis then play tennis. If you like to run then run. If you like to hike or bike then do it. If you like to cross country ski, knock yourself out. People are most likely to follow through on the things they like to do. You don't have to coax, bribe, or threaten someone to do something they enjoy doing.

You can also keep your love alive by cross training with a few different workouts. Mix up your workout routine so it doesn't get boring and monotonous. If you cross train by rotating through a few different activities then you are less likely to get burned out. A few years ago I took up roller-blading to swap out with running and biking. It was a different workout and it helped me develop my balance for a winter ski trip. The wipeouts were a little painful but I was a quick learner. I picked up some roller blades for about $20 at Wal-mart. Man did I get my money's worth out of those! There are tons of activities you can do to keep entertained and fit: jump rope, jump on a trampoline, play soccer, basketball, street hockey, touch football, ultimate Frisbee, bike, skateboard, rock climb, canoe, kayak, or dance. Don't get bored, get active.

Some people leave their love of exercise due to an injury. Injuries unfortunately happen. If you stretch and take normal precautions when exercising you can reduce your chances of sustaining an injury. However, if you do get one it is important to take some time off to heal. But don't throw the baby out with the bath water. While you are nursing a knee or ankle find something else to do like swimming or rowing. Most gyms have rowing machines. Get hooked up to one until you can get back to your regular activity. Or find a pool and learn how to swim. There is nothing more vigorous on the heart and lungs than swimming. It is also low (really no) impact and you

Top Mistakes People Make in the Gym

The all-or-nothing approach. Not having a full hour to exercise is no reason to skip your workout. Research shows that even 10 minutes of exercise can provide important health benefits.

Unbalanced strength-training programs. Most people tend to focus on certain muscles, such as the abdominals or biceps, because they have a greater impact on appearance or it is where they feel strongest. But to achieve a strong, balanced body, you have to train all the major muscle groups.

Bad form. The surest way to get injured in a gym is to use bad form. For example, allowing the knee to extend beyond the toes during a lunge or squat can put undue stress on the knee, and using momentum to lift heavy weights or not exercising through a full range of motion will produce less-than-optimal results.

Not progressing wisely. Exercising too much, too hard or too often is a common mistake made by many fitness enthusiasts. Rest and gradual progression are important components of a safe and effective exercise program.

Not enough variety. Too many people find a routine or physical activity they like—and then never change it. Unchanging workouts can lead to boredom, plateaus and, worse case, can lead to injury or burnout.

Not adjusting machines to one's body size. Most exercise equipment is designed to accommodate a wide range of body types and sizes. But it's up to you to adjust each machine to your body's unique needs. Using improperly adjusted machines will lead to less-than-optimal results and increase your risk of injury.

Focusing on anything but your workout. The importance of being "mindful" of the task at hand cannot be overstated. Reading or watching TV can adversely affect the quality of your workout because the distraction can literally slow you down.

Not properly cooling down after your workout. Too many people wrap up their workouts and head straight to the showers. Instead, take a few minutes to lower your heart rate and stretch your muscles. This not only improves flexibility, but also helps prepare the body for your next workout.

Poor gym etiquette. This can range from simply being rude—lingering on machines long after you are done or chatting loudly on your cell phone—to poor hygiene and not wiping your sweat from machines once you're finished. Always be considerate of other exercisers.

Not setting realistic goals. Unrealistic and vaguely stated goals are among the leading causes of exercise dropout. The key is to establish a training goal that is specific and appropriate for your fitness and skill levels—something a bit challenging but not overly difficult.

By The American Council on Exercise

can do it for the rest of your life. Your body will eventually heal and you will have to endure some pain while retraining your muscles or ligaments. They will be sore but you can work through it. Hundreds of thousands of people have returned to running, biking, tennis, skiing, basketball, track, and everything else after going through reconstructive surgery for blown out or torn body parts. Don't give up, get up.

I met a guy named Todd at our local park. He was doing laps on a hand pedaled bicycle that was made for paraplegics. I helped him load his bike into his truck and we talked for a little while. He lost the use of his legs at 15 years of age due to a motorcycle accident. Apparently he is a champion at heart because he didn't let it ruin his life. He told me he competes in 10kK races, duathlons, and triathlons (some iron man distance). He swims the first part, bikes the second part on his special bike, and wheel chairs the third part. I don't know what he did prior to his accident, but I guess he decided it wasn't going to keep him from staying in shape. He has some massive arms. He is married and has two kids. Go Todd! Despite his setback he seems to be loving life and keeping fit.

Don't give up on your fitness and your body. If you have tasted the goodness of feeling and looking healthy then make a decision to do it your entire life. If it is time to return to the good life then dust off those sneakers, lace 'em up, put on those gym shorts, and hit the road. Your body will thank you. Your spouse will thank you. The kids will thank you. Even your co-workers will thank you. Return to your love of fitness.

Faith in Action: Take your strength training routine to the next level. Purchase some free weights or a multi-exercise machine and develop a repertoire of six to eight strength training exercises that focus on different muscle groups. Include chest muscles, back muscles, abdomen muscles, biceps, triceps, shoulders, and leg muscles. Perform two sets of each exercise. Alternate days of strength training with aerobic exercise, taking one day off per week.

29.

You gotta want it

—⁓—

Faith

Matthew 5:6 "Blessed are those who hunger and thirst for righteousness, for they shall be satisfied."

If you really, really want to know God, you will find Him. If you really, really want to follow Him and do what is right, you will find the way. Jesus promised that if we were hungry enough and thirsty enough, we would be satisfied. The problem with an unfulfilled spiritual life does not rest on God's fault. The problem is an internal lack of hunger for righteousness. David said in **Psalm 42:1 "As the deer pants for the water brooks, so my soul pants for you, O God."** There was no stopping his passion for the Lord. He was so zealous for God that he thought anything was possible. He wrestled a bear and a lion because he knew God was on his side. When he saw Goliath taunting the armies of God he was offended because his Israeli brothers were so chicken. He ran to the battle, in the name of the Lord, with a slingshot and no armor and defeated the giant. He wrote numerous songs to the Lord because he was in love with Him and was hungry for more of Him.

When we are hungry enough for something we go for it. When I fell in love with my wife, nothing could stop me from wanting to be with her. I brought her gifts, wrote her love notes, talked with her on the phone, took her out to dinner, changed the oil in her car, washed her flea ridden dogs, and spent as much time around her as possible. I loved her and wanted to be with her. It is amazing all the things I put off or put on the back burner to focus on her.

Many times in life we find something that we are passionate about and we go for it. It might be a sport, a hobby, a car, a sports team, a house, or something else that rocks our boat. When we get hungry for something we commit time, attention, and finances to achieving it. If we make up our mind that we want it, we will do whatever it takes and then some, to get it.

The problem all too often is...we pursue the wrong thing. Many people are willing to make Jesus the Savior of their life, but not the Lord. Acknowledging Jesus as your Lord means that you are submitting to His service and worship. Your new mission in life is to please your King. You are at His beck and call and live to bring His kingdom forward. It is not a burden or struggle, but rather your delight because you are passionate about Him. Finding this place requires devotion to Him. It may require laying down some idols. If you want to know the Lord you will need to remove some distractions and spend some quality time with Him. Like any great love story, the more you know the person the more you want to be around them. The more you spend time with them the deeper you fall in love. Read His words, spend time with him in prayer and worship, and spend time with His people who are a reflection of Him. Passion starts with a seed that is planted and watered.

And if you really want to lay hold of God and His will you can follow in the footsteps of Jesus and the apostles-fast and pray. Fasting is a great way to quiet your flesh, loose the cords of bondage that may be snaring you, and strengthen your spirit. There are many examples in the Bible of men and women fasting to lay hold of God and His power. Fasting is a great way to show the Lord you are serious and are focused on Him alone. The times that I have fasted I have noticed a breaking and freedom from the fleshly nature and temptation as well as more clarity and power in spiritual things. The Lord is available to those who earnestly seek Him.

Fitness

I sometimes get very tired of people saying they just can't lose weight. They say they eat pretty healthy or they eat barely anything at all and they still can't lose weight. The truth of the matter is that these folks are just not being honest with themselves. Losing weight is a simple mathematical equation. You must burn more calories than you consume. You can lose weight two ways, eat less or exercise more. If you exercise more, you cannot eat more or you will stay the same weight. There is no magic diet or secret formula for losing weight. Eat less and exercise more.

Besides not being honest with themselves, many people make excuses or blame others for their lack of progress. My wife and I have heard every excuse in the book: no time, too much work, the kids, my selfish spouse, a slow metabolism, menopause, etc. People who don't exercise regularly, lose weight, or quit smoking just don't want to. They don't want it bad enough. They are not passionate about it. If they wanted to, they could do it. They just don't want it bad enough.

On the side of my filing cabinet in my office I have a picture of myself with two fifth grade twins that I had the pleasure of coaching in PE. KC and Whitney were remarkable athletes and had hearts of true champions. KC recorded the fastest mile I have ever timed for a fifth grader, five minutes and forty seven seconds (5:47). He returned two days later to try and beat his record but fell short by a few seconds. KC, Whitney, and their third grade brother Michael were the pictures of health. They were always smiling, they radiated true beauty, and they were always up for a challenge. All three were nationally ranked tennis players. One thing they did absolutely blew my mind. They would often jog the mile distance to school (at 7:20 am) while their parents drove their back packs and dropped them off in the office. This feat is rarely heard of in children this age. Their determination to live a fit life and excel earned them a place in my hall of fame.

If you want to make a change in your life or set a goal on something, you have to do it with all your heart. You have to hunger and thirst for it. It has to be your intense focus that you will not be deterred from. Jesus said in **Matthew 11:12 "....the kingdom of heaven suffers violence, and violent men take it by force."** I think He was trying to get His people fired up. Jesus was not mamsy-pamsy and He didn't want His followers being apathetic about life either. If you want to achieve something you will need to get violent about it.

I have probably met at least 50 people in the last twenty years who have waited until they were divorced before they started losing weight. Most were about 20-30 pounds over weight. They didn't care what they looked like after they were married. But when they lost their spouse they decided that they better get with it and lose weight. When they wanted it bad enough, they made it happen. Most people just don't want it bad enough.

When I coach little league baseball I often have to deal with players who are apathetic about practice, making plays, getting a hit, or even winning. They show up for practice and want to clown around and talk with friends and goof off instead of drill to become better at the game. When they step up to the plate they don't have any hunger in their eyes for a hit. They are fearful of the ball or the pitcher and take half-hearted swings or go down looking (strike out without even swinging). Getting them hungry for the game and competitive in a positive sense becomes a great challenge. They lack internal motivation and I, as the coach, must instill it in them. Running laps for making mistakes on the field gives them a little fear of messing up and creates a small amount of desire to make the play. However, the driving force is still not what I am looking for. My strategies for developing an internal hunger and drive for success include setting up small goals that they can achieve, giving them tons of praise for doing something right on the field, engaging them in small contests where they can compete and win (and taste the victory), and teaching them to love the game and admire talented and skilled players. Many people face the same problems in getting motivated to exercise.

In the movie *Facing the Giants,* the coach of a high school football team encouraged his players to live for the glory of God. He told his players to do everything possible in their power and strength and let God do the rest. He pushed his players to give 100% of

Herschel Walker

Herschel Walker became famous as the 1982 Heisman Trophy winner. At age 12 he prepared for his sports career by performing 100,000 push-ups, 100,000 sit-ups, and sprinting thousands of miles during the course of one year. He came from a poor high school that couldn't afford expensive weights so push-ups and sit-ups became his fitness routine. He scored 85 touchdowns as a running back and led his team to state championships in football and track while maintaining an A average. He was valedictorian of his class and the most sought after high school football player in the nation.

His career highlights include:
- 10 NCAA game records
- 15 Southeastern Conference records
- 30 University of Georgia records
- Heisman Trophy in 1982
- USFL rushing record of 233 yards
- 2,411 yards rushing in a single professional season
- USFL rushing leader in 1983 and 1985
- NFL personal best of 173 yards rushing
- Dallas Cowboys single season receiving record of 76 receptions and single game record of 282 total yards
- Led NFL running backs in receptions and yards per carry in 1988
- Led the NFC in 1988 with 1,514 rushing yards
- First NFL player to ever achieve 700 yards rushing and receiving in a single season
- Became the 10th NFL player to gain 2,000 yards from scrimmage
- In 1990 led the NFL in combined yards
- Was a member of the 1992 U.S. Olympic Bobsled Team

From Academy of Achievement and Herschel's Famous 34

themselves, believe that anything was possible with God, and don't hold back because of fear or doubt. Their hard work, determination, and faith defeated the giants that stood in their way of victory.

If you want to get in shape, lose weight, quit smoking, or achieve some other health related goal, you have to want it. You have to want it real bad and do whatever it takes to get there. If you want it bad enough I know you will commit your time, attention, and resources to making it happen. With all of your effort, and help from the Lord, you will succeed.

Faith in Action: Fast for one day. Drink nothing but water. During morning prayer, state the purpose of your fast to the Lord. (Lord, I am fasting today to break my addiction to...Lord I am fasting today to find the answer to this question...) Spend some spiritual time during the day reflecting on God's plan for your life and the purpose of your fast.

30.

Misinformation

—⌇⌇⌇—

Faith

Matthew 7:15 "Beware of the false prophets who come to you in sheep's clothing, but inwardly are ravenous wolves. You will know them by their fruits."

J esus often warned His disciples and followers about false prophets and hypocrites. He understood the dangers of following a lie and made every effort to expose falsehood. Jesus condemned those who did not practice the truth. He was so passionate about the truth that He was very blunt and direct to those who were not walking in it. He often rebuked the religious leaders of the day because they were holding on to lies and resisting the truth. One of Jesus most powerful rebukes was in **John 8:44** where He said **"You are of your father the devil, and you want to do the desires of your father. He was a murderer from the beginning, and does not stand in the truth because there is no truth in him. Whenever he speaks a lie, he speaks from his own nature, for he is a liar and the father of lies."** Here He made it very clear that if you speak lies you are working for the devil. Wow, not a place I would want to be.

Unfortunately, deception, lies, corruption, and falsehood are commonplace in our society and world. There are many false religions that deceive billions of people. Some followers are very willing to die a radical death for beliefs that are founded on lies. There is no way to sugarcoat the indisputable truth. Jesus is the only way to God. If you are offended by this statement, then you are offended by God. Jesus is the narrow gate that leads to life. All alternate routes are lies. God Almighty, the Creator of heaven, earth, and mankind revealed Himself in a specific way to man and created a plan of salvation for everyone. He prepared the gift of salvation, the ultimate sacrifice, His Son the Messiah. God is not schizophrenic and He did not reveal Himself in totally different ways to different cultures. It would be crazy for God to pretend He was a different being to different people groups. Why would He do that? He is God. He is the Creator. He is all powerful, all knowing, and all good. **1Corinthians 14:33** says **"for God is not a God of confusion, but of peace..."** There is a true way to know Him and have a relationship with Him. That way is through Jesus His Son and through the Holy Scriptures, the Bible. If you want to dispel misinformation read the Old and New Testament and you will know the truth.

Besides the misinformation of world religions we also have to beware of deceivers within the Christian faith. There have been many ministers who have either knowingly or unknowingly deceived many. Some deception is small and is construed for the purpose of greed or power. These ministers have a goal of getting rich or becoming famous by twisting the words of the gospel. The truth becomes distorted and the minister goes off on a tangent until he falls into some serious sin. In the end, those who have been deceived feel cheated.

When I was in my twenties, I went to hear a Christian comedian speak at a mega-church. He shared his testimony that he was a former Satanist who had been saved. He told some of the horrors of his past life and how Jesus' power had changed him. Besides his testimony he shared many funny jokes. We, the congregation, believed his every word and were inspired by what he said. A few years later the story surfaced that he was a fake and had never been a part of any satanic cult. He had deceived many for the purpose of drawing a crowd and I guess, making some money. When I was listening to him, I hung on every word and had no idea he was feeding me a line. What a disappointment to find out later that he was a deceiver!

Besides lies created for personal gain, there is a deeper deception which is created by the devil to mislead many into false religion or cult groups. Leaders of these cult groups have been duped into promoting themselves to deity status and have created all kinds of sick and twisted doctrines. Their deception is serious and results in people devoting themselves to a lie that may end in death. Jesus said in **Matthew 15:14 "...if a blind man guides a blind man both will fall into the pit."**

Wisdom, knowledge, and instruction are everywhere. There is a lot of good teaching and preaching available that can change our life in a powerful way. However, it is important to differentiate between the wisdom of the world and godly wisdom. It is important to know the difference between good information and misinformation. There are plenty of fools spouting off psycho-babble that has absolutely no basis of sound wisdom or knowledge. The alarming fact is that these deceivers speak with such conviction and determination. Some are quite convincing and mislead many. Jesus warned that there would be many false prophets who would arise and mislead many. Think about how many religions there are in the world and how many different sects of each religion exist.

We must be careful what we listen to and who we believe. When in doubt, we must compare what we are hearing to the Word of God, the Bible. If what we hear doesn't match up with scripture, we need to run the other way or stand up and refute the misinformation.

As Christians, we must be resolute about knowing the truth. We must be diligent to identify and avoid the false prophets who propagate lies and misinformation. We must study the Word of God, apply it to our heart, and act upon it. We must have a humble heart before the Lord that is eager to do His will. In **John 8:31-32** Jesus promised **"If you continue in My word, then you are truly disciples of Mine; and you will know the truth, and the truth will make you free."**

Don't blindly follow any preacher. Get in the Bible, get before the Lord, and figure out for yourself what God has said. His Holy Spirit will be your teacher and lead you into all the truth.

Fitness

There is a lot of good health and fitness information. There is also a lot of health and fitness misinformation. Merriam-Webster's Dictionary refers to misinformation as "bad, wrong, unfavorable, suspicious, opposite, or lack of" information. The health and wellness industry consumes billions of dollars each year and many deceivers have entered it to make a quick buck. There are plenty of bad diet plans, diet pills, exercise equipment, weight loss strategies, healing techniques, herbal remedies, vitamins, alternative medicines, surgeries, and the like that have been fabricated to make money and have no solid scientific ground (truth) to stand on. Some of these bad ideas are a big waste of money and others are down right dangerous to our health. It is important that health consumers discern between good and bad information.

Recently a friend told me of an herbal remedy that she was taking to cure a physical ailment she has suffered from for awhile. She was excited about the remedy and read me a laundry list of things that it cured. The herb was about $35 per bottle. It was pricey but I guess she won't have to buy anything else since it cures almost everything…yeah, right! If it sounds too good to be true, it probably is too good to be true.

There are many things that have big claims for success that may not deliver on the promise. Sometimes these things are touted with a lot of hype and promises of super success. Sometimes new "breakthroughs" have testimonials from people who have had incredible success. Sometimes these products come with money back guarantees that really don't follow through with their promise. Buyers need to beware! We need to be careful who we listen to in regards to our health, wellness, and fitness. Some products may indeed give us some health benefit. But the benefit may be much smaller than promised and may not be financially worth it.

The best way to be able to discern the truth from the lies is to begin reading up on whatever you are contemplating. There are tons of books on every topic under the sun. There are many great websites that will give you solid information for free (there are also plenty of bad ones). When you begin reading, you need to go

---

Medline Plus Guide to Healthy Web Surfing

What should you look for when evaluating the quality of health information on Web sites?

Know who is responsible for the content. Is it a government website, non-profit organization, professional organization, health system, commercial organization, or an individual? Does the site list contact information?

Focus on the quality of the site. Does the site have an editorial policy? How is the information approved? What does it say about the writers or authors?

Be a cyber skeptic. Quackery abounds on the Web. Does the site make health claims that seem too good to be true? Does it promise quick, dramatic, miraculous results? Does the site use sensationalism?

Look for the evidence. Rely on medical research, not opinion. Does the site rely on testimonials? Can these testimonials be tracked down?

Check for current information. Look for dates on the site and information.

Beware of bias. What is the purpose of the site? Who is providing funding?

Protect your privacy. Health information should be confidential. Does the site have a privacy policy for the information they collect?

Consult with your health professional before making medical decisions.

From **U.S. National Library of Medicine
National Institutes of Health**

---

to the experts first. In every field there are recognized authorities or governing bodies. These governing bodies set up standards by which all information must be scrutinized and synthesized. Anything that is not sound advice is discarded or labeled as experimental. Proven success and experimental trials are two totally different things. Peer review journals offer articles that have been through the scrutiny of other experts in the field. Articles often published in these journals have been substantiated with some clinical studies and research.

It is best to find reliable sources that offer sound advice that is balanced in approach and success. There are no silver bullets or magical success methods in health and fitness matters. The body is a complex organism that responds to prolonged care. If we take care of our body and exercise it and feed it good stuff, it will be pretty healthy. Adjusting our health by gimmicks or pills or surgery is risky business. What allegedly worked for someone else might not work for us. Diligent, long-term, comprehensive care is the best way to go.

I believe in some forms of alternative medicine and healing. I believe in taking vitamins. I believe in the power of God to heal and help in recovery when sick or injured. I have seen a chiropractor. I have been to a massage therapist. I have tried herbs such as barley green and a few others. Some of these things have proven effective in promoting my health. I have friends who have experienced successes in other things. I also believe that God has given us doctors and medicines to help us when our body needs help recovering. However, the most sound health advice, which is agreed upon by everyone in the health and wellness field is….eat healthy foods and exercise every day.

Before biting into the latest fitness fad, diet program, diet pill, or herbal remedy get your facts straight. Practice the basics of vigorous daily exercise, eating right, not smoking, limiting alcohol, staying off drugs, and other healthy, safe habits. If you are considering some additional means after you have done the basics, read up on your plan of action. Make well-informed sensible decisions about your health and you will live a long and healthy life.

Faith in Action: Surf on the web and find ten reputable websites that provide a variety of information on health topics (healthy eating, exercise, strength training, medical advice, research) that are of interest to you. Bookmark the sites and refer back to them often for reliable information. Don't forget to check us out on the web at www. forwewalkbyfaith.net where you can find links to our favorite websites.

31.

The Strength Which God Supplies

—⟋ℳ⟍—

Faith

1 Peter 4:11 "Whoever speaks, is to do so as one who is speaking the utterances of God; whoever serves is to do so as one who is serving by the strength which God supplies; so that in all things God may be glorified through Jesus Christ, to whom belongs the glory and dominion forever and ever. Amen."

The Christian life is a balance of giving everything we have in us to the task at hand and surrendering to the Lord and letting His strength take over on the inside of us. We must be diligent to give 100% of our effort to what God has called us to do. But at the same time we must remember that our life, gifts, and talents are from Him and that He gives us the strength and spiritual power to operate in them. **Philippians 2:13 says "for it is God who is at work in you, both to will and to work for His good pleasure."**

If we don't honor God as the source of our gifts and as the source of our strength, then we are not glorifying Him. If we make achievements in our own strength then we, in essence, are glorifying ourselves. We are in essence saying 'Look at what I did by my own hands. I am the man (or woman)! I am self sufficient and need no one.' **Psalm 127:1 says "Unless the Lord builds the house, they**

labor in vain who build it; unless the Lord guards the city, the watchman keeps awake in vain." If we don't tap into God's strength and give Him the glory, our pursuits and efforts are in vain.

When my wife and I owned a daycare center there were many times when we hit rock bottom and knew if the Lord didn't come through for us we were done. Several times we didn't have anywhere else to go or any resources left and all we could do is pray and ask the Lord to help us out. He always did. Whether it was the mortgage, or the taxes, or payroll, or low enrollment, or busted pipes flooding the place, or disgruntled workers, or disgruntled parents, or a broken septic tank pump, or dealing with burdensome state childcare inspectors-God always poured out His grace, strength, and provision to make it through. We actually developed a strong faith in Him that reasoned something like this: "Lord we know you have called us to serve these children and staff in a Christian setting. You know we are doing this to glorify you. We have this problem and we know you can fix it. You have helped us many times in the past and once again we ask for your help now. Please help Lord! Thank you for your faithfulness and the victory we have over the enemy. Amen." When you are doing what God has called you to do and you are doing it for the right reasons, He is always there to help out.

The heavyweight boxing champion Evander Holyfield had the following passage sown on the back of his boxing robe: **Phil. 4:13.** It says **"I can do all things through Him who strengthens me."** When he entered the ring Christian music that exalted God was trumpeting on the speakers. He fought with God's strength. When he was finished fighting he humbly gave glory to God for helping him.

When we surrender our life to Christ and put our faith in His salvation on the cross we become born again. Jesus called it being born of the Spirit. God's Spirit comes to live on the inside of us and He begins to work in our lives and clean us up. This process of cleaning up is called sanctification. Paul wrote in **Philippians 1:6 "For I am confident of this very thing, that He who began a good work in you will perfect it until the day of Christ Jesus."** If God is working in us to change our desires and fill us with the fruit of His Spirit, then He gets the glory for changing us. His power works in us and makes us more like Him.

Problems arise when things start going good and we take over and start leading the way without Him. We forget that He is the one changing us on the inside. We forget that it is His strength and gifts that have gotten us to where we are. We start making our own plans and thinking more highly of ourselves than we ought to. Paul wrote in **Galatians 3:3 "Are you so foolish? Having begun by the Spirit, are you now being perfected by the flesh?"** When Christians and even ministers forget that God is their strength, they make wrong turns, bad decisions, get burned out, and eventually fall or backslide. Pride comes before the fall.

What do you do when you fall? You have to get back up. But before you get off your knees you may want to take some time to repent before the Lord and humble yourself. Acknowledge to your heavenly Father that your life is His. Let Him know that you realize that everything you have and everything you are has come from Him. Let Him know that you don't want to go another step without His guidance and strength. Cast all your cares and anxieties on Him and ask Him to take care of them. Ask Him to help you through. Ask for His strength. **1Peter 5:6-7** says **"Therefore humble yourselves under the mighty hand of God, that He may exalt you at the proper time, casting all your anxiety on Him, because He cares for you."**

He will hear you and answer you. He desires to be your refuge, your strength, your tower, your fortress, your deliverer, and your very present help in time of trouble. Live life in His strength and you will be victorious!

Fitness

In your fitness pursuits you are going to hit the wall. You are going to come to places where you feel like you just can't go on. The wall might be physical exhaustion. The wall might be an injury. The wall might be stress from all of life's trials and complications. The wall might be schedule conflicts. During these tough times you must be able to tap into the strength which God supplies. You must drain yourself of your own abilities and strengths, and tap into His. There is a place where we can step into His divine power and continue onward. David said in **Psalm 18:29 "For by You I can run upon a troop, and by my God I can leap over a wall."**

There are two different occasions mentioned in the gospels where Jesus' disciples were in trouble on the water. They were physically straining at the oars of the boat and they cried out to Jesus for help. Once He was asleep on a cushion and they woke Him thinking they were going to drown. Another time Jesus was walking by them on the water and they cried out to Him. Both times He saved them. The first time He rebuked the storms and they ceased and the second time He got in the boat and the wind stopped. When we are on the journey of life and we are physically straining, we can cry out to Jesus and He will help us.

During my Physical Education studies I learned how to canoe in my outdoor education class. At Christmas break a friend and I decided to paddle about 18 miles down the Chattahoochee River. We put in the frigid racing water just below the dam and started our journey. The dam was at full release and we only made it about ¾ mile before we hit a submerged tree and were capsized. As we were plunged into the fifty degree water, all I could do was pray "Help me Jesus" and hang onto the canoe. As we floated several hundred yards downstream getting cold real quick, we shouted out plans for an exit strategy. The paddles took off in front of us and were gone but we wanted to save the canoe since it was a rental. We decided to push the canoe towards a fallen tree and ram it into it and try to get out of the water there. Somehow my friend got in front of the boat and when we hit the tree he got his leg pinned between the boat and the tree. As the boat filled with water and the back lifted into the air, he started to go under as the front submerged. All I could do was cry out to the Lord for help and wrestle with the boat to try and set him free. By God's divine grace we were able to get his leg out and make it safely to shore. He later told me that he had seen his life flash before his eyes and that all he could remember was that he was thankful that he had kissed his wife and kids goodbye that morning. He had thanked me for saving his life but all I could do is thank the Lord for saving both of us by the strength which He supplies.

Before each run I usually say a brief prayer to the Lord to ask for His strength to run *faster, higher, and stronger* (the Olympic motto).

Once I have committed my way to Him, I am off. On occasion I will become very winded or begin to cramp. On those times I begin to confess Philippians 4:13 while I run. I draw on His strength and ask Him to help me make it to the end. During the marathon I hit the biggest wall ever and did not think I would make it. I thought I would have to drop out. Yet somehow, after much prayer, He enabled me to continue on.

I know many people who begin an exercise routine after years of inactivity face many complaints and resistance from their body and mind. They begin to wheeze like every breath may be their last. Their heart is pounding out of their chest. Their legs are screaming in pain and they feel like they may collapse at any second. Thoughts race through their mind about the impossibility of ever getting back into shape again. The only way of completing the task is to call out for God's strength. Taking care of your body is His will and He will give you the strength to carry on if you ask Him and believe for His grace.

Beside physical exhaustion, injuries are another setback that will require God's strength to endure. When I get injured or become sick the first thing I do is PRAY. When my wife is injured or sick, we PRAY. When my son or daughter is injured or sick, we PRAY. Prayer enables us to step into God's strength and His healing power. Our family doctor is a second plan of action for us. Doctor Jesus comes first. We use our faith, common sense, and sometimes modern medicine to get through injuries and sickness.

My most common injury is throwing my back out. It has happened several times over the past years and after prayer I take measures to look after it's healing. My usual plan is rest, ice, heat, and traction. My traction involves hanging from my chin up bar and letting my legs dangle for about 45 seconds. When my back is hurt badly, I hang several times a day. If you have back problems please give traction a try. If I incorporate it into my daily stretching, I usually have no problems with my back. When I neglect my stretching, I usually suffer. During times of injury I cry out to the Lord for His healing and strength to recover quickly. Why should I rely on my own strength and the hands of the doctors when He is available?

Back Pain Facts

- Stress is the leading risk factor for back pain and injury
- Between 60-80% of North America will suffer from back pain or injury at some point in their lives
- Back pain is the leading cause of inactivity for people under age 45.
- Approximately 5% will experience pain that last six months or longer.
- 80-90% will recover in 3-6 days
- Besides stress individual risk factors include: lack of sleep/fatigue, emotional instability, family problems, substance abuse, lack of physical activity/too much physical activity, poor muscle endurance and poor trunk muscle stabilization, excessive weight
- Sedentary jobs have the highest risk of disk herniation
- To prevent back injuries: exercise, strengthen core muscles, lift correctly

<u>From American College of Sports Medicine</u>

Treatments for Low Back Pain

- Rest for no more than 2-3 days
- Medicines such as non steroidal anti-inflammatory drugs or acetaminophen may be helpful
- Passive modalities such as ice, heat, massage, ultrasound, electrical stimulation, traction, and acupuncture may help with pain
- Spinal manipulation (chiropractic care) may also decrease pain
- Injections such as epidurals or nerve root injections may be done by doctors
- Surgery is done only when other options have been met

From American Academy of Orthopaedic Surgeons

When you hit the wall of exhaustion, injury, or stress I hope you will call on the Lord and enter into His strength. It is free to those who humbly ask. When we are weak, He is strong on our behalf. We are able to overcome obstacles, barriers, and setbacks when we humble ourselves before Him and enter into the strength which God supplies.

Faith in Action: Take a few minutes to think about some of the trials you have encountered in the past. Did you hand them over to the Lord? Did He help you? Create a Philippians 4:13 Journal where you record all the trials and victories you have experienced in life. When you hit rough times read it and charge up your faith in God's strength.

Appendix-Scripture List

—ᴡ—

Psalm 34:8 "O taste and see that the Lord is good..."

Mark 5:19-20 "Go home to your people and report to them what great things the Lord has done for you, and how He had mercy on you." And he went away and began to proclaim in Decapolis what great things Jesus had done for him; and everyone was amazed."

Psalm 94:14 "For the LORD will not abandon His people, nor will He forsake His inheritance."

Proverbs 22:6 "Train up a child in the way he should go, even when he is old he will not depart from it."

Job 8:7 "Though your beginning was insignificant, yet your end will increase greatly."

Proverbs 27:17 "Iron sharpens iron, so one man sharpens another."

Philippians 3:13-15 "Brethren, I do not regard myself as having laid hold of it yet; but one thing I do: forgetting what lies behind and reaching forward to what lies ahead, I press on toward the goal for the prize of the upward call of God in Christ Jesus."

1Peter 4:10-11 "As each one has received a special gift, employ it in serving one another as good stewards of the manifold grace of God. Whoever speaks is to do so as one who is speaking the utterances of God' whoever serves is to do so as one who is serving by the strength which God supplies' so that in all things God may be glorified through Jesus Christ, to whom belongs the glory and dominion forever and ever. Amen."

1 Corinthians 1:26-27 "For consider your calling, brethren, that there were not many wise according to the flesh, not many mighty, not many noble; but God has chosen the foolish things of the world to shame the wise, and God has chosen the weak things of the world to shame the things which are strong...."

Mark 10:43-45 "...whoever wishes to become great among you shall be your servant; and whoever wishes to be first among you shall be slave of all. For even the Son of Man did not come to be served, but to serve, and to give His life a ransom for many."

3. The 5F's
Matthew 6:21 "for where your treasure is, there your heart will be also."
Matthew 6:33 "Seek first His kingdom and His righteousness; and all these things shall be added to you."
Exodus 20:2-3"I am the LORD your God, who brought you out of the land of Egypt, out of the house of slavery. You shall have no other gods before Me

Exodus 20:12"Honor your father and your mother, that your days may be prolonged in the land which the LORD your God gives you."

Proverbs 22:6 "Train up a child in the way he should go, even when he is old he will not depart from it."

1Corinthians 6:19-20 "Or do you not know that your body is a temple of the Holy Spirit who is in you, whom you have from God, and that you are not your own? For you have been bought with a price: therefore glorify God in your body."

John 13:35 "By this all men will know that you are My disciples, if you have love for one another."

Proverbs 17:22 "A joyful heart is good medicine..."

4. Check Up Time

Psalm 26:2 "Examine me, O LORD, and try me; test my mind and my heart."

Psalm 19:12-14 "Who can discern his errors? Acquit me of hidden faults. Also keep back Your servant from presumptuous sins; Let them not rule over me; then I will be blameless, and I shall be acquitted of great transgression.
Let the words of my mouth and the meditation of my heart be acceptable in Your sight, O LORD, my rock and my Redeemer."

1John 1:9 "If we confess our sins, He is faithful and righteous to forgive us our sins and to cleanse us from all unrighteousness."
Psalm 51 "1Be gracious to me, O God, according to Your lovingkindness;
　　　According to the greatness of Your compassion blot out my transgressions.
　2Wash me thoroughly from my iniquity
　　　and cleanse me from my sin.
　3For I know my transgressions,
　　　and my sin is ever before me.
　4Against You, You only, I have sinned
　　　and done what is evil in Your sight,
　　　So that You are justified when You speak
　　　and blameless when You judge.
　5Behold, I was brought forth in iniquity,
　　　and in sin my mother conceived me.
　6Behold, You desire truth in the innermost being,
　　　and in the hidden part You will make me know wisdom.
　7Purify me with hyssop, and I shall be clean;
　　　Wash me, and I shall be whiter than snow.
　8Make me to hear joy and gladness,
　　　Let the bones which You have broken rejoice.
　9Hide Your face from my sins
　　　and blot out all my iniquities.
　10Create in me a clean heart, O God,
　　　and renew a steadfast spirit within me.
　11Do not cast me away from Your presence
　　　and do not take Your Holy Spirit from me.
　12Restore to me the joy of Your salvation
　　　and sustain me with a willing spirit.

13Then I will teach transgressors Your ways,
   and sinners will be converted to You.
14Deliver me from bloodguiltiness, O God, the God of my
salvation;
   Then my tongue will joyfully sing of Your righteousness.
15O Lord, open my lips,
   that my mouth may declare Your praise.
16For You do not delight in sacrifice, otherwise I would give it;
   You are not pleased with burnt offering.
17The sacrifices of God are a broken spirit;
   a broken and a contrite heart, O God, You will not despise.
18By Your favor do good to Zion;
   Build the walls of Jerusalem.
19Then You will delight in righteous sacrifices,
   in burnt offering and whole burnt offering;
   Then young bulls will be offered on Your altar."
Proverbs 14:16 "A wise man is cautious and turns away from evil,
but a fool is arrogant and careless."

5. Glorify God in Your Body
1 Corinthians 6:19-20 "Or do you not know that your body is a
temple of the Holy Spirit who is in you, whom you have from God,
and that you are not your own? For you have been bought with a
price: therefore glorify God in your body."

Luke 24:49 "And behold, I am sending forth the promise of My
Father upon you; but you are to stay in the city until you are clothed
with power from on high."

Acts 2:17 "'And it shall be in the last days,' God says, 'That I will
pour forth of My Spirit on all mankind...'"

2 Corinthians 6:14-18 "Do not be bound together with unbelievers;
for what partnership have righteousness and lawlessness, or what
fellowship has light with darkness? Or what harmony has Christ
with Belial, or what has a believer in common with an unbeliever?
Or what agreement has the temple of God with idols? For we are
the temple of the living God; just as God said, "I WILL DWELL
IN THEM AND WALK AMONG THEM; AND I WILL BE THEIR
GOD, AND THEY SHALL BE MY PEOPLE. "Therefore, COME
OUT FROM THEIR MIDST AND BE SEPARATE," says the Lord.

"AND DO NOT TOUCH WHAT IS UNCLEAN; and I will welcome you. "And I will be a father to you, and you shall be sons and daughters to me," says the Lord Almighty.

Matthew 7:6 "Do not give what is holy to dogs, and do not throw your pearls before swine..."

Haggai 2:9 "The latter glory of this house will be greater than the former...."

6. Abundant Life
John 10:10 "The thief comes only to steal and kill and destroy; I came that they may have life, and have it abundantly."

Mark 9: 23 "All things are possible to him who believes."

Acts 10:38 "You know of Jesus of Nazareth, how God anointed Him with the Holy Spirit and with power, and how He went about doing good and healing all who were oppressed by the devil, for God was with Him."

Mark 1:40-41 "And a leper came to Jesus, beseeching Him and falling on his knees before Him, and saying, "If You are willing, You can make me clean." Moved with compassion, Jesus stretched out His hand and touched him, and said to him, "I am willing; be cleansed."

3John 1:2 "Beloved, I pray that in all respects you may prosper and be in good health, just as your soul prospers."

7. Wisdom is crying out
Proverbs 1:20-33
²⁰Wisdom shouts in the street, She lifts her voice in the square;
²¹At the head of the noisy streets she cries out;
at the entrance of the gates in the city she utters her sayings:
²²"How long, O naive ones, will you love being simple-minded?
And scoffers delight themselves in scoffing
and fools hate knowledge?
²³"Turn to my reproof, Behold, I will pour out my spirit on you;
I will make my words known to you.

[24]"Because I called and you refused, I stretched out my hand and no one paid attention;

[25]And you neglected all my counsel And did not want my reproof;

[26]I will also laugh at your calamity; I will mock when your dread comes,

[27]When your dread comes like a storm And your calamity comes like a whirlwind,

When distress and anguish come upon you.

[28]"Then they will call on me, but I will not answer; they will seek me diligently but they will not find me,

[29]Because they hated knowledge, and did not choose the fear of the LORD.

[30]"They would not accept my counsel, they spurned all my reproof.

[31]"So they shall eat of the fruit of their own way, and be satiated with their own devices.

[32]"For the waywardness of the naive will kill them, and the complacency of fools will destroy them.

[33]"But he who listens to me shall live securely, and will be at ease from the dread of evil."

Proverbs 1:7 "fools despise wisdom and instruction."

Proverbs 13:20 "He who walks with wise men will be wise, But the companion of fools will suffer harm."

Matthew 7:24-27 "Therefore everyone who hears these words of Mine and acts on them, may be compared to a wise man who built his house on the rock. And the rain fell, and the floods came, and the winds blew and slammed against that house; and yet it did not fall, for it had been founded on the rock. Everyone who hears these words of Mine and does not act on them, will be like a foolish man who built his house on the sand. The rain fell, and the floods came, and the winds blew and slammed against that house; and it fell—and great was its fall."

Proverbs 1:32 "the complacency of fools will destroy them."

1 Corinthians 13:11 "When I was a child, I used to speak like a child, think like a child, reason like a child; when I became a man, I did away with childish things."

8. Love Yourself

Psalm 139:13-16 "For You formed my inward parts; You covered
me in my mother's womb. I will praise You, for I am fearfully and
wonderfully made; Marvelous are Your works, and that my soul
knows very well. My frame was not hidden from You, when I was
made in secret, and skillfully wrought in the lowest parts of the
earth. Your eyes saw my substance, being yet unformed. And in Your
book they all were written, the days fashioned for me, when as yet
there were none of them."

John 3:16 "For God so loved the world that He sent His only Son,
that whosoever will believe in Him will not perish but have everlasting life."

Matthew 11:28 "Come unto me all you who are weary and heavy
laden and I will give you rest."

Luke 15:4-7 "What man among you, if he has a hundred sheep
and has lost one of them, does not leave the ninety-nine in the open
pasture and go after the one which is lost until he finds it? When
he has found it, he lays it on his shoulders, rejoicing. And when he
comes home, he calls together his friends and his neighbors, saying to
them, 'Rejoice with me, for I have found my sheep which was lost!'
I tell you that in the same way, there will be more joy in heaven over
one sinner who repents than over ninety-nine righteous persons who
need no repentance."

Matthew 22:39 "You shall love your neighbor as yourself."

9. Desire, Discipline, Delight

Matthew 16:24-25 ""If anyone wishes to come after Me, he must
deny himself, and take up his cross and follow Me. For whoever
wishes to save his life will lose it; but whoever loses his life for My
sake will find it."

John 3:3 "Truly, truly, I say to you, unless one is born again he
cannot see the kingdom of God."

Psalm 37:5 "Commit your way to the LORD, Trust also in Him, and
He will do it."

1 Corinthians 9:27 "I discipline my body and make it my slave, so that, after I have preached to others, I myself will not be disqualified."

10. The weapons of our warfare

Ephesians 6: 10-17 "Finally, be strong in the Lord and in the strength of His might. Put on the full armor of God, so that you will be able to stand firm against the schemes of the devil. For our struggle is not against flesh and blood, but against the rulers, against the powers, against the world forces of this darkness, against the spiritual forces of wickedness in the heavenly places. Therefore, take up the full armor of God, so that you will be able to resist in the evil day, and having done everything, to stand firm. Stand firm therefore, HAVING GIRDED YOUR LOINS WITH TRUTH, and HAVING PUT ON THE BREASTPLATE OF RIGHTEOUSNESS, and having shod YOUR FEET WITH THE PREPARATION OF THE GOSPEL OF PEACE; in addition to all, taking up the shield of faith with which you will be able to extinguish all the flaming arrows of the evil one. And take THE HELMET OF SALVATION, and the sword of the Spirit, which is the word of God."

Revelations 12:11 "and they overcame him (Satan) because of the blood of the Lamb and because of the word of their testimony."

Mark 16:15 "Go into all the world and preach the gospel to all creation."

11. Watch over your heart

Proverbs 4:23 Watch over your heart with all diligence, for from it flow the springs of life.

Matthew 15:17-19 "Do you not understand that everything that goes into the mouth passes into the stomach, and is eliminated? But the things that proceed out of the mouth come from the heart, and those defile the man. For out of the heart come evil thoughts, murders, adulteries, fornications, thefts, false witness, slanders."

Matthew 12:36-37 "But I tell you that every careless word that people speak, they shall give an accounting for it in the day of judgment. For by your words you will be justified, and by your words you will be condemned."

Mark 9:47 "If your eye causes you to stumble, throw it out; it is better for you to enter the kingdom of God with one eye, than, having two eyes, to be cast into hell..."

Matthew 7:17-20 "So every good tree bears good fruit, but the bad tree bears bad fruit. A good tree cannot produce bad fruit, nor can a bad tree produce good fruit. Every tree that does not bear good fruit is cut down and thrown into the fire. So then, you will know them by their fruits."

12. Enduring Tribulation

Romans 5:3-5 "And not only this, but we also exult in our tribulations, knowing that tribulation brings about perseverance; and perseverance, proven character; and proven character, hope; and hope does not disappoint, because the love of God has been poured out within our hearts through the Holy Spirit who was given to us."

John 16:33 "In the world you have tribulation....."
John 10:10 "The thief (devil) comes only to steal and kill and destroy...."
Proverbs 24:16 "For a righteous man falls seven times, and rises again..."

John 16:33 "In the world you have tribulation, but take courage; I have overcome the world."

13. Don't Follow the Crowd

Matthew 7:13-14 "Enter through the narrow gate; for the gate is wide and the way is broad that leads to destruction, and there are many who enter through it. For the gate is small and the way is narrow that leads to life, and there are few who find it."

Matthew 5:16 "Let your light shine before men in such a way that they may see your good works, and glorify your Father who is in heaven."

John 6:38 "For I have come down from heaven, not to do My own will, but the will of Him who sent Me."

14. Persistence

Luke 11:9-10 "So I say to you, ask, and it will be given to you; seek, and you will find; knock, and it will be opened to you. For everyone who asks, receives; and he who seeks, finds; and to him who knocks, it will be opened."

Luke 11:5-8 "Suppose one of you has a friend, and goes to him at midnight and says to him, 'Friend, lend me three loaves; for a friend of mine has come to me from a journey, and I have nothing to set before him'; and from inside he answers and says, 'Do not bother me; the door has already been shut and my children and I are in bed; I cannot get up and give you anything.' I tell you, even though he will not get up and give him anything because he is his friend, yet because of his persistence he will get up and give him as much as he needs."

Matthew 7:6 "Do not give what is holy to dogs and do not throw your pearls before swine...."

15. Sowing and Reaping

Galatians 6:7-8 "Do not be deceived, God is not mocked; for whatever a man sows, this he will also reap. For the one who sows to his own flesh shall from the flesh reap corruption, but the one who sows to the Spirit shall from the Spirit reap eternal life."

2 Corinthians 9:6 "he who sows sparingly will also reap sparingly, and he who sows bountifully will also reap bountifully."

Matthew 6:20 "........store up for yourselves treasures in heaven..."

Galatians 5:19-21 "Now the deeds of the flesh are evident, which are: immorality, impurity, sensuality, idolatry, sorcery, enmities, strife, jealousy, outbursts of anger, disputes, dissensions, factions, envying, drunkenness, carousing, and things like these, of which I forewarn you, just as I have forewarned you, that those who practice such things will not inherit the kingdom of God."

16. Iron sharpens iron

Proverbs 27:17 Iron sharpens iron, so one man sharpens another.

1 Thessalonians 5:11 "Therefore encourage one another and build up one another, just as you also are doing."

Ecclesiastes 4:9-10 "Two are better than one because they have a good return for their labor. For if either of them falls, the one will lift up his companion. But woe to the one who falls when there is not another to lift him up."

Matthew 18:19 "Again I say to you, that if two of you agree on earth about anything that they may ask, it shall be done for them by My Father who is in heaven."

Proverbs 27:6 "Faithful are the wounds of a friend, but deceitful are the kisses of an enemy."

Proverbs 12:27 "the precious possession of a man is diligence."

17. It's Never too late to start
Romans 4:18-21 "In hope against hope he believed, so that he might become a father of many nations according to that which had been spoken, SO SHALL YOUR DESCENDANTS BE." Without becoming weak in faith he contemplated his own body, now as good as dead since he was about a hundred years old, and the deadness of Sarah's womb; yet, with respect to the promise of God, he did not waver in unbelief but grew strong in faith, giving glory to God, and being fully assured that what God had promised, He was able also to perform."

Deuteronomy 34:7 "Although Moses was one hundred and twenty years old when he died, his eye was not dim, nor his vigor abated."

Isaiah 43:18-19 "Do not call to mind the former things, or ponder things of the past. Behold, I will do something new, now it will spring forth; will you not be aware of it? I will even make a roadway in the wilderness, rivers in the desert."

Joshua 14:7,10-11, "I was forty years old when Moses the servant of the LORD sent me from Kadesh-barnea to spy out the land, and I brought word back to him as it was in my heart"....... "Now behold, the LORD has let me live, just as He spoke, these forty-five years, from the time that the LORD spoke this word to Moses, when Israel walked in the wilderness; and now behold, I am eighty-five years old today. I am still as strong today as I was in the day Moses sent me; as my strength was then, so my strength is now, for war and for going out and coming in."

18. I don't feel like working out today
Mark 14:38 "Watch and pray, lest you enter into temptation. The spirit indeed is willing, but the flesh is weak."

Galatians 5:16 "But I say, walk by the Spirit, and you will not carry out the desire of the flesh."

James 1:6-8 "for the one who doubts is like the surf of the sea, driven and tossed by the wind. For that man ought not to expect that he will receive anything from the Lord, being a double-minded man, unstable in all his ways."

Galatians 5:24 "And those who are Christ's have crucified the flesh with its passions and desires."

Romans 8:13 "for if you are living according to the flesh, you must die; but if by the Spirit you are putting to death the deeds of the body, you will live."

1Corinthians 9:27 "But I discipline my body and bring it into subjection, lest, when I have preached to others, I myself should become disqualified."

19. Fathers of the Faith
Philippians 4:9 "The things you have learned and received and heard and seen in me, practice these things, and the God of peace will be with you."

Hebrews 11:33-38 "who by faith conquered kingdoms, performed acts of righteousness, obtained promises, shut the mouths of lions, quenched the power of fire, escaped the edge of the sword, from weakness were made strong, became mighty in war, put foreign armies to flight. Women received back their dead by resurrection; and others were tortured, not accepting their release, so that they might obtain a better resurrection; and others experienced mockings and scourgings, yes, also chains and imprisonment. They were stoned, they were sawn in two, they were tempted, they were put to death with the sword; they went about in sheepskins, in goatskins, being destitute, afflicted, ill-treated (men of whom the world was not worthy), wandering in deserts and mountains and caves and holes in the ground."

Hebrews 12:1 "Therefore, since we have so great a cloud of witnesses surrounding us, let us also lay aside every encumbrance and the sin which so easily entangles us, and let us run with endurance the race that is set before us..."

20. No Condemnation
Romans 8:1-2 "Therefore there is now no condemnation for those who are in Christ Jesus. For the law of the Spirit of life in Christ Jesus has set you free from the law of sin and of death."

Revelations 12:10 Satan is called the "accuser of the brethren."

Proverbs 24:16 "For the righteous man falls seven times and rises again but the wicked stumble in time of calamity."

Hebrews 10:39 "But we are not of those who shrink back to destruction, but of those who have faith to the preserving of the soul."

1John 4:8 "God is love."

Philippians 4:13 "I can do all things through Him who strengthens me."

Proverbs 21:19 "It is better to live in a desert land than with a contentious and vexing woman."

21. Setting Goals
Philippians 3:14 "I press on toward the goal for the prize of the upward call of God in Christ Jesus."

22. Bondage
John 8:34 "Jesus answered them, "Truly, truly, I say to you, everyone who commits sin is the slave of sin.""

Romans 1:28-32: "And just as they did not see fit to acknowledge God any longer, God gave them over to a depraved mind, to do those things which are not proper, being filled with all unrighteousness, wickedness, greed, evil; full of envy, murder, strife, deceit, malice; they are gossips, slanderers, haters of God, insolent, arrogant, boastful, inventors of evil, disobedient to parents, without understanding, untrustworthy, unloving, unmerciful; and although they know the ordinance of God, that those who practice such things are worthy of death, they not only do the same, but also give hearty approval to those who practice them."

James 1:14-15 "But each one is tempted when he is carried away and enticed by his own lust. Then when lust has conceived, it gives birth to sin; and when sin is accomplished, it brings forth death."

Romans 6:12-14 "Therefore do not let sin reign in your mortal body so that you obey its lusts, and do not go on presenting the members of your body to sin as instruments of unrighteousness; but present yourselves to God as those alive from the dead, and your members as instruments of righteousness to God. For sin shall not be master over you, for you are not under law but under grace."

2Corinthians 12:9 "And He has said to me, "My grace is sufficient for you, for power is perfected in weakness. ""

2 Corinthians 6:17 "Therefore, COME OUT FROM THEIR MIDST AND BE SEPARATE," says the Lord." AND DO NOT TOUCH WHAT IS UNCLEAN; And I will welcome you."

23. Train up a child
Proverbs 22:6 "Train up a child in the way he should go, even when he is old he will not depart from it."

Psalm 118:24 "This is the day the Lord has made, let us rejoice and be glad in it."

Proverbs 20:15 "There is gold, and an abundance of jewels; but the lips of knowledge are a more precious thing."

Mark 9:42. "Whoever causes one of these little ones who believe to stumble, it would be better for him if, with a heavy millstone hung around his neck, he had been cast into the sea."

24. Truly Good things
Genesis 1:31 "God saw all that He had made, and behold, it was very good."

Ephesians 1:18-19 "I pray that the eyes of your heart may be enlightened, so that you will know what is the hope of His calling, what are the riches of the glory of His inheritance in the saints, and what is the surpassing greatness of His power toward us who believe."

Genesis 1:29-31 "Then God said, "Behold, I have given you every plant yielding seed that is on the surface of all the earth, and every tree which has fruit yielding seed; it shall be food for you; and to every beast of the earth and to every bird of the sky and to every thing that moves on the earth which has life, I have given every green plant for food"; and it was so. God saw all that He had made, and behold, it was very good."

25. We are judged by our deeds
2 Corinthians 5:10 "For we must all appear before the judgment seat of Christ, so that each one may be recompensed for his deeds in the body, according to what he has done, whether good or bad."

Luke 6:46 "Why do you call me Lord, Lord and do not do what I say?"

James 2:14-18 "What use is it, my brethren, if someone says he has faith but he has no works? Can that faith save him? If a brother or sister is without clothing and in need of daily food, and one of you says to them, "Go in peace, be warmed and be filled," and yet you do not give them what is necessary for their body, what use is that? Even so faith, if it has no works, is dead, being by itself. But someone may well say, "You have faith and I have works; show me your faith without the works, and I will show you my faith by my works.""

Revelations chapters 2&3"I know your deeds..."

Acts 7:56 "Behold, I see the heavens opened up and the Son of Man standing at the right hand of God."

James 1:22 "But prove yourselves doers of the word, and not merely hearers who delude themselves."

26. Appearances
1Samuel 16:7 "for God sees not as man sees, for man looks at the outward appearance, but the LORD looks at the heart."

2 Chronicles 16:9 "For the eyes of the Lord move to and fro throughout the earth that He may strongly support those whose heart is completely His."

Isaiah 40:7-8 "The grass withers, the flower fades, when the breath of the LORD blows upon it; surely the people are grass. The grass withers, the flower fades, but the word of our God stands forever."

27. Keeping things in perspective
Philippians 4:11-13 "Not that I speak from want, for I have learned to be content in whatever circumstances I am. I know how to get along with humble means, and I also know how to live in prosperity; in any and every circumstance I have learned the secret of being filled and going hungry, both of having abundance and suffering need. I can do all things through Him who strengthens me."

1 John 2:15-17 "Do not love the world nor the things in the world. If anyone loves the world, the love of the Father is not in him. For all that is in the world, the lust of the flesh and the lust of the eyes and the boastful pride of life, is not from the Father, but is from the world. The world is passing away, and also its lusts; but the one who does the will of God lives forever."

1 Timothy 6:7-9 "For we have brought nothing into the world, so we cannot take anything out of it either. If we have food and covering, with these we shall be content. But those who want to get rich fall into temptation and a snare and many foolish and harmful desires which plunge men into ruin and destruction."

28. First Love
Revelations 2:4-5 "But I have this against you, that you have left your first love. Therefore remember from where you have fallen, and repent and do the deeds you did at first; or else I am coming to you and will remove your lamp stand out of its place—unless you repent."

Isaiah 42:3 'A bruised reed He will not break and a dimly burning wick He will not extinguish.'

Mark 4: 18-19 "And others are the ones on whom seed was sown among the thorns; these are the ones who have heard the word, but the worries of the world, and the deceitfulness of riches, and the desires for other things enter in and choke the word, and it becomes unfruitful."

Colossians 1:27 "Christ in you, the hope of glory"

29. You gotta want it
Matthew 5:6 "Blessed are those who hunger and thirst for righteousness, for they shall be satisfied."

Psalm 42:1 "As the deer pants for the water brooks, so my soul pants for you, O God."

Matthew 11:12 "….the kingdom of heaven suffers violence, and violent men take it by force."

30. Misinformation
Matthew 7:15 "Beware of the false prophets who come to you in sheep's clothing, but inwardly are ravenous wolves. You will know them by their fruits."

John 8:44 "You are of your father the devil, and you want to do the desires of your father. He was a murderer from the beginning, and does not stand in the truth because there is no truth in him. Whenever he speaks a lie, he speaks from his own nature, for he is a liar and the father of lies."

1Corinthians 14:33 "for God is not a God of confusion, but of peace…"

Matthew 15:14 "…if a blind man guides a blind man both will fall into the pit."

John 8:31-32 "If you continue in My word, then you are truly disciples of Mine; and you will know the truth, and the truth will make you free."

31. The Strength Which God Supplies
1 Peter 4:11 Whoever speaks, is to do so as one who is speaking the utterances of God; whoever serves is to do so as one who is serving by the strength which God supplies; so that in all things God may

be glorified through Jesus Christ, to whom belongs the glory and dominion forever and ever. Amen.

Philippians 2:13 "for it is God who is at work in you, both to will and to work for His good pleasure."

Psalm 127:1 "Unless the Lord builds the house, they labor in vain who build it; unless the Lord guards the city, the watchman keeps awake in vain."

Philippians 4:13. "I can do all things through Him who strengthens me."

Philippians 1:6 "For I am confident of this very thing, that He who began a good work in you will perfect it until the day of Christ Jesus."

Galatians 3:3 "Are you so foolish? Having begun by the Spirit, are you now being perfected by the flesh?"

1Peter 5:6-7 "Therefore humble yourselves under the mighty hand of God, that He may exalt you at the proper time, casting all your anxiety on Him, because He cares for you."

Psalm 18:29 "For by You I can run upon a troop, and by my God I can leap over a wall."